Praise for "A Crocus in the Desert"

"With a heart to help hurting women, Nancy Williams has crafted a sensitive yet powerful tool for those dealing with infertility. Saturated in Scripture and teeming with real-life testimonials, Nancy gently leads the reader on a journey from heartache to hope–ever whispering, "You are not alone."
—LeAnne Blackmore, Author and Bible Teacher

"Nancy Williams has written a wonderfully helpful book of devotionals for women confronted with the experience of infertility. Writing from her own experiences, and those of others with this life challenge, she draws from the depths of God's grace and truth to provide wisdom, comfort, and hope to others. We pray that the God of hope will use this book to bring peace, joy and hope to many."
—Dr. and Mrs. Jim Richter, Pastor/Wife, Presbyterian Church in America

"Longing for a baby? Grab this book! 'A Crocus in the Desert' offers encouragement and hope through the stories of others who have traveled through the same despair and hunger you feel. This down-to-earth book filled with stories, short devotions, prayer, and Christian Scripture is a balm that undergirds and encourages your journey. Read it! You will no longer feel you are alone!"
—Elizabeth B. Brown, Author and Speaker

"Nancy Williams is a devout Christian who has felt the burden for women experiencing infertility. She relates first-hand the longing to birth a child. However, she found her rest and comfort in her relationship with her Lord. He has sustained her over the years and has given her an understanding of the pain and frustrations of barren women. This is a book that will bring comfort and direction for those who need a vibrant story of barrenness."
—Willette Ericson, retired Christian educator and missionary

"Informative, insightful, and written from the heart, 'A Crocus in the Desert' addresses infertility and its myriad physical, mental, and spiritual implications. Scientific and medical advancements are also requiring new thought in the moral and ethical realms. Nancy Canestrari Williams offers hope and guidance through *these many complex issues with Scripture, prayer, and purposeful stories from others' experiences with infertility. I would recommend this book for those seeking to understand the emotions and struggles with infertility, our relationship with God and His promises, and how we are to fulfill our purpose according to His will."*

—Samuel V. Lewis, M.D. OB/GYN, State of Franklin Ob/Gyn Specialists; Chairman, Department of Surgery, Franklin Woods Community Hospital; Medical Director of Agape Women's Services

"This is a soft and gentle book, yet it's filled with encouragement for those whose desire to bear children for God's glory is yet unfulfilled. Read it, and see how God can turn your sadness into a song of praise."

—Michele King, Care Services Director, Summit Leadership

A Crocus in the Desert

Devotions, Prayers, and Stories for
Women Experiencing Infertility

NANCY CANESTRARI WILLIAMS

Lightbourne Creative
Johnson City, Tennessee

© Copyright 2019—Nancy Canestrari Williams
Lightbourne Creative

Print ISBN: 978-1-7331231-1-2
Library of Congress Control Number: 2019907300

All rights reserved. No part of this publication may be reproduced or transmitted for commercial purposes, except for brief quotations, without written permission from the author or publisher.

Churches and other noncommercial interests may reproduce portions of this book without the express written permission of Lightbourne Creative, provided that the text does not exceed 5 percent of the entire book, and that the text is not material quoted from another publisher. When reproducing text from this book, include the following credit line: "From *A Crocus in the Desert*, by Nancy Canestrari Williams, published by Lightbourne Creative. Used by permission."

Scripture taken from the New King James Version®. Copyright © 1982 by Thomas Nelson. Used by permission. All rights reserved.

For more information, go to lightbournecreative.com
Johnson City, Tennessee

Back cover portrait credit: Mary Pierce Hogue
Logo/illustration and "Wild Ones" font credit: Alyssa Boyér Sprouse

Dedicated to Dr. Carrie Beth Swanay, my awesome boss and a much-beloved professor at Milligan College. You have nurtured so many students in the Communications Department in your decades of faithful instruction—they have been your children. You are an inspiration to all of us.

Table of Contents

A Letter to My Readers
Introduction—"A Crocus in the Desert"
Chapter 1—Why Is This Happening to Me?
Chapter 2—A Royal View of God
Chapter 3—God's Incredible Gift: Jesus Christ
Chapter 4—The Blessing of Marriage
Chapter 5—The Joy of Having Children
Chapter 6—Unfulfilled...Finding Peace in Prayer
Chapter 7—Seeking God in the Pit of Despair
Chapter 8—The Shame Game
Chapter 9—Fury and Forgiveness
Chapter 10—From Fear into Faith
Chapter 11—For the Man of the House
Chapter 12—Is He Ready for "Dadhood"?
Chapter 13—Keeping the Love Flame Burning
Chapter 14—Coping with Conflicts
Chapter 15—Becoming a "Jewel" Wife
Chapter 16—The Privilege of Prayer Time
Chapter 17—Dealing with In-Laws, Outside Pressures
Chapter 18—Getting Your Financial House in Order
Chapter 19—The Church and You
Chapter 20—The Sisterhood of Friendships
Chapter 21—Motherhood in Your Workplace/Career
Chapter 22—New Biotechnology for Infertility
Chapter 23—Is Adoption an Option?
Chapter 24—Branching Out: Fostering and Mentoring
Chapter 25—When Grief Overwhelms
Chapter 26—The Crucible of Faith
Chapter 27—Listening to God, Following His Will
Chapter 28—The Sacrifice of Praise
Chapter 29—The Beauty of Christian Contentment
Our Story: From Siberia, With Love
The Good News of God's Grace
Acknowledgments
Footnotes
About the Author

A Letter to My Readers

Dear friend,

You are not alone.

You might think you're completely alone in this trial, but it's not true. That's a lie from Satan, and as my pastor/friend Jim Richter is fond of saying, "It smells like smoke and comes straight from the pit."

In fact, you represent a significant percentage of the population: an estimated 10 to 18 percent of couples have difficulty conceiving and/or carrying a pregnancy to delivery.[1] That puts you among one in 10 to one in six women around you.

Infertility is nothing new. In the Bible, in the earliest accounts of the bloodlines of man, are the stories of Sarah, Hannah, Elizabeth, and others, all of whom experienced an unmet desire for children at some point in their lives.

Infertility is nothing new in the United States today, either. And it may be a growing problem here as more women delay marriage and childbearing in return for education and career.

I assume you're reading this book because you are (or a close loved one is) struggling with childlessness and infertility. It's not an easy subject to address, and you may have difficulty talking about it with others. I know. I've been there, too.

My own journey through infertility began with a "late" marriage at 34. My husband was certainly worth the wait, but it meant we had to get our show on the road pretty quickly if we wanted to have any children. I'll never forget my ob/gyn physician's comment about my "advanced age" at 36...I thought I was still young!!

Nine months of trying on our own, testing, two surgeries (for endometriosis and ovarian cancer), six months of crash-landing into artificially-induced menopause (what fun), followed by powerful ovulation-inducing drugs (on one ovary), and bingo! We were pregnant with our beautiful daughter, Elizabeth. God had answered our prayers with a resounding "yes."

And then He said, "No." Two more years of infertility, and we closed the doors permanently with my hysterectomy. I would bear no more children. (There is more to our story, which you can read at the end of this book.)

Infertility was a huge trial for me—going through hormonal upheaval and suffering through the aftermath of surgery—all while working in a high-pressure environment (FedEx), attending a church that we jokingly called "Our Lady of Perpetual Fertility" since nearly every eligible female was pregnant, and coping with the pressures on our young marriage. And it was all in silence when dealing with the outside world. Mark and I didn't share it with our friends. It was too personal and private.

That feeling of isolation adds to the emptiness. When it seems that the rest of the women in the world can get pregnant at the drop of a hat, it is so easy to feel alone, worthless, insufficient, broken.

What I didn't know at the time was that if I had just counted six to 10 women down the pew, in all directions, I would have found sisters in this struggle. Once I began to open up about my battle with barrenness, I suddenly found many others who had dealt with this before me...they, too, had not shared it much with others. In a strange twist against our communicative natures, women tend to suffer in silence when it comes to infertility.

I actually started on this book research more than two decades ago, in the middle of waiting for children, and then put it aside. The subject was so painful and raw at the time that I couldn't wrap my brain around it.

God tapped me on the shoulder for years, reminding me that it was gathering dust in my filing cabinet, but I ignored Him. Lots of other projects, more fun to write, got in the way. So, I buried it, much as the faithless servant buried his master's talent in the ground (*Matthew 25:14-30*).

Finally, God wooed me to go with Him to a writers' retreat in the mountains of North Carolina, and I knew I needed to take my old book notes with me. As I looked out my window that weekend into the sun-dappled green leaves of apple trees and poplars, I was overwhelmed with His presence and love. The time for this book had come.

Ultimately, it's not my work. It's really an edited collection of the voices of women who have already walked the path of infertility ahead of you. These are ordinary women, from the Bible and among my friends. They're not spiritual giants. They are women like you. Some have children now; some remain childless.

I promised my friends anonymity so that they would feel free to share their experiences honestly. Listen to their stories—they are your sisters in this walk.

This book is intended for anyone going through the struggle of infertility or for those who have loved ones suffering under the burden. And while written from an American perspective, my hope is that women in other countries can learn from the eternal, universal truths of Scripture.

It's by women and for women. So, if you're a man reading this, take a look at Chapters 11 and 12 (aimed at helping women understand how infertility affects men). Perhaps the rest of the book will give you insights into some of the emotions that your wife is experiencing, too.

Also, this book is specifically written with married women in mind. If you're a single, childless woman reading this book—whether by widowhood, divorce, or having never married—I sincerely apologize. I was single for a long time, and I know you carry the double burden of being childless and alone. But I hope you will bear with the chapters and comments that deal with marriage. Perhaps they may prepare you for marriage in the future or at least help you sympathize with the infertility burdens that married women endure.

This book offers no talisman for fertility. There are no magic words to chant, no wand to wave, no oil for anointing, no special prayer that is going to do the trick and bring children into your home.

Its purpose, ultimately, is to draw you closer to the God who is omnipotent and omnipresent. He is all-powerful, is always with you, sees you and hears you, knows you from the inside out. After all, He made you. And He loves you deeply.

If you are not a Christian, perhaps this time of walking through prayer will introduce you to Jesus Christ in a way that you have not seen Him before. May His Holy Spirit breathe new life, comfort, peace, and purpose into your soul.

So please, from my heart to yours, know that you are not alone. God is with you. And, you are surrounded by a great "cloud of witnesses"—people who care about you, those who have gone before you, those who right now are also walking the path of infertility. They are all cheering you onward, encouraging you to finish the race, fight the good fight, and take comfort in the unreleasing grasp of our Savior's hand as He pulls you through this.

You are loved!

INTRODUCTION

A "Crocus in the Desert"

"The wilderness and the wasteland shall be glad for them, and the desert shall rejoice and blossom as the rose; it shall blossom abundantly and rejoice, even with joy and singing." (Isaiah 35:1-2a)

If you live anywhere close to an urban environment, only the brightest of the stars penetrate the glow of streetlight overhead. But if you live in a dry desert, oh my—what an incredible performance you can witness every night, with whole galaxies and millions of stars parading across the heavens' black velvet curtain.

A few years ago, our family went to Sedona, Arizona, which is surrounded by a starkly beautiful terrain of shaded rocks and mountains. I insisted that we go away from the nighttime glow of town to a place where we could park the car, turn out all the lights, and get out to look at the sky. After our eyes adjusted to the darkness, the star visibility was astonishing. The Milky Way was truly milky, and stars upon stars bombarded our eyes like millions of fireworks exploding.

We couldn't have seen this from our comfortable hotel. To witness the majesty of God's universe unshielded from the trappings of civilization, we had to go into the desert.

Infertility (or "barrenness," the typical word in the Bible for it) is a desert. It offers nothing, just emptiness and sterility. No fruit, no productiveness, no results. It conjures up emotions of being desolate, bleak, bare, lonely. Sound familiar?

Thus, infertility in Scriptures and ancient cultures was a curse from God. It represented being in an isolated place, dry and parched. It meant certain death.

The Arabah (the Hebrew word used in the verses above from Isaiah), then and now, is such a place, more than 100 miles long and located at the border of Israel and Jordan, just south of the Dead Sea. Its name means "sterility" and "desert."[1] It also served as a hiding place for David and his men *(1 Samuel 23:24)*, a kind of no man's land.

A woman who had no children, in Bible times and onward, was considered to be worthless, without blessing. Her infertility was seen as a reproach, a judgment from God for her sin or some other shortcoming.

There are three things that are never satisfied, four never say, "Enough!": the grave, the barren womb, the earth that is not satisfied with water—and the fire never says, "Enough!" (Proverbs 30:15b-16)

Conversely, having children (and having many children) meant being blessed by God. It represented fruitfulness, the virility of men, abundance, life, legacy. Those with children could sit smugly satisfied that they rested squarely in the favor of God. His light shone upon them brightly. Their sun would set on a completed job and purpose.

We who experience infertility sit on the outside, looking in. We are out of control of our situation. We cannot create a child.

So, what *can* we do? We can talk with the One who loves us and is in charge of our lives.

Before you were born, God ordained your days and His purposes for you *(Jeremiah 1:4-8)*. He is with you always.

Prayer is not a last resort when all else fails. We must go to Him first for everything. Right after giving His disciples His "Lord's Prayer" model, Jesus *commanded* them to pray. The words "ask," "seek," and "knock" are in the imperative voice *(Luke 11:9-13)*, which means they're commands, not options.

How do we talk with Him? How do we get started?

One popular pattern for prayer is ACTS—adoration, confession, thanksgiving, and supplication. Let's look at each of these in order:

❖ *Adoration*

When we come to God on our knees, our first words to Him should be in praise to Him simply for who He is. In the first breaths of Hannah's beautiful prayer in Scripture for receiving Samuel as her son, she proclaims that there is no one holy like the Lord. *"For there is none besides You, nor is there any rock like our God" (1 Samuel 2:2).* Hannah goes on to praise Him as the God of knowledge by whom actions are weighed. He is the Lord of infinite power, who kills and makes alive, makes poor and makes rich, and yes, allows the barren to have children.

As you start your own prayers to God, always begin with true worship of His kingship, His strength, His love, His grace. Come before Him as the princess who adores her royal Father, telling Him all the ways that He is wonderful and expressing how much she admires Him. We take the attention off ourselves and focus entirely on Him.

Pause at this juncture to revere God and think of nothing else. Learn what it means to love Him with all your heart, soul, mind, and strength.

❖ *Confession*

Here is where shame must be addressed. Go straight to the feet of this all-powerful, all-present God. Guess what? He already knows what you've done, what has happened to you. He knows everything you're going to say before you open up your box of thoughts. He is ready to listen, ready to forgive, ready to heal the gaping wounds.

Read through Psalm 51 where you'll find David's soul-wrenching confession of his sin against God. Pour out your anguish before Him. Name your sins and acknowledge them. Ask God to wash you clean, purge all of your sin, create in you a clean heart, keep His presence with you, restore the joy of His salvation, and uphold you by His generous Holy Spirit.

This is a tell-all moment just between you and God. You don't have to air your dirty laundry before the world, because God will have it all clean by the time you're done.

❖ *Thanksgiving*

Your prayer doesn't stop after confession—otherwise, you'd still be wallowing in the guilt and shame. After all, you've just told the Creator of the universe that you have done something wrong (or failed to do something right) and acted as a loathsome worm.

Instead, you're going to commit an act of absolute faith. Thank God for His forgiveness. Say "thank you" over and over. You haven't deserved His forgiveness. You haven't escaped the earthly consequences of your transgressions. But you *have* escaped His eternal punishment if you have accepted His Son's sacrificial payment on the cross. Thank your Heavenly Father for His gift of life. Thank Jesus for paying the ultimate cost. Thank His Holy Spirit for abiding with you.

This is the moment when shame is undone. When you accept what God has done for you, when you embrace His great love and understanding, it is the most liberating experience in your entire life.

As Jesus said in John 8:32, you shall know the truth at that moment, and the truth shall set you free. You are now free to rejoice, free to rest in His comfort, free to move forward.

❖ *Supplication*

Now it's time to lift up your requests before the throne of God. Supplication means praying humbly and earnestly. You have adored God, confessed to Him, and thanked Him. Now it's time to ask Him for the desires of your heart and for the needs of others. Hannah had no qualms about asking God for a child, and neither should you. You are forgiven, and you can approach God now with a fresh start.

When you pray, ask with confidence. Our Lord hears you, and that alone should be comforting. The Scriptures tell us that His desires are for our best interests. "*And we know that all things work together for good to those who love God, to those who are the called according to His purpose*" (*Romans 8:28*). When we raise our hands to God, the Giver of all good gifts, He stoops to hear us. What an incredible portrait of a loving Father!

Never forget, however, that God has three answers to prayer: "yes," "no," and "wait." He may open a door for you. He may close it permanently. He may keep the door shut for only a certain period of time. Whatever His answer, place your full trust in His loving plans for you. They are always for His glory and His kingdom, which are for your good.

Ask God, too, to change your dreams. Ask Him to help you focus your vision on Him and His purposes for you. Ask the Holy Spirit to fill You with His comfort, guidance, and power.

Now, take a look back to the verse from Isaiah at the beginning of this section—you'll find an exquisite promise from God. The "rose" mentioned here is *chabatstseleth* in Hebrew.[2] It is uncertain as to its specific species—it's translated in another Bible version as "crocus," a plant similar to the narcissus, or described as meadow-saffron. A crocus emerges from a bulb, hidden in the winter-worn earth until rainfall and sunshine cause it to burst forth in beauty and radiance. The crocus is the first sign of spring and represents new life.

God's word offers you hope—that this "desert time" in your life is but a season and that, in time, he will cause the barren place in your heart to blossom abundantly. He wants to show you His beauty in your life...how He is making all things beautiful in His time.

Begin your prayer journey with Him right now—pray through this psalm as your opening conversation:

"O God, You are my God;
Early will I seek You;
   My soul thirsts for You;
my flesh longs for You in a dry and thirsty land
where there is no water.
   So I have looked for You in the sanctuary,
to see Your power and Your glory.
   Because Your lovingkindness is better than life,
my lips shall praise You.

Thus I will bless You while I live;
I will lift up my hands in Your name.
My soul shall be satisfied as with marrow and fatness,
and my mouth shall praise You with joyful lips.
When I remember You on my bed,
I meditate on You in the night watches.
Because You have been my help,
therefore in the shadow of Your wings I will rejoice.
My soul follows close behind You;
Your right hand upholds me." (Psalm 63:1-8)

Amen!

MY AUNT LIZY'S STORY:

My great-aunt Elizabeth "Lizy" Ridley Hackworth was a powerhouse woman...a visionary with relentless energy in bettering the lives of others. She founded libraries, drove a bookmobile (well into her 80s), ran for public office, taught in a one-room schoolhouse, developed educational materials, fostered civil rights (way before it was cool), and pretty much invested her life in helping young children. I was one of them.

But one of the greatest disappointments of her life was that she could not have children to live and grow with her. Both of her young sons died as infants...one at birth and the second at 10 months. It was never clear why she was not able to bear healthy babies.

Lizy was advised by her doctor to never get pregnant again.

"The two years following the death of my children were traumatic ones for me," she said. "The shock of losing my babies and knowing that I could never have a child of my own threw me into a deep depression. I was only 30 years old. I had to try to learn how to live again.

"One afternoon, a knock came at my front door, and I found my pastor and his wife standing there. It wasn't unusual for them to come to my home...they were friends.

"Others who had come offered consolation, but my pastor and his wife challenged me. They urged me to attend an upcoming Christian workers' training program. I told them I wasn't interested, but they continued to talk about what might be in the future for spiritual growth guidance for children.

"Their visit was a success because for the next four years I traveled throughout the region, developing church leaders' awareness of the need for guiding children in Christian nurture.

"After serving the church, I went back into public school teaching for fourth graders. From the first day, I accepted each child as my opportunity to help him or her have a fuller, happier life.

"I never had a bad child. I never had a child I could not love. Every child had a special place in my heart. Each child had his own story to share with me."

My Aunt Lizy died in September 2001 at the age of 97. It was a great privilege to know her and see how God used her to have a positive impact on citizens throughout our state in the 20th century, continuing today. Her love for Christ kept her going, despite childlessness, widowhood, and total blindness. She still inspires me even now.

CHAPTER 1

Why Is This Happening to Me?

"Then God blessed them, and God said to them, "Be fruitful and multiply; fill the earth and subdue it...." (Genesis 1:28a)

"O LORD, our Lord, how excellent is Your name in all the earth! ...When I consider Your heavens, the work of Your fingers, the moon and the stars, which You have ordained, what is man that You are mindful of him...? For You have made him a little lower than the angels and You have crowned him with glory and honor." (Psalm 8:1a,3-4a,5)

The waiting room at your ob/gyn office, full of infants, new moms, and pregnant bellies...

The baby food aisle at your grocery store...

The new mom holding her baby in the church pew, who turns to you and says, "You need one of these!"...

Television shows about babies or even diaper commercials...

The umpteenth baby shower for someone else...

The empty seats at your own kitchen table....

If you're experiencing infertility, or if you've lost a child to miscarriage, you know how any of these experiences can trigger an instant flow of tears.

You cover your face, flee the scene, and run to a place of solitude—where you lift your hands to heaven and wail, "Why is this happening to me?"

We weep not only for what we have lost but also for that which we have never possessed. Infertility is perhaps more grievous than the death of a loved one, for we may keep fond memories of the person we have lost. There are no memories, though, for a vanished dream.

This hunger for something we cannot grasp is at the heart of our burden. Our arms ache to hold a child...our very own child. Instead, infertile women may carry an armload of emptiness, bewilderment, envy, anger, and despair. Our dreams of having children have gone from sweet wishes to nightmarish torments.

So, if you're wandering in the desert of infertility right now, you're probably asking the same questions I once asked: "Why me? Why us?"

To go deeper, let's look at the miracle and tragedy of creation...how God made us, how He views us, and what happened to mess it all up.

Before King David ruled over Israel, he was a simple shepherd who was entranced by the beauty of God's universe. Picture him lying on his back alone on a remote wilderness hillside, hearing the murmurs of sleepy sheep, and gazing at the night sky. As he pondered the work of God's fingertips, he mused, "What is man that you would care anything about him, much less visit him?"

David understood he was absolutely nothing in the vast expanse of God's creation...smaller than a grain of sand in an endless ocean. He grasped the infinite hugeness and supremacy of the Maker of the universe and lived in fear of Him. Yet he spoke with God and chased after God's heart. David understood the value that God places on humankind, the pinnacle of His creatures on Earth.

"You have made man only a little lower than the angels," David said, "and You even crowned him!"

Long before King David or you and I ever contemplated the stars, God was busy handcrafting and speaking into existence His extraordinary Earth. He created humankind, male and female, to be His very own people. He made us in the image of His Three-in-One personhood—the Father, His Son Jesus Christ, and His Holy Spirit.

God made Adam first, shaping him from the dust of the ground and breathing life into his nostrils. God set Adam in the Garden of Eden, to work it and take care of it. Because our Father God already experienced the joy of fellowship with Jesus and His Spirit, He desired for Adam to enjoy companionship, too. So, He put Adam under general anesthesia, removed a rib, and sculpted Eve from it, bringing her to Adam when he woke up.

Can you imagine how Adam felt when he first saw Eve? I'll bet he said, "Wow!" Adam beheld a perfectly formed reflection of himself, a lovely helper for his work and his true soul mate. He saw Eve immediately as a part of himself—bone of his bones, flesh of his flesh. He also saw in her a reflection of his Friend, God.

It was an amazing, instantaneous marriage, two people coming together in perfect harmony: one man, one woman, blended from the start as husband and wife. Adam and Eve lived as holy and happy people in peace. For this reason, in future generations, God planned for each man to leave his mother and father and be united with his wife, and the two would become one flesh, encircled in the Holy Spirit. God commanded them to be fruitful and multiply, to fill the earth with other holy and happy people.

Of course, we all know what happened next. Eve was deceived, even as we are today, by Satan's treachery and Eve's pride, and Adam followed suit. Eve tossed away priceless gifts...a perfect relationship with God and a perfect relationship with her husband. Up to that time, her marriage with Adam was unspoiled. Satan's sabotage corrupted everything from that time forward.

Worst of all, Adam and Eve became separated from God's presence, driven out of the Garden of Eden. As their children today, we struggle with alienation from God by our own sin.

"In essence, when Adam and Eve sinned they lost a true knowledge of God," said pastor Neil T. Anderson. "In God's original design, knowledge was relational....When they sinned and were banished from the garden, Adam and Eve lost their relationship with God."[1]

We would love to follow God's original plan and obey His command to multiply today. There are many obstacles, unfortunately, standing in the way. Our generation still reels from the long-term effects of Adam's and Eve's original sin—divorce, disease, infidelity, abortion, misapplied birth control or sterilization, miscarriages, and of course, infertility.

What do we do now? God's design was for us to be holy and happy, to be fruitful and multiply, to have families who would do His desire and His holy will. Why did He allow His beautiful creation to be deceived and fall apart? How do we fulfill His purposes if we are facing infertility? How do we satisfy our God-programmed intense craving for children?

We can't answer those questions. Only God knows. If we have that passionate desire to have children, it's because God has placed it there...God has wired us that way because it's what He wants for us.

We're stymied. We can't go back to the Garden. But we can start our journey afresh, here and now, in renewing our friendship with God. The first thing we need to do is call upon the Lord.

If you're reading this book, you may be dealing with infertility right now. You're reaching out for lifelines in every direction, grasping at any hope. You may have already prayed to God for years, with no results. Like Eve, you may have found that your relationship with God has become tarnished, distant, cold.

Adam and Eve continued to talk with God after they sinned, and their descendants over the millennia have talked with Him, just as He has spoken through them. But we live in a day and age when we don't hear His voice as clearly. Too many things crowd Him out. Our hearts are crusty, our ears are broken, our vision is polluted. We can't see the stars.

But if you open His word and read carefully, you will hear the gentle whisper of your loving Creator, calling you to enter His throne room. He invites you to sit at His feet, cross-legged as a child. With your head down and weeping if you must, pour out your heart before Him.

Ask Him to stand by you in this trial. Ask Him to be your Guide, your Stay, your Father who hears your pleas and your cries. As you enter this study on infertility, seek to hear your Father's voice through His word as well as through these messages, your prayers, and the stories of other women, so that every day you will know *you are not alone.*

Your Father God does walk with you and will hold your hand every step along the way...through every tear, every trial, every confrontation, every disappointment. He has promised to be with you until the end. Cry out to Him, talk with Him, plead with Him through the name of His Son, Jesus. Listen for His response. Pursue His presence, even in the darkness and desert.

He, too, is pursuing you...the pinnacle of His creation.

PRAYER:

Great and mighty God, as I start this spiritual trek, please let me come before You with awe and reverence. I applaud You, the mighty Creator of the universe, Architect of Earth, Maker of our people, Designer of me. Everything You have created is beautiful, astonishing, and magnificent. O Lord, I praise You today for the excellence of Your name and glory in all the earth and above the heavens!

When I consider Your heavens, the work of Your fingers, who am I that You are mindful of me, to visit me? Help me to see that You have crowned me with glory and honor, greater than all Your earthly creatures and only a little lower than the angels. When I see my reflection in a mirror, help me to recognize that I am worth so much more to You than I can imagine...You have numbered even the very hairs of my head.

Now, as I sit or kneel here, as if inside Your great throne room, I ask You to comfort me with Your Holy Spirit. Remind me that You are here with me...You are eternal, all-knowing, present everywhere.

Even before I speak, O God my Father, You know what I need. You search my heart and understand all the intent of my thoughts. I pray You will hear my cries and give ear to my pleadings. Show me, Lord, how to walk this difficult path with You in Your grace. Let me know more about You so that I may serve You with a loyal heart and a willing mind.

When I fail to see the beauty of Your masterpiece creation in me, unable to see beyond the sin-marred image in the mirror, open my eyes to see myself the way You see me...Your child, Your precious work of art.

And so, I offer up honor to You—for Your beautiful creation of mankind, Your perfect plan, and Your great love and mercy to me. I ask these things in Jesus' name, Amen.

(Psalm 8:1,3-8; Luke 12:7; 1 Chronicles 28:9)

FOR REFLECTION:

❖ Today (or later this week), take at least one hour or more to escape to God's exquisite creation of nature. This can be as dramatic as hiking to a waterfall or as simple as sitting on an urban park bench. Look for the wonder of His handiwork in a wildflower or the ragged face of a stony cliff. Whisper your praise to God, or shout out a hallelujah to Him if you're alone! Record your thoughts here afterward:

_____
_____
_____
_____

❖ Read Psalm 8 aloud as a prayer to God. How does David exalt God's name and character?

_____
_____
_____
_____

❖ Check out a library book of nature photos, or page through a website of nature photography. Or search for images taken of deep space by satellite cameras. Pause to reflect on the majesty of God, His miracle of the human body, and our smallness in the vast universe. Write a thank-you note to God for creating you and caring about you.

_____
_____
_____
_____

NATALIE'S* STORY:

Shortly before I was married, I underwent emergency surgery to remove a tumor. From the final pathology report, I was diagnosed with a rare genetic disease. Although my case is mild, it is genetic—with a 50 percent chance of having a child with it. We were also told that it would be life-threatening for me to carry a baby with my disease. Evan (my fiancé at the time) and I felt that God had revealed this to us to protect us; consequently, I had a tubal ligation before we were married. As difficult as not having children is, Evan and I are confident in God's sovereign plan for us.

The Holy Spirit has revealed things to me about God's character that have definitely shaped my views of myself. In seeking to find out WHY this has happened to me, God has revealed more of His character to me. He is completely perfect, holy, powerful, and sovereign, and He lovingly controls every detail of my life. He created me with infertility for a purpose and has known me before I was even formed. Not only is His plan perfect, but I have learned to trust Him with my worries and anxieties about not having a child.

My Christian friend, Fiona, helped me to realize that my inability to be pregnant was, in a sense, the death of my plan for my life. I needed to go through the grieving process in order to accept God's plan for my life. It was instrumental for my emotional health to allow myself to be sad, to cry, to be angry...I couldn't work past the pain without allowing it to come. In addition, my family kept encouraging me by reminding me that God has something incredible planned for Evan and me. Because I have been shown unconditional acceptance, love and encouragement, I try to do the same for others in dealing with infertility. Most importantly, I try to have a shoulder to cry on, a sympathetic ear to listen, and a heart that is willing to break for another's pain.

It is crucial to know that God is sovereign, that His plans (although they may hurt) are far better for us than our own plans. Realizing that He is in control of every situation enables us to desire what He would have us learn and experience.

(*All names for "stories" shared in Chapters 1-29 have been changed for anonymity.)

CHAPTER 2

A Royal View of God

"Who is like You, O Lord, among the gods? Who is like You, glorious in holiness, fearful in praises, doing wonders?" (Exodus 15:11)

"He shall judge the world in righteousness, and He shall administer judgment for the peoples in uprightness." (Psalm 9:8)

"Therefore the Lord will wait, that He may be gracious to you; And therefore He will be exalted, that He may have mercy on you. For the Lord is a God of justice; blessed are all those who wait for Him." (Isaiah 30:18)

I'm a hopeless Anglophile—which means I love all things about England, especially the royals. I've watched the televised royal weddings and followed news about the Queen's family over the years. It's all fascinating to me, even though I will never meet any of them.

Like the English royalty, God is sovereign. But what does *sovereign* mean?

Dictionaries tell us that a sovereign is an absolute ruler, a king, the highest royalty. A sovereign is someone who is in charge of everything. The top dog. The president of the country. The monarch of the world. Or, in God's case, the King of the universe.

Sovereign is also an adjective. It means to be in charge...to be the one who executes commands, who administers judgments, who designs and charts the course of the future for his subjects.

The concept of being in charge implies there are people to be ruled, subjects who need governing, and providence from the person in command. A sovereign reigns over people.

God is the ultimate Sovereign. He is sovereign over the magnitude of space. He is in charge of the stars, shaping their orbits and their paths through space.

He is sovereign over every aspect of life on Earth, even in the nitty gritty of things. He is sovereign over everything from the devastating power of hurricanes to the tiniest flutter of a gnat wing. He is sovereign over microscopic life, including each singular embryonic cell from which He created each of us, from which He creates all of His children.

God is sovereign over your life, your marriage, your children-to-be. He is sovereign over your past, your present, your future. He is completely in charge of you. You are wholly dependent upon His Holy Spirit for your next breath.

In that case, what control do we have in our lives? That's a touchy subject theologically, with lots of debate about God's will versus the free will of man.

A sidebar in the *New Geneva Study Bible* attests that "God's rational creatures...have free agency, that is, the power of personal decision as to what they will do. We would not be moral beings, answerable to God the Judge, if it were not so....God's control over our free actions...is as complete as it is over anything else; but how this can be we do not know."[1]

God ultimately has His hand upon you—if He has called you and you have given your heart to Him, He will not let go. You cannot fall out of His hand or run away from Him. You cannot mess up His plans for you. He is too powerful for that.

Because He is good, God's motives are always for our good. He is holy. That means He's pure, unspotted, unpolluted, crystal clear. In His holiness, He cannot tolerate any sin. Nothing wrong can come from Him or come before Him. He rules His kingdom in righteousness.

That also makes Him a God of judgment. He cannot let the guilty go unpunished. God will see His justice meted out for the sins and problems of the world. And that is the rub for us.

The rain falls on the just and the unjust. The rain of infertility is falling on you, whether there is some issue or private sin in your past that has led to your infertility, or whether you have followed a godly path and still have problems.

The truth is that eventually we must face the fact that we are all sinners. Not one of us is good. We're all daughters of Eve, and we share in her sin. Our human race is contaminated, you included. You, God's beautiful creation, are completely besmirched.

Commit only one tiny sin a day, and you're a sinner, as loathsome as a cake made with two good eggs and one rotten egg. You are inedible. God will throw you out. You are unable to save yourself, no matter how many good works you try to do.

In your sin, you cannot approach God. But while God exudes purity and righteousness as our judge-king, He has another complementary trait incorporated into His entire being. He is a God full of mercy—He is the very essence of love.

He does not desire to squash us between His fingers because we haven't been perfect or because He flippantly and randomly decides which people to squash. Quite the contrary, He has beautiful and wonderful plans for our good and not for evil: *"For I know the thoughts that I think toward you," says the Lord, "thoughts of peace and not of evil, to give you a future and a hope." (Jeremiah 29:11)*

In God's master plan, He has allowed you to be right here, right now, where you are. In His great mercy, He will abstain from sentencing you to that which you deserve, your ultimate judgment.

If you are reading this book and trust in Jesus, God has already plucked you from the gates of hell. Mercy is like deserving to go to the electric chair for something bad you've done and finding out the judge sent his son instead. God sent His Son Jesus to die on a cross, to pay the penalty for your sin. He has pardoned you from what you deserve. You can go free now. His mercy means His judgment is now withheld.

But wait, there's more! The luxury of grace. If, in addition to letting you go free, that same judge also awarded you a hundred billion dollars, that's grace—unmerited favor.

Grace is what Christ bestows upon you as a gift. Not only does He give you freedom, He gives you abundant life. Through His death on the cross, Christ offers you blessings beyond all you could ever request or imagine...not in the things of earth but in the wealth of heaven. He presents you with the gift of eternal life. He becomes your Forever Friend.

If you really think about it, none of us deserves to be a parent. There is nothing you have done or can do to deserve the gift of a child.

In His grace, God provides us children...children of our own, children we adopt, children we foster, or children whose lives we can influence for good. Maybe all of the above. In any event, it's all *grace*, all from Him.

He is the Provider of children. He's the only One who can provide. That's why you must trust Him and talk with Him every day about the children you desire to have or encounter in your life. And unlike the distant English royals, God meets with us personally and even calls us His close friends!

If you have accepted that Jesus Christ is your Savior and have decided to follow Him, He alone is the source of your self-worth. Your identity no longer depends on motherhood or marriage, even though these are good things.

As you walk through this journey, recognize God's orchestration in it and praise Him for His mercy and grace. Open your eyes to consequences He has allowed you to escape. Look for His abundant blessings in your everyday life. Look for His abundant life all around you. Thank Him for everything.

Rejoice that you have a Sovereign you can approach and love!

PRAYER:

Lord, I come before You, recognizing indeed that You are sovereign over my life. You are the Rock, a God of truth and without injustice—all of Your work is perfect, and all of Your ways are justice. I praise You for Your great goodness and the multitude of Your lovingkindnesses, according to Your mercies, and for all that You have bestowed on me.

I praise You, too, for Your mercy and grace. Let me understand You, that You are the Lord, exercising lovingkindness, judgment, and righteousness in the earth—You delight in these. Give me a heart to know You; let me be among Your people with You as my God. Let me give You my whole heart.

Forgive me for my sins; forgive me for doubting Your plan in my circumstances. Do not remember the sins of my youth, nor my transgressions; according to Your mercy, remember me, for Your goodness' sake, O Lord. Let me hope in You, for with You are mercy and abundant redemption.

As You walk me through this journey, I pray that You will make me more and more aware of Your mercy and grace poured out over me. Thank You for Your great love for me. As You provide children—whoever they are, wherever I find them, whatever role they play in my life—I pray that I will see them as a gift from You. Make me, I pray, a better servant to You day by day. Show me Your mighty hand at work in my life, so that I may learn to rejoice and praise You in all things. In Jesus' name, Amen.

(Deuteronomy 32:4; Isaiah 63:7; Jeremiah 9:24, 24:7; Psalm 25:7; Psalm 130:7)

FOR REFLECTION:

❖ Make a list of at least three amazing gifts you have received from God in only the past 24 hours, including joys, ordinary blessings, and any problems you may face. Praise Him for His good gifts and those difficulties He is using to remold and reshape your heart.

❖ Read 1 Chronicles 29:11-12. How does knowing God as your all-powerful, majestic King affect your attitudes, fears, and life purpose?

_____

_____
_____
_____

❖ Think of one small way to be a servant to God by helping one other person, outside of your regular activities today, and do it. Pray for that person to see God's blessing through you. Describe what you did and what the results were.

_____
_____
_____
_____

🙢 🙢 🙢

CAROLINE'S STORY:

As of this writing, I have lived about 434 months. Out of these, there is one month whose time and details stand still in my mind. It was an intensely emotional month, and a time of growth and learning. It was the month of Bethany.

After Bethany's birth with Down Syndrome and other medical issues, we quickly knew the reality that only God was in control—neither Frank and I nor even the doctors who seemed so certain of their course of action. We were totally dependent on Him, which was truly wonderful reassurance. After only one month of life, Bethany passed from our arms into His.

But this was far from a tragedy, for we were witnessing God at work. He turned sorrow into joy, answered many prayers, and showed us continual love by surrounding us with people to care and comfort us.

Frank and I look back at our brief time with Bethany as a unique gift from the Lord who keeps on giving.

For months after her death, my arms would ache (yes, actually ache!) to hold a baby of our own. So you can imagine how joyous we were afterward to be pregnant last fall. Certainly this baby would be perfect—after all, I deserved it, didn't I? Instead, I miscarried. I have never known such despair as after this miscarriage. I literally could not speak, and in my mind, "Why me?" drummed.

But then the Lord chided, "Why not you?" My thoughts went to the dear women I knew who had never held their own babies. He dragged me out of my selfish pit and back to the living. And as time went by, He removed the ache from my arms. I could look at big pregnant bellies and new babies without jealous arms or a yearning heart. God was so good to show that mercy to me!

Still, there are times when a line of a hymn or a sudden memory will cause tears to flow for Bethany. But I don't mourn—she's at the best home there is, and she's healthy there.

We treasure the memories of our dear daughter, but we also look forward to our new daughter who will join us soon from China. Just as God has reaffirmed many times that Bethany was no tragedy, He moved us to see a truly tragic situation: babies without families to love them or share the love of our Lord with them.

Our challenges of this past year seem so much smaller than many around me. But we couldn't have gotten through them and felt so hopeful and joyous without deep faith in Jesus Christ. Staying focused on Him has been, at times, the real challenge. When I miscarried this spring, I grasped onto Psalm 25, and it was the Lord who did not allow me to sink into despair. He has carried me a lot this year—and in truth, His solutions are not the ones I'd have chosen. But I have seen that His way is best.

CHAPTER 3

God's Incredible Gift: Jesus Christ

"For by grace you have been saved through faith, and that not of yourselves; it is the gift of God, not of works, lest anyone should boast. For we are His workmanship, created in Christ Jesus for good works, which God prepared beforehand that we should walk in them." (Ephesians 2:8-10)

"Yet in all these things we are more than conquerors through Him who loved us. For I am persuaded that neither death nor life, nor angels nor principalities nor powers, nor things present nor things to come, nor height nor depth, nor any other created thing, shall be able to separate us from the love of God which is in Christ Jesus our Lord." (Romans 8:37-39)

If you've experienced infertility for a while, your experience may be like this:

You've asked, pleaded, demanded, cried, begged, prayed for a gift you've wanted more than anything—a child of your own. Month after month, year after year, you've come before the throne of God with your request, only to walk away empty-handed. You've trusted, doubted, trusted, doubted, trusted—a cycle repeated over and over again.

You've shaken your fist at heaven, you've sobbed on your knees. "Life!" you've cried. "All I want is one little life to be mine! Surely it's not too much to ask!!" But the ceiling, the skies are stone-cold silent.

C. S. Lewis felt the same way during intense grief.

"When you are happy, so happy that you have no sense of needing Him,...you will be—or so it feels—welcomed with open arms," Lewis wrote. "But go to Him when your need is desperate, when all other help is vain, and what do you find? A door slammed in your face, and a sound of bolting and double bolting on the inside. After that, silence....the same thing seems to have happened to Christ: 'Why hast thou forsaken me?' I know. Does that make it easier to understand?

"Not that I am...in much danger of ceasing to believe in God. The real danger is of coming to believe such dreadful things about Him."[1]

The story of the prophet Elijah tells of a time when he asked God to withhold rain from rebellious Israel, and the heavens overhead became as hard as brass. For three years, the country lay infertile, incapable of producing any fruit. Finally, Elijah prayed for relief, and God sent a roiling storm, a sky black with clouds and wind, with a heavy rain to refresh the earth.

But you're not seeing your prayers answered. "How long, O Lord? How long will you make me wait and suffer?" Your quest for a child becomes your life's focus...it colors every decision you make, every moment with your husband, and every painful encounter with other moms, especially in your own family.

What if, however, God has already given you at least one answer to your pleas? What if He has set before you a priceless gift you haven't opened?

God gave a very unexpected pregnancy to an unmarried young woman named Mary. It was a gift of life she hadn't requested or even imagined. But she offered herself as a faithful servant to God, accepted the Fatherhood of His Holy Spirit, and humbled herself to become the mother of Jesus. On Christmas, God gave her the ultimate gift—the Savior of the world as a newborn baby.

Mary went on to have other children, with Joseph afterward, but her firstborn was like no other child. Jesus had come into Mary's life to transform her, to give her an eternal life with Him.

God had sent Jesus as His gift not only to Mary but the rest of the human race as well. Can you imagine how Mary felt, raising this Son for her God, wondering how all of God's plans would be fulfilled in Him? Don't you suppose she trusted, doubted, trusted, doubted, trusted—over and over again, especially when this innocent Son she loved so much was murdered on the cross? Did He have to die like that? How could His life possibly be fulfilled as God's gift now?

But, on Easter morning, Mary could better understand the Person whom God had entrusted to her. Jesus was alive, and death was conquered! What she had heard and believed from the beginning was now reality. Jesus had paid the price to offer eternal life for the entire world and for her personally.

That same gift, bought with sacrificial love, is now available to you. Will you accept what Jesus has to offer? It is, indeed, a gift because you can't earn it or pay for it. You can only close your eyes, hold out your hands, and take it as the helpless beggar that you are.

Now, open your eyes to see what's inside God's gift: eternal life—assurance that Jesus is holding a place for you in His mansion in heaven, a place at His table prepared for His wedding feast; and abundant life here—a daily walk with Jesus through His Holy Spirit, with an outpouring of the fruits of love, joy, peace, patience and more.

As you stand here, holding out your hands to receive this extraordinary gift, you may be wondering what it means to have this promise while you are still on earth. Imagine this: as you extend one hand to receive it, Christ gently takes hold of your other hand. He has you firmly in His grasp and will not let go of you.

You will stumble, but you will never fall. You will have pain and conflict, but you will be able to endure through His strength. You may doubt, but you will be reassured by His word. You may take a wrong road, but you will not stay on it long before He turns you around in the right direction. Following His lead, you will never get lost. His path, His commandments, and His ways are sure.

You will sin, but you will find its hold on you loses its strangling power over time. When Christ puts new clothes of righteousness upon you, you find yourself eager to keep them unsullied. Yet when you fail Him, you find forgiveness...new mercies every morning.

As with any astonishing gift, you'll be too excited about it to keep the news to yourself. Once you've stepped into your new shoes as a Christ-follower, you become aware of others who need His love, too. Step out in faith, in courage, to take His life-giving message to others.

Dig deeper into this gift, uncovering new jewels within it, by reading from God's word. Some of the passages are easy to accept, but some are hard; the Christian life isn't a guarantee of health, wealth, and pain-free existence. Rather, you've entered a new world where suffering is to be expected...Satan hates to let a new believer go unscathed. Your infertility could be his trap to rob you of your joy in the Lord.

However, God has an abundant life waiting for you through the sacrifice of His Son on the cross. He will never leave you nor forsake you.

What's even more amazing is that Jesus considers you His "treasure"—regardless of whatever sins, warts, shortcomings, inadequacies you have to offer in return. He *treasures* you.

Heather DeJesus Yates (don't you just love her name?) explained this well in her book, *All the Wild Pearls*. Yates described Him as a diver in search of beautiful pearls:

"Jesus gave it all up, to dive to earth for us," she wrote. "Not because of a duty, but because He sought a treasure. His motivation was not the praise of man, but a heart full of love for people who were screaming, whether we knew it or not. Just as pearl divers risk their lives to dive because they know there is treasure beneath the frigid and dangerous dark depths, Jesus saw us as His treasure, and only He could retrieve us....

"We can know that whatever we are to Him, and to God, whatever value we must hold must be great if it was worth Him diving to a dusty, ungrateful, unhinging earth, just to have us as His own."[2]

You've asked for a life to be your own. Jesus stands ready to give you Himself as the Way, the Truth, and *the* Life. Isn't that a gift worth opening and treasuring every day?

🍂 🍂 🍂

PRAYER:

O Heavenly Father, how much I want this gift, right now! Please take me into Your kingdom of love as I accept Jesus Christ as my Lord and Savior!

You alone are capable of leading me, guiding me, loving me through infertility. You are my Creator God, Savior Son, Comforting Spirit. You are the reason I live, breathe, rejoice, and ache for Someone beyond myself.

I know that salvation is found in no one else but You, Jesus Christ, for there is no other name under heaven by which I must be saved. Your whole purpose in coming to our fallen earth has been to seek and save the lost. Thank You for seeking me.

In light of the sins I have committed, I struggle with believing I can be saved. But You have promised us that things impossible for us to accomplish are all possible with You. You have said that if I confess that Jesus is Lord and believe in my heart that You raised Him from the dead, I will be saved from death and will be promised an eternal home in heaven.

So, I accept that I am a complete mess—a sinner, full of wrongdoing, fraught with doubts, angry at myself, heartbroken at my selfishness. Please accept me, just as I am, through Your abundant grace and pardon. Empty me of myself; fill me back up to overflowing with the fountains of living water that will wash me white as snow.

As I believe in You, I know that You will fill me with an inexpressible and glorious joy, the end result of my faith and the salvation of my soul.

Bless me with Your peace, Your assurance, and Your delight as You carry me and hold my hand in the days and years ahead. In Jesus' wonderful name I pray, Amen.

(Acts 4:12; Luke 19:10; Matthew 19:25-26; Romans 10:9; 1 Peter 1:8-9)

FOR REFLECTION:

❖ Read Isaiah 9:6, John 1:1-18, 2 Peter 1:16-17, and 1 John 4:9-10. What words in these passages do you find that describe who Jesus is and what His character is like?

❖ Write a short "love letter" of your own to Jesus, asking Him to be your Savior, dedicating your life to Him, renewing your love for Him. Confess your sin and acknowledge that you are incapable of saving yourself. Thank Him for His gift of grace. Ask Him to show you how to follow Him in the days ahead.

❖ Think of someone else among your friends, family, and acquaintances who does not know Christ. Pray now for that person, for God to prepare his or her heart to hear the Good News about Jesus. Ask God to give you an unexpected opportunity to share His love with that person and talk about the reason for the joy in your own heart.

🍎 🍎 🍎

LAUREN'S STORY:

Four years of infertility, three miscarriages...that's my story. I have an autoimmune disease and have gone through a variety of medications, treatments, and diagnostic tests, anticipating laparoscopic surgery next.

The world sees infertility as the body's way of preventing overpopulation. But I feel inadequate to my husband and less of a woman. Without a support group, I feel left all alone.

Having children is a very strong desire of ours, so it's hard to deal with, especially knowing what the word of God tells us in Luke 1:37, that nothing is impossible with God. It's also difficult to read about Sarah, Hannah, Elizabeth, and all the other women of the Bible who have given us examples of their strong faith in hard times—God met their needs, why not mine? To stand on the truth of God's word and walk in faith, yet be realistic at the same time, is a very fine line to walk.

No one can walk this for you. This is between you and the Lord. You will *only* survive with God, continually running to Him and leaning on His word and promises. You *will* have bad days, but in those days come joy, character, a renewed hope, and an increased love in your relationship with Christ. To conceive is our desire, but a strong relationship with Christ and changing into His image is more profitable to us.

This walk is not easy. You cannot do it alone. You need Christ, and you need a wall of *true* Christians you can count on to constantly lift you up and point you to Christ in all of life's circumstances. If I didn't lean on Christ hundreds of times a day, I wouldn't make it.

Through infertility I have learned, like Paul, to be content when I have everything and when I have nothing...content to know only the love of God can only fill this void. I am joyful now, instead of being envious and jealous, when others get the blessings I desire. The fruits of the Holy Spirit come through me more strongly now. My faith is deeper for having been tested. I *know* now I will follow God, no matter what....

CHAPTER 4

The Blessing of Marriage

"This is my beloved, and this is my friend, O daughters of Jerusalem!" (Song of Solomon 5:16b)

"Many waters cannot quench love, nor can the floods drown it. If a man would give for love all the wealth of his house, it would be utterly despised." (Song of Solomon 8:7)

"Though one may be overpowered by another, two can withstand him. And a threefold cord is not quickly broken." (Ecclesiastes 4:12)

Remember when you first met your husband? How you felt on your wedding day? For most couples, those are giddy days. Finally, you've met someone with whom you completely connect. He is absolutely perfect for you.

Fast-forward to the present, and maybe you still feel a bit giddy about him occasionally...just not all the time. Marriage is a long road trip with ruts, bumps, fender benders, and oftentimes plain old grouchiness. It doesn't always feel like a blessing. There are times when it would be so easy to just give up.

Marriage at its best, though, is a companionship of purpose. It is designed and instituted by God for His plans—for a man and woman to work in harmony together to glorify Him, not themselves. A Christian marriage should reflect the unity of the Trinity and the mystery of the love between Christ and His church.

When was the last time you and your husband talked about your "marriage mission"? How do you think God has specifically designed your marriage to serve Him? Have you even thought about it?

You and your man got ready for a wedding, maybe made some career adjustments, talked about how many children you'd like to have, planned for where you wanted to live, maybe even started looking around at schools. You've dreamed together, played house together, traveled together, had lots of fun together. And now, it's time to grow your family, adding those adorable kids. They're going to be perfect!

But, what are you doing together to advance God's kingdom on earth? How has God given you talents and resources as a couple, not just for being parents, but for making a difference for His glory?

Maybe it's time for you and your husband to sit down and talk about being more than just parents. If you've felt God's call for you to become a mother and your guy is likewise led to be a father, that's a great calling. You're on your way to becoming godly parents who will nurture your children in the admonition of the Lord—your desire is to raise children who will follow Jesus.

And what if He's calling you to do more? Ask your husband to sit down with you and pray about your marriage as a mission. How would it be different? What would God want you to do if children never arrive?

Would you be saving money for a bigger home, or would you both work on building a home for a needy family? Would you spend your vacation at the beach or working in the yard, or would you travel overseas for a disaster relief trip? Would you go on a date to a restaurant or take a meal to a shut-in? Would you focus on the urgency to have children of your own, or would you take time to tutor side-by-side at a community center for inner-city youth?

None of these choices are bad...they are choices we make as couples every day. You may already be involved in a local or national ministry in separate organizations. Would you find greater satisfaction together by working in the same ministry?

The key is writing your very own marriage mission statement. Most organizations have some sort of mission statement, a motto that shapes their activities, plans, and purposes. They evolve, too, as time goes by.

Here's an example: "Our marriage will be centered around loving and serving Jesus Christ: spending time together in worship, prayer, leading others to Christ, working hand-in-hand at a Christian ministry and in our church, and leading our family to a growing faith."

Or, here's what my husband Mark came up with as a mission statement:

"A mutually loving, honoring relationship—respecting the husband, loving the wife. Working to meet each other's needs in a God-honoring way. Working together to support/encourage children and extended family. A will to negotiate and compromise in decision-making. To continue to the end."

When you define your marriage mission in terms of serving God, what happens? Having children may still be high on your to-do list, but it no longer becomes the top priority. Seeking God's will and advancing His kingdom becomes your primary goal as a couple. The pressure's off. Being parents could be only one of the ways you serve Him.

The amazing result is a tremendous blessing from God. If you are focused purely on waiting for God to send you children, you are missing out on His good gifts for you along with joy in your marriage.

Perhaps God is calling you both to step out of your comfort zone and do something dramatic. Some counselors refer to that as a BHAG—Big Holy Audacious Goal. Maybe God is calling you to do more than you think you can!

What if, though, your husband isn't a Christian? Or he's overcommitted to his work and only wants to rest when he gets home? What if he's unwilling to talk about a marriage mission? Would that make you feel robbed of the chance to serve God together?

If he really loves you, even a nonbeliever can't argue with your desire to spend some quality time with him. You and your husband need plenty of time for just chilling out together, taking walks, going on getaway trips, and celebrating what you have together.

You could always talk with your pastor or some Christian friends, asking them to invite you and your husband to be part of an evening or weekend service project. When your guy sees the joy of Christians working together in harmony and laughter, he might change his mind about serving others with you.

But that can be hard if you and your husband are experiencing conflicts about infertility or other issues. If you're struggling to simply get through the day without fighting or if the effort of holding your marriage together is exhausting, look for a Christian counselor to help both of you iron out disagreements.

God wants you to work on building a marriage with walls that shut out the noise from the world, walls that are strong from attacks by outsiders who seek to pull you two apart. The battles within marriage are difficult enough!

God planned marriage to be physically enjoyable, full of intimacy and bonding. Nurture your time with your husband in a way that makes you two stronger together as husband and wife than the sum of your separate activities.

Seek the blessing of God in your marriage. You and your spouse are a team that God has put together. God wants you to be "happy and holy," the way Adam and Eve were created. And even though we won't ever achieve it fully here on earth, we can definitely be happier and holier in loving Him together in our marriages.

What a blessing that will be, indeed!

PRAYER:

Father God, I praise You for creating the institution of marriage. I thank You for providing me with a husband (now, or perhaps in the future) and for pairing me with someone who will daily bless me or send me running to You in prayer, to follow You more closely. I bless You for being the Author of good marriages and the Perfecter of our faith in marriage. You are love.

Thank You for being the third strand in the marriage cord that binds my husband and me more tightly together. God, whether my marriage is strong today or in shambles, I invite You to come build up what is good and help repair whatever is broken.

I confess that I have not always laid our marriage on the sacrificial altar to You. Forgive me for times when I have viewed our marriage as a convenience or self-serving arrangement, not as a mission/ministry in service to You. Forgive me for trying to "fix" my husband or for pressing selfishly for my own way. I no longer have authority over my body, nor does my husband over his—we belong together and owe each other our allegiance and submission.

Bless my husband and me with Your presence. Bless us with time together that is calm, peaceful, and renewing. Bless us with a marriage that reflects the unity of Your own Trinity.

Show us how to nurture each other. Give us unexpected time, freed from responsibilities, that we can devote purely to our marriage. Build walls around us that will keep out worldly foes and attacks. Guard our marriage from the wiles of Satan; lead us not into his temptation because of lack of self-control. Help us to give to each other the affection that we owe to each other. Do not let us part ways, but reconcile us when we have conflicts. You have called us to peace.

Show us how to minister to others together. Make us a team that works together, not fighting over selfish whims but dedicated to sharing the same purpose in serving You. Broaden our vision for what we can achieve together with You and for You. Show us where and how You would have us to serve.

As my husband and I go to bed this evening, give us both a spirit of peace and joy in our marriage. Help us to leave anger, petty disputes, or selfish feelings outside of our bedroom. Sanctify our marriage bed and our daily work together for Your glory. Use us as partners for the advancement of Your kingdom. In Jesus' name, Amen.

(1 Corinthians 7:3-5,10-11,15b)

🍎 🍎 🍎

FOR REFLECTION:

❖ Write down a "mission statement" for your marriage. Ask your husband to do the same, separately from you. Then, come together and compare your thoughts. Edit the two approaches together in your discussion so that you both agree on how to best serve each other and God.

_____

_____

_____

❖ Remember (if you can!) some of the things you promised when you said your marriage vows to your husband. Write down one of those vows and ways you could live it out daily in your marriage.

_____

_____

_____

❖ Plan a date night at home or off-work day away with your man. Choose a place or activity where you will have the opportunity to talk and spend "quality" time together (for example, a walking tour or drive through the countryside instead of a movie). Set some ground rules: make discussion of having children, criticism, and negative words all off-limits. Use this time to simply get to know each other better. Write down ideas below for how you could arrange this.

_____

_____

_____

❦ ❦ ❦

DARCI'S STORY:

I knew from age 18 I had endometriosis. When I married at 29, we knew we could have some difficulty, so we began trying to get pregnant the first year. I had all the infertility testing, plus four laparoscopy surgeries with laser treatment (primarily for the pain). God miraculously provided for all of our medical expense on a very low salary. He used these experiences—the tests, financial struggles, pain of surgery, etc.—to draw us closer to each other, too.

We adopted Brooke after four and half years of marriage. Then I became pregnant with Renee a year later, and then we had Zachary after nine years of marriage. We had hoped to have more. That wasn't God's plan.

From the beginning, Cody and I felt called to be very open about our infertility situation. Not everyone can or necessarily should be that way—but we felt led to do so. We headed off a lot of problem conversations by being so open. We took the initiative to share with others, which helped them to be more comfortable around us. We have learned to ask others in hard situations what is helpful and what is not helpful. Infertility became an opportunity for outreach to others—who in turn have ministered to us. You can learn from others as they share their difficulties. Most are eager to open up.

It's also good to remember that infertility is not the only "hard" situation. Cody and I poured ourselves into ministry and found that the Lord gave us a real love for singles. They so long to marry—we have that blessing, they don't. It helps one see things in perspective. So many others have more difficult situations than we do. It's important to keep your focus on what God *has* given, not on what He has *not* given.

CHAPTER 5

The Joy of Having Children

"Then Elkanah her husband said to her, "Hannah, why do you weep? Why do you not eat? And why is your heart grieved? Am I not better to you than ten sons?" (1 Samuel 1:8)

"But we were gentle among you, just as a nursing mother cherishes her own children." (1 Thessalonians 2:7)

Do you ever feel guilty about wanting a child so badly? Are there moments when you feel that God isn't giving you children because it's such a selfish wish?

First of all, there's nothing wrong with wanting a child. We have God's specific commandment in Genesis 1 to be fruitful and multiply, and God has planted that desire firmly in our hearts. Otherwise, there'd be no future for the human race!

We women grow up playing with baby dolls and cuddling stuffed animals. Then somewhere in our child-bearing years, the desire to be a mother can kick in pretty strong. We're uniquely programmed to conceive, give birth and to have maternal instincts—they're not just reserved for the lesser animals on our planet. And while men can desire children, too, there's a deeper emotional level for us because it's part of our DNA, our chemical responses, and our cultural upbringing.

And who doesn't like the thought of having a sweet child to cuddle, feed, bathe, dress up, kiss, show off, and play with? Never mind the realities of sleepless nights, spit-up soaked shirts, poopy diapers, colic, fevers, endless crying. We are fired up and ready to get busy in motherhood.

So, let's look at some of the "selfish" joys of parenthood, according to the Bible.

First, children are a reward from God. But it's not because of anything we've done to deserve them. He gives us the beautiful gift of children because we are His children first. Our children become His children, too.

If you have been called by Jesus Christ to love Him, trust Him, and serve Him, you can be assured that you are among God's "very own people."

King David decides to build a temple for God's ark of the covenant, which is still housed in the tabernacle tent at that time. But when he hears from the prophet Nathan that God doesn't want him to build the temple but simply prepare for it, David goes into the tent and sits down before the ark. Like a child before a loving parent, David ponders how the amazing God of the universe would stoop to care for him.

"For You have made Your people Israel Your very own people forever; and You, Lord, have become their God." (2 Samuel 7:24) David sees that God's people are His forever, and your children—if they accept Jesus Christ, too—will become part of that continuing heritage. What an incredible joy that will be!

Along those lines, children are greatly to be desired because they are the pinnacle of all of God's good gifts to us. He is our Jehovah Jirah, our Provider for what we need—our daily bread, clothing, shelter, work, health.

And He is also the Father of Lights—*"Every good gift and every perfect gift is from above, and comes down from the Father of lights, with whom there is no variation or shadow of turning. Of His own will He brought us forth by the word of truth, that we might be a kind of firstfruits of His creatures." (James 1:17-18)*

Jesus, as God's Son in human form, explains how His Heavenly Father gives good gifts to His children.

"Ask, and it will be given to you; seek, and you will find; knock, and it will be opened to you. For everyone who asks receives, and he who seeks finds, and to him who knocks it will be opened. Or what man is there among you who, if his son asks for bread, will give him a stone? Or if he asks for a fish, will he give him a serpent? If you then, being evil, know how to give good gifts to your children, how much more will your Father who is in heaven give good things to those who ask Him!" (Matthew 7:7-11)

It isn't wrong to want God's good gifts or to ask for them...it is the right thing to do, and He commands us to ask, seek, knock. It is never selfish when we ask God to bless us with gifts that will draw us closer to Him, that will cause us to serve Him and seek His counsel, that will drive us more often to our knees before Him, that will give us constant obligation to praise and thank Him. Children will do all of those things.

We must always ask, however, in light of His will. When we submit ourselves completely to His plans for us, He sometimes gives us closed doors...or He gives us doors to open that we weren't expecting. He also gives us the right heart for parenting, as a means of serving Him and not ourselves.

Jesus Christ's great commission to us is to go and make disciples of all nations...teaching them to observe all that He commanded us. We could certainly start in our own homes with our own children. But if that's not an option, you could always lead other children in love by telling them about God's good news.

In a final caveat, however, you must beware of the dangers of idolatry. When wanting a child becomes so all important that it consumes your life, you have transformed a good desire from God into idolatrous worship of something else.

Satan, the author of lies, is highly effective at twisting our healthy desires away from God toward his crafty purposes. To avoid his devilish traps, keep your eyes focused on your Heavenly Father. As David did, go in and sit before God's presence in prayer. Talk with Him, pour your heart out before Him, rest in His loving arms. Place your desires before Him, and ask Him to funnel your own will into His perfect will for you.

Ask, seek, knock. He is waiting for you, ready to bestow His good gifts upon you.

PRAYER:

O Holy Father, You are indeed the Father of Lights, in Whom no secret is hidden. I praise You for Your generous spirit, for being our Jehovah Jirah Provider. I love You for who You are, my Father who seeks only my good.

Jesus, prompt me to ask, seek, knock on God's heavenly door; but give me Your Holy Spirit of faith, that I may trust in Your perfect will...wisdom, that I may be prudent in asking for the right things...patience, that I may wait for what is best...love, that I may be generous to others.

If You desire for us to be parents, please let my husband and me receive Your heritage of children and rejoice in them as Your gifts. Let us never take our children for granted...they are precious jewels in Your sight.

Jesus, let me have a cup of Your living water today, recognizing that You have already given me many blessings. Fill me up with thanksgiving, that I may focus on all the good in my life and regard the cup as overflowing, not half empty with infertility.

Change my desires so that I will seek You for my life instead of Your gifts. Tune my heartstrings to the chords of praise that resonate with Your own song of love over me. Let me rest in Your loving arms, content and trusting that You, the Father of Lights, will provide gifts that are good and perfect for me...in Your timing.

I ask that, if You make me a mother of children, You will provide me with the love, patience, and desire to raise them as Jesus-followers, too. Remove all idolatry from my heart.

If it is not in Your plans for me to become a mother, please work in my heart to accept this, come to peace with it, and find my joy in You. Let my resolve to praise You in everything be unwavering. In Your Son's name I pray, Amen.

(Ecclesiastes 5:19; John 4:10; Psalm 23:5)

FOR REFLECTION:

❖ Examine your heart before the Lord; make a list of three reasons why you strongly desire to have children (there are no good or bad answers). Take each reason before Him in prayer, asking Him to bring your heart into submission to His will.

_____

_____

_____

❖ Read Proverbs 22:6 and Ephesians 6:4. What do those verses require of parents? How does that affect your purpose in having children?

_____

_____

_____

❖ Satan likes to drive a wedge between us and God through our sins, idolatry, and doubts. Read 1 Timothy 2:8 and James 1:6. How does doubting God's ability or His will for your life steer you off-course in your prayers? How does trusting God's plans keep you grounded?

_____

_____

_____

CATELYN'S STORY:

My letter to a friend whose long-awaited adoption fell through at the last second:

Dear Molly,

When I see you in passing by, there's never a time or place to talk. I've wanted to tell you how I ache for your loss and disappointment with the baby. I can't begin to imagine how you guys must have felt or the grief you have experienced and continue to experience. This parenting stuff can be heart-breaking.

I don't know if you knew our story (it continues to be in progress). Our first child came very easily, and the pregnancy was uneventful. Since we were getting older, we "decided" (ha!) to have another fairly quickly. After a year and a half, we sought medical advice. They couldn't find much wrong with either of us, but we started treatment anyway. Again, no pregnancy.

Everyone was asking (it seemed to be daily), "So when are you guys gonna have number two? You're not getting any younger...." "You don't want Jud to be an only child, do you?"

The frustration mounted. Then, the last year there were two pregnancies and two miscarriages. There was no answer to the "whys" that plagued us. We could only trust God. And it was amazing to us how God was *with* us and never left us! (We believe He hurt, too.)

After the second one (ectopic), I felt bad for five weeks...it was hot, and I felt gross and sad. But when my health returned, I remembered experiencing life and joy in a heightened way. We went camping a lot, and I really saw the stars, the clear water, the sun, the evergreens. It was like God gave me *more* life in the losses. I realized how very precious life is, and I looked at my loved ones differently. No, I didn't have "number two," but I wanted to stop looking at what I didn't have and enjoy the gifts I had—*for the day*. My contentment increased, even though there was still a longing inside. God knew my ache, but He was teaching me to enjoy the grace He had given in the here and now.

Not long ago, my doctor suggested a blood test to see if the miscarriages were related to an inability to carry. The tests came back negative, indicating they just happened for all the reasons they happen. At that point, Will and I decided we couldn't *do* anything else...that if God wanted to give us another, it would just have to happen. And He did provide!

This pregnancy has been so different for us—no home tests or rushing to the doctor...no telling the world...just a quiet "thank you" to God each day and many prayers to deal with our ever-present fear of loss right now. And we continue to wait on God.

CHAPTER 6

Unfulfilled...Finding Peace in Prayer

"And she [Hannah] was in bitterness of soul, and prayed to the Lord and wept in anguish." (1 Samuel 1:10)

"But as it is written: 'Eye has not seen, nor ear heard, nor have entered into the heart of man the things which God has prepared for those who love Him.'" (1 Corinthians 2:9)

Many Christian women experiencing infertility turn to the story of Hannah and her predicament...what a great story of hope! It's an extraordinary passage in its emphasis on a woman of faith and perseverance in the fervency of prayer. God answers her, but there is a price to pay for her vow.

Read 1 Samuel 1:1-18, then let's see what we can learn from Hannah.

Hannah's infertility is an issue with multiple ramifications. She lives in a time when childlessness is seen as a curse upon her. Other women might shun someone so obviously cursed by God, lest the curse spread to them as well.

The "barren womb" is a slow-acting social poison, and only one other woman in the Bible—the one with the constant flow of blood, healed by Christ—is worse off in her position within polite society. Hannah hurts from the inside out.

Not only does she experience the pain of being less acceptable and the sorrow of being childless, she is hounded by the nearest other woman, Peninah. Her husband Elkanah has two wives, and Peninah has the satisfaction of bearing him children.

My sister-in-law K. B. Ballentine is a talented poet who wrote of the childless woman surrounded by mothers:

"Other women were made to mother
arms held open at the door
cookie dough ready to heat and serve...

I can sterilize the bathroom and the bath
pack toys and stiff blankets into tiny boxes
listen to the crooning radio

There are no days to honor me
no groups to join with tales to tell
no hands reaching out, no voices calling"[1]

Peninah is described as Hannah's "rival." When she sees that Elkanah loves Hannah a bit more than he loves her, she doesn't miss an opportunity to remind Hannah that she is the fertile one. Peninah makes Hannah's life doubly miserable.

Hannah has some consolation in that Elkanah treats her admirably and tenderly. It isn't enough, though, to counter the weight of her burden; perhaps this makes things worse because she cannot repay his kindness by giving him children.

Year after year, the entire family goes up to the tabernacle at Shiloh, the house of the Lord before the temple was built in Jerusalem. On the way, Peninah goads Hannah with incessant verbal jabs, making Hannah tearful and unable to eat.

After the others have finished their dinner, Hannah slips away to go to the shrine, a place where she can speak directly to God in prayer, trusting that He is present there with her.

When Hannah prays, her heart is full of torment. She cries out to God silently, teardrops streaming down her face. She moves her lips, but her words are inaudible. She has pleaded with God for years, but this time she approaches the Lord of Hosts in complete humility, as His maidservant, and vows that if God will give her a son, she will give him to the Lord for all the days of his life.

This is a staggering vow. Hannah wants a child so badly that she is willing to keep him for only a short time before giving him away for good. She is desperate, begging God to simply give her a few crumbs of time with her baby for the privilege of bearing her husband a child. She does not dare pray this aloud, because her husband could make her vow legally null and void if he heard it...and no man at that time would see the point in giving up a son.

To add insult to injury, the Shiloh priest Eli sees Hannah's lips moving and her discomposure. He thinks she's drunk, and he flippantly criticizes her, heaping salt upon her raw wounds. Hannah has pretty much hit rock bottom.

How long have you carried the burden of infertility in silence? For Hannah, it has been years. You may have endured this a long time, too. You bear the scars of careless words from other highly fertile women. You know the deep bitterness of soul...the despair of unanswered prayers, the silence from heaven...the compounded injury of not being able to return your husband's love with the gift of a child.

What can you learn from Hannah in the midst of misery? First, Hannah shows a remarkable capacity for meekness. Centuries before Jesus Christ would utter His Beatitudes, blessing the meek and promising them an inheritance of the earth, Hannah displays the same kinds of genuine, godly humility. She suffers without complaint.

There is no indication in the passage that Hannah lashes back at Peninah, who seems to be a first-class bully in the method women handle best—with malicious words. Hannah perseveres, without letting a prideful ego create further strife in the household. She doesn't counter the jabs with her own assertions that Elkanah loves her more...she doesn't try to one-up Peninah.

Second, Hannah is sorrowful in prayer to the point of fasting. This isn't the same, perhaps, as intentional fasting, but it indicates the sincerity of her prayers. She does not appear to be angry at God, only grief-stricken in view of her plight. She neither eats nor rests until she has laid her burden at the feet of the Lord.

Third, Hannah takes her problems directly to the Lord. She appeals not for release from the taunts of Peninah or for a curse upon this woman for those catty remarks, but Hannah gets straight to the point. She pleads with God, "Please remember me." She bows herself before the Lord of heaven as a slave before her master, begging for mercy. She doesn't want God to forget her.

Does God hear our prayers? The truth is that God does hear our prayers. Scripture affirms this over and over in many places, but in this particular passage, Eli is the one who affirms this truth to Hannah.

After she humbly defends herself against Eli's insensitive remarks, declaring she isn't drunk but has poured out her abundant complaint and grief before the Lord, Eli turns around. For one moment in his career, Eli serves as a comforter to Hannah. He commands her to go in peace and pronounces a blessing upon her, calling upon God to answer her prayer.

Finally, Hannah trusts that God will answer her prayers. She has persevered in praying. She leaves the shrine and goes back to the feast to eat, her face no longer sad. At the end of her distressed prayers with God and the encouragement she receives from Eli, Hannah is indeed at peace. She goes back to her difficult situation with the rest of the family. You have the impression that she is no longer bowed down under the weight of her burden but standing tall in the confidence that God hears her.

We'll look at Hannah again in the next chapter, but think for a moment about what Hannah is teaching us.

Can you look at your own infertility situation with true humility? Can you let the careless comments of others go without rebuttal or without making excuses?

Have you taken your requests directly to God? Have you physically gone down on your knees in prayer? Have you fasted along with your prayers? Have you and your husband joined hands in praying and fasting together?

C.S. Lewis observed grief up close and personal in the losses of his life. He wrote, "If you've been up all night and cried till you have no more tears left in you—you will know there comes in the end a sort of quietness."[2]

Have you walked away from your tears and prayers with a deeper trust in God? When the darkness of night begins to fade in the rising of dawn, look for Jesus with you. Rejoice in His love. Claim His promises of His peace that He has left for you. Trust His plans. Like Hannah, go back to the life you know. And wait...for God to show you how He answers prayer in His way, in His timing.

🍒 🍒 🍒

PRAYER:

Dear God, I praise You for being the God who hears. You, the God of our fathers, have said, "I have heard your prayer, I have seen your tears; surely I will heal you." Please, recall that promise from Your Scriptures, and consider my plight.

You have promised to hear my prayers, so I trust that You will fulfill Your good plans for me, according to Your will and Your timing. Let me be like Your Son, Jesus, who, in the days of His earthly life, when He had offered up prayers and supplications, with vehement cries and tears to You, learned obedience by the things which He suffered. As I suffer, Lord, hear my cries, too...yet teach me over and over to obey You.

Even though I weep and lament, I pray that You will turn my sorrow into joy. Hear, from Your dwelling place in heaven, my prayers and supplications, and forgive me when I sin against You.

Father, do not forget me. Help me through my times of unbelief, and help me to be Your maidservant in all that I do. Walk with me through the valley of misery, and hold my hand. Be my Vision, my Comforter, my Confidence. In Jesus' name, Amen.

(2 Kings 20:5; Hebrews 5:7-8; John 16:20; 2 Chronicles 6:39)

❦ ❦ ❦

FOR REFLECTION:

❖ What inspires you about Hannah's story? How can you implement her same ways of dealing with this struggle in your own life?

_____
_____
_____
_____

❖ Read Psalm 34:17 and Psalm 69:33. How do these reassure you that God hears your prayers?

_____
_____
_____
_____

❖ How have times changed for women over the centuries? What social pressures do you face now, in general? Do you currently face any peer pressures over your infertility? If so, write a prayer that God will help you overcome stressful situations with His courage and peace.

_____
_____
_____
_____

❦ ❦ ❦

JADE'S STORY:

My infertility process was full of self-pity. Baby showers were tough…birth announcements from friends having the third kid were excruciating!

Nosy relatives and friends had all kinds of things to say. We learned to laugh at this, but it was rarely fun to experience the questions: "Why don't y'all have any kids yet?" "When are y'all gonna figure out where babies come from?"

I used to have a collection of "advice" magazine/newspaper articles people would send me out of the blue—things like, "Don't eat chocolate," "Briefs cause infertility in men (as in, he better wear boxer shorts!)," and all sorts of hilarious junk I wish I still had.

The only method I had for coping was prayer. How did God use this? He pointed me to an extended study of the sovereignty of God and thereby formed in my soul a deep trust in Him. He used the Word to teach several things:

Infertility is an example of a fiery dart from the evil one, and I was challenged to lift the shield of faith (*Ephesians 6:16*). I lifted the shield in several ways by putting myself in circumstances where I would be around children. I taught children's church for a year and did a weekly songtime/Bible lesson at the daycare across the street. I felt I kept a realistic look at children by being around them. Also, to truly rejoice at baby showers, I started giving them! I signed up at the church to be the person who did this.

One month I complained to the Lord that I was "caught" in a monthly cycle that felt like bondage—*something He had set up!* Then I read a passage in Zephaniah 3:18 that I took as a promise: "*I will gather those who sorrow over the appointed assembly, who are among you, to whom its reproach is a burden.*" I felt He had spoken that He would take away the burden of infertility—I didn't take it as a promise for kids, but that He knew the load I was carrying and would grant me peace in the midst of the storm.

CHAPTER 7

Seeking God in the Pit of Despair

"And Hannah prayed and said: 'My heart rejoices in the Lord; my horn is exalted in the Lord. I smile at my enemies, because I rejoice in Your salvation.'" (1 Samuel 2:1)

"I waited patiently for the Lord; and He inclined to me, and heard my cry. He also brought me up out of a horrible pit, out of the miry clay, and set my feet upon a rock, and established my steps. He has put a new song in my mouth— praise to our God; many will see it and fear, and will trust in the Lord." (Psalm 40:1-3)

"Let not the floodwater overflow me, nor let the deep swallow me up; and let not the pit shut its mouth on me." (Psalm 69:15)

Have you found yourself in the "pit of despair"? Do you feel as if you've been pinned down and had years of your life sucked away, much like the hero Westley in the 1980s movie, *The Princess Bride*?

Or maybe you're slogging along in the Slough of Despond. That's from one of the greatest books of all time, *The Pilgrim's Progress*, by John

Bunyan.* On his journey of faith, the central character, Christian, is a new convert who falls into a miry bog:

> "This miry Slough is such a place as cannot be mended; it is the descent whither the scum and filth that attends conviction for sin doth continually run, and therefore is it called the Slough of Despond: for still as the sinner is awakened about his lost condition, there ariseth in his soul many fears, and doubts, and discouraging apprehensions, which all of them get together, and settle in this place; and this is the reason of the badness of this ground."[1]

Christian tumbles through the mud, "grievously bedaubed with the dirt," and cannot get out because of his burden of sin. He is finally plucked out of the mire by Help, a friend who comes along at the right moment.

When our plans for having children are frustrated, we are caught in the same muddy mess. Our feet no longer run swiftly to joy. We plod through our work and daily activities, burdened with the weight of despondency. Our situation may look hopeless. We turn away from our friends, our family, our husbands...we turn away from God.

Or we can turn to Him. He has kept our tears in His bottle, and He has not forgotten us. In fact, He is trying to get our attention. As C. S. Lewis said, "God whispers to us in our pleasures, speaks in our consciences, but shouts in our pains. It is His megaphone to rouse a deaf world."[2]

Author Heather Holleman described despair as the complete loss of hope. "It's a haunting feeling that you're trapped and that something is irreversibly, permanently lost," Holleman observed in her book, *Guarded by Christ*. "It's a mired down, quicksand feeling that you're sinking into an abyss of regret and loss....

"It's an indescribable, suffocating, unseen pain. It's a kind of wrongness inside, an estrangement from yourself, and a colorless void....Everything hurts, both inside and out. And the worst part is that you can't imagine any relief."

Holleman went on to give practical, spiritual ways to "open the window" from despair into delight. She learned to trust and seek Jesus, the One who "binds up our broken hearts, frees us from darkness, comforts us, provides for us, gives us beauty in places of ruin, and pours out joy."[3]

From many millennia earlier, we find a similar personal experience in Scripture.

Let's look back at Hannah's response to despair. Read 1 Samuel 1:19-2:11. We find that Hannah goes back to the shrine in the morning to worship and back to normal living in her dysfunctional household. And what happens? *The Lord remembers her.*

Hannah conceives, bears a son, and names him Samuel, because she has "asked for him from the Lord." The name Samuel means "heard by God."

Can you imagine Hannah's incredible joy? It is tinged, however, with the realization that she must make an excruciating decision—does she keep her sacrificial vow to release her firstborn to the Lord's service, or does she keep this precious baby all to herself?

Hannah remains true to her word, and she bravely tells Elkanah that Samuel is meant to serve before the Lord forever. Surprisingly, Elkanah assents to her wishes and tells her to do what seems best to her, as long as the Lord confirms this decision.

After just a few blissful years, Hannah weans Samuel and fulfills her vow. She and Elkanah take Samuel and sacrificial animals to Eli, where Hannah reminds the priest that she is the one who had prayed there. "For this child I prayed," she says, "and the Lord has granted me my petition which I asked of Him." She lends Samuel to the Lord for as long as the boy lives.

Oh, my...could you do that? After receiving the gift she had sought from God for so long, Hannah gives it away. She releases Samuel into the Lord's hands. Can you imagine walking away from the shrine, seeing your little boy holding Eli's fat hand, knowing this priceless child will never return to your home? It would be unbelievably gut-wrenching. And there are no guarantees that Hannah will ever have other children to replace Samuel.

It would be so easy for Hannah to fall back into that Slough of Despond. Her story should be followed by painful and anguished declarations before God, her regrets, a new abundance of tears.

Instead, what follows is a beautiful soliloquy: Hannah's prayer of praise, thanksgiving, acceptance. Her obedient response foreshadows the "Magnificat" song of praise by Mary, who tells of God's incredible strength, mercy, and provision after discovering she will become the mother of Christ.

"My heart rejoices in the Lord...I rejoice in Your salvation," Hannah says. "No one is holy like the Lord, for there is none besides You, nor is there any rock like our God" (1 Samuel 2:1-2).

Hannah's entire focus is on the Lord. She sees herself not as a mother bereft of her little boy but as a woman who is in the hands of a mighty God. "Even the barren has borne seven," she says, a number representing completeness for her in the birth of her only child.

Hannah has been made alive out of death, made rich out of her poverty, raised from the dust and ash heap. She is a beggar who has been set among princes to inherit the throne of glory. She recognizes that it is all the Lord's doing.

The story could end there, but we find that God smiles upon Hannah and rewards her faithfulness. As Hannah returns year by year to the sacrifice at Shiloh with Elkanah, she is able to see Samuel and each time bring him a little robe that she makes for him as he grows. Eli blesses the couple with a prayer that the Lord will give them more children in return. Eli's prayer is fulfilled: Elkanah and Hannah have three more sons and two daughters.

What becomes of Samuel? He grows in stature and in favor with both the Lord and men. He becomes a mighty prophet, anointing King Saul and then King David. He is a forerunner of Jesus Christ who will grow up in the same way, dedicated to God's service. Hannah's commitment and submissive sacrifice become God's way of blessing the people of Israel.

When you find yourself in the doldrums of infertility, go back and read Hannah's prayer aloud. Follow her example. Begin with praising God for who He is, what He has accomplished, and what He will do. Give thanks for His holiness, His unchanging love, His power, His blessings. Ask Him to give you strength and to anoint you with His integrity.

Promise God that, if He bestows children upon you, you will turn them over to Him every day of their lives. Recognize that they are always His first and that as a mother you are merely a steward of them for a brief time.

Then, dry your tears, face the day, and go in His grace. Just as King David did as he pleaded with God to lead and guide him, declare to your Holy Father that He is your rock and fortress...proclaim in praise to Him, *"For You are my strength. Into Your hand I commit my spirit; You have redeemed me, O Lord God of truth." (Psalm 31:4b-5)*

He will pluck you from the Slough of Despond. He will always walk with you.

PRAYER:

Heavenly Father, I praise You for who You are—the God of knowledge, who breaks down and builds up. I praise You for what You have accomplished and what You will do. I thank You for Your unchanging love for me, Your power over me, Your blessings to me.

My heart rejoices in You; I smile at my enemies and my affliction because I rejoice in Your salvation. No one is holy like You...You are my Rock, the God of knowledge, and You weigh my actions.

You strengthen those who stumble, fill the hungry, and give completeness to infertile women. You reign over life and death, You bring down and You lift up, You make poor and make rich. Please lift me up when I am poor in spirit and sitting in ashes, and set me in high places to inherit Your riches of grace and peace.

You who created our world will guard the feet of Your saints and silence the wicked in darkness. You break Your adversaries in pieces and thunder against them from heaven. O Great Lord, give me strength and build me up...hear my prayer.

Let all those who seek You rejoice and be glad in You; let such as love Your salvation say continually, "The Lord be magnified!" I am poor and needy, and yet You think of me. You are my help and my deliverer; do not delay, O my God.

Make me a Hannah in my faith, trust, and hope in You. Make me Your maidservant, ready to humbly serve You at all times. If You bless me with children, help me to trust You with them, all the days of their lives. Let me rest in You. In Jesus' name, Amen.

(1 Samuel 2:1-10; Psalm 40:16-17)

*Author's note: *The Pilgrim's Progress* is a wonderful allegory of the Christian life, and if you've never read it, pick it up when you're done with this study. There are modern translations that make it easy to read, but the old English original version is delightful, too.

❦ ❦ ❦

FOR REFLECTION:

❖ Read Hannah's prayer and vow again in 1 Samuel 1:11. Do you think you could give up your first-born child to go work in a temple for the Lord? It's an admirable thought, but do you think you could do the same? Why or why not?

_____

_____

_____

_____

❖ Read verses 1-3 of Psalm 40 again at the beginning of this chapter. For what purpose does God pull us out of the miry pit?

_____

_____

_____

_____

❖ Think of a time in the past (or right now) when you have found yourself in a miry bog. If in the past, write a thankful prayer to God for bringing you out of it. If you are in a Slough of Despond right now, ask God to pull you out of it or send His agent (a friend?) to help lift you up.

🐞 🐞 🐞
NATALIE'S STORY (CONTINUED FROM CHAPTER 1):

Although the circumstances leading up to my situation are different from most infertile women, the emotional distress is not. There have been too many hardships to list. However, the feeling of inadequacy, that my body failed me, and ultimately, that God in some way failed me have been the underlying root of all my pain. My intense envy of pregnant women crippled my ability to pray or to spiritually grow for a long time. I now realize that my envy and jealousy stemmed from feeling like less of a woman. God has truly comforted me and shown me how Evan and I will be incredibly blessed through adoption.

Evan and I coped with our situation with prayer, prayer, and more prayer. I am blessed to have a husband who is thankful for WHO I am—not what I can do. He has never encouraged my negative feelings but has done his best to comfort me; Evan has been faithful to remind me that he would much rather have me with no children than to not have me at all. Through prayer and time, God has healed our pain by giving us the overwhelming desire to adopt a baby.

Our focus is not on what we can't have but on what we can do to make our dream of having children happen. We pray for financial discipline, for God's timing, and our patience in waiting for His timing, and we pray for the decisions and spiritual growth of our baby's birth parents. This has made the decision to adopt our preference rather than a second choice. Also, about a year ago, a couple from our church asked Evan and me to be the godparents of their two precious children. Evan and I were completely impatient for God's timing in our adoption plans, so these children have been an answer to prayer for us.

In the first years after my tubal, my response to insensitive people was completely wrong. People say things like, "Be glad that you can't get pregnant." "You can always adopt (this used to hurt a lot more than it does now)." "When are you and Evan going to start a family?" or "When you breast feed your baby...." Often, my eyes would well up with tears, or I would just walk out of the room, or I might reply that "I can't have a baby." It is still painful that people are insensitive, but I am much better at holding my tongue. I realize that most people are not trying to be insensitive—they don't know. I try to remind myself that I, too, have unintentionally hurt others. It is still painful, but the passage of time has made it possible for me to move past it more quickly.

God has blessed me with a loving, faithful, patient husband who shares my excitement for adopting a baby. The void of not being able to carry a child inside me has been filled by the joy of knowing that God has created another woman somewhere to carry her baby for me, a baby she may allow Evan and me to love and raise in her place.

CHAPTER 8

The Shame Game

"The sacrifices of God are a broken spirit, a broken and a contrite heart—these, O God, You will not despise." (Psalm 51:17)

"Do not fear, for you will not be ashamed; neither be disgraced, for you will not be put to shame; for you will forget the shame of your youth...." (Isaiah 54:4a)

"Blessed is he whose transgression is forgiven, whose sin is covered. Blessed is the man to whom the Lord does not impute iniquity, and in whose spirit there is no deceit. When I kept silent, my bones grew old through my groaning all the day long. For day and night Your hand was heavy upon me; my vitality was turned into the drought of summer. Selah. I acknowledged my sin to You, and my iniquity I have not hidden. I said, 'I will confess my transgressions to the Lord,' and You forgave the iniquity of my sin. Selah." (Psalm 32:1-5)

What if you're "damaged goods"?

In the second season of the wildly popular television series, *Downton Abbey*, Lady Mary knows she has to confess to her beloved Matthew that she has already engaged in sexual activity. "I have fallen," she admits, shaking her head. "I am impure."[1]

Her previous sexual liaison, scandalous by Edwardian era standards, has forced her to the brink of an unloving marriage to another man. But Matthew is willing to turn his back on her past—and his own—in order to look forward to their own happiness together.

You may have married your husband under those very circumstances. It's also possible that you're worried about your own past and its effects on your infertility.

That past abortion or several abortions may have scarred your reproductive organs. Perhaps a sexually transmitted disease has worked its havoc on the delicate structure where life is created…in you or in your husband. A birth control device to prevent pregnancy before you were married has decreased your fertility.

Maybe it was a single affair. Or your first experimentation with sex. Or a bunch of former lovers in the mix. Or even sexual abuse.

Maybe it wasn't a big problem at the time. You were enjoying what you felt was a natural pursuit in life, the pleasures of sexual activity in a single life. You kept yourself from getting pregnant, or you took care of the inconvenience if you did. You were just keeping pace with everyone else. Or you were hiding the truth from yourself and others about past abuse.

Now, you're not so sure that freestyle sex was a good thing. Instead of being a happy participant in the freedom of the sexual revolution, you are one of its casualties. Instead of keeping an abusive situation buried, you have seen it exposed as a rotting corpse from your memory.

The vultures of past sins—yours or someone else's—have now come home to roost.

So, let's name this feeling that has swept over you like chills during a horror show—it's called shame. Wherever you find shame, Satan has been there. He has had you right where he wanted you, and now he's laughing with gleeful derision. Extra-marital sex, abortion, sexual abuse, and their prevalence in our culture are among the devil's finest achievements.

When infertility arises from misconduct of the past, the sorrow can be unbearable. You can blame yourself or blame your husband. You can blame the lovers of your past or blame the media culture—especially magazines and movies that extol the virtues of promiscuous sex. You can blame your home background or an abuser. You can even blame God or His church for letting you down.

I encourage you, though, to place the blame squarely on its source—the sinful nature of mankind and its origin in Satan. We are all fallen creatures, including us as daughters of Eve who have inherited our proclivity toward sin from her. When God gave His top ten commandments to Moses, He put adultery right after murder in His list of "do-nots." God ordered our lives around marital faithfulness, which included reserving sex until marriage between a man and a woman.

Neil T. Anderson said an emotional by-product of sin is shame as well as hiding from the truth: "Before Adam and Eve disobeyed God they were naked and unashamed *(Genesis 2:25)*. God created them as sexual beings....When they sinned, however, they were ashamed to be naked and they had to cover up *(Genesis 3:7)*. Many people mask the inner self for fear that others may find out what is really going on inside. When dominated by guilt and shame, self-disclosure is not likely to happen."[2]

As the adage goes, sin takes us further than we intended to go, keeps us longer than we intended to stay, and costs more than we intended to pay. There are always consequences to sin, either immediately or long-term. God does not always protect us from the earthly penalties we must pay, whether inflicted upon us by others or by ourselves.

King David was no exception. Read his gut-wrenching story in 2 Samuel 11:1 through 12:23.

This man after God's own heart—the king of everything, the victorious ruler at the height of God's blessings, husband already to a harem of beautiful wives—commits a lowlife sin. He sleeps with the wife of his loyal warrior, Uriah, and gets her pregnant. Then David arranges to have the poor guy killed in battle to cover up the sin.

It's an ugly story with an ugly ending. The son whom David and Bathsheba conceived together is struck by God in punishment for David's sin.

David knows from the moment this royal prince is born that the young child is doomed to die. Nathan, David's personal prophet, has already revealed it to him from God. In a brazen display of courage, Nathan confronts David after Uriah's death with an accusation from God.

Instead of sending Nathan to the dungeon, however, David finds himself experiencing an emotion that is new to him: shame. His response is a remarkable, simple, humble statement—"I have sinned against the Lord." One imagines that it is uttered in a trembling whisper.

David recognizes that his sin, initially against Bathsheba and Uriah, is really a rebellion against God's commands. The Lord who has blessed him so richly has been disregarded for a one-night stand and a casual murder.

When the babe becomes ill, David pleads with God. He refuses to eat and lies all night on the ground. It's no good. David's sin ends in his son's death. Bathsheba, the compromised woman, is now bereft of both her first husband and her child.

What about Bathsheba? The Bible doesn't give us any indication about her feelings during this time. Was she complicit in the affair? Women didn't have any real rights at this time, and the king was *king*...whatever he wanted, he could have. She might have been dragged up to his chambers against her will.

Whether she had ulterior motives or an inability to refuse the king, Bathsheba has to watch as her first husband and then her son both die. On top of that, all the palace staff—and consequently, the entire community—know that Bathsheba is a fallen woman. She wears the badge of an adulterated woman and would be avoided by all the other wives. She falls under the burden of shame.

We don't know about her faith in God, but He does not forget Bathsheba. As David repents, he does not reject his new wife Bathsheba but comforts her instead. God blesses their union with the birth of another son: Solomon, a child who would grow up with great wisdom. We know that God loved Solomon because He sent word by Nathan, who called the baby Jedidiah, "Beloved of the Lord." God has covered Bathsheba's shame by giving her a son who will be loved by Him, much as He has loved Solomon's father David. Perhaps she will be accepted by others, too, over time as Solomon grows to become the new king.

Are you weighed down by a burden of shame? Take heart...even if there is no foreseeable cure for your infertility, there is a remedy for shame: God's forgiveness and unconditional love.

Treatment begins with prayer. Start with adoration, once again praising God for who He is. Then, the most difficult part is also the most redeeming—confess your sins to the One who created you and ask for His forgiveness, not only for yourself but for anyone who has wronged you. This calls for genuine sorrow over your past indiscretions as well as genuine forgiveness of others.

God loves these prayers, and as you turn your heart toward Him, thanksgiving to Him wells up naturally as an automatic response in your soul. He is the God who forgives when our hearts are laid bare before Him. Through His forgiveness, the Holy Spirit is able to breathe new life into your soul.

Once you confess and recognize that God has forgiven you, it's time to forgive yourself...otherwise, you're acting as if His forgiveness is not effective, as if you're a higher judge than He is. Remind yourself that the host of angels in heaven are shouting "Forgiven!" in echo of God's pronouncements! Shout "Forgiven!" to yourself anytime that guilt pokes you with reminders.

Make no mistake—we are in a spiritual battle against the forces of evil, against the slings and arrows that Satan throws our way. Keep on the armor of God, especially a prayer covering, asking Him to guard you at all times.

Do you need a safe place to talk about shame issues? Christian psychological counselors can help you work through past problems that continue to haunt you, showing you ways to accept what is in the past and move forward in your relationships.

We'll look a little longer at forgiveness in the next few pages. But for just this moment, stop and talk to the King of Glory. Adore Him, admit your erring ways to Him, speak your gratitude to Him, and hand over your needs and wishes. He is waiting to sing His love song over you in return.

PRAYER:

O my Father, You are holy, enthroned in the praises of Your children. Even as the angels cry out day and night to each other, I shout to You, "Holy, holy, holy are You, Lord of hosts; the whole earth is full of Your glory!"

I give thanks to You, O Lord, for You are good...Your mercy endures forever. If I walk in the light as You are in the light, I have fellowship with other believers, and the blood of Jesus Christ Your Son cleanses me from all sin.

However, if I say that I have no sin, I deceive myself, and the truth is not in me. And so, I fall on my knees before You now to confess my sin and my unfaithfulness to You...I have walked contrary to the ways You commanded me to follow. I have neglected to follow You and instead followed my own desires. Have mercy upon me, O God, for I am a miserable, wretched sinner! I am helpless to save myself!!

You have promised, though, that if I confess my sins, humble myself, and accept my guilt, You will be faithful and just to forgive my sins and to cleanse me from all unrighteousness...and You will remember Your covenant promises to me from of old.

Therefore, having these promises, help me in this very moment to remove all filthiness of my flesh and spirit by repenting and turning toward You, so that Your Son Jesus Christ may establish my heart blameless in holiness before You, my God and Father.

Even now, as I am set free from sin and become Your servant instead, I can enter Your gates with thanksgiving and into Your courts with praise. I thank You and bless Your name! I will praise Your name with a song and will magnify You with thanksgiving.

I come before You now with my petition, in light of Christ's redeeming love, asking You to provide me the gift for which You have given me a longing...a child to love and nurture. I pray that You will hear the pleas of Your maidservant, someone who longs to serve You here on earth as a mother.

You are the Giver of good gifts—please continue to work in my heart by planting good seeds there. As I walk closer with You, help me to recognize Your will for my life. Give me patience, an open heart for seeking to glorify You, and a submissive spirit that will accept all that You have planned for me, whether or not I have children of my own.

In Jesus' Holy name and for Your glory, Amen.

(Psalm 22:3; Isaiah 6:3; Psalm 136:1; 1 John 1:7-9; Leviticus 26:40-42; 2 Corinthians 7:1; 1 Thessalonians 3:13; Romans 6:22; Psalm 100:4; Psalm 69:30; Ephesians 4:7-8)

❦ ❦ ❦

FOR REFLECTION:

❖ Read David's grief-stricken prayer to God in Psalm 51. Which words or phrases resonate with you? How does David ask God to cleanse and forgive him?

_____
_____
_____
_____

❖ Think of times in the past when you have sinned against God. As you confess these silently to yourself, write down the words "God forgives me" several times on the lines below.

_____
_____
_____
_____

❖ Read Isaiah 51:3. What does it mean to you to accept God's forgiveness? How will that change your attitude toward yourself and toward others?

_____
_____
_____
_____

❦ ❦ ❦

MEGAN'S STORY:

I first discovered there was a problem after Larry and I had been married about two years. I was on the pill for half a year, and then like most couples, hoped I'd be pregnant in the next six months. Nothing. By our second anniversary, I talked with my gynecologist, who put me on the basal thermometer, which I did for nearly eight months. It showed I was ovulating, and we would try at the right times, but still no pregnancy. At this time, Larry and I were checked thoroughly—no problems for him, but I had scarring on my tubes, a tilted uterus, and irregular periods. My doctor put me on a fertility medication, but my emotions were on a rollercoaster, I had migraines, and couldn't sleep. I took a break for a few months and then tried an ovulation kit to predict the best time. Three months later, my period was late. I was so nervous, it took two pregnancy kits to convince me it was really true...both were pink and positive. Only a few days later, I woke up with extremely bad cramps and had a miscarriage. I didn't get out of bed for two days. I went to see my doctor to make sure everything was okay, and it was...but for me, I became very bitter and angry at myself and my body.

Finally, I had a laparoscopy just for one more "look." They found several cysts which were removed and noticed the scarring. My doctor was puzzled...but I had a secret that I had not shared with him.

Shortly after the miscarriage, I shut down—spiritually, emotionally, and physically. I found a wonderful Christian counselor I could open up to.

I felt God was "punishing" me because of past mistakes in college. My senior year, I had an abortion and almost bled to death. My miscarriage brought back similar pain and experiences, and I was having flashbacks. The past was something I had tried to bury and keep hidden. I started having suicidal thoughts again, just like in college. Though Larry knew of my past (I told him before we were married), the counselor was the first person I had told. That was helpful, but not healing.

Even though my doctor mentioned we could try in vitro fertilization (IVF), neither Larry nor I felt comfortable with that. So, Larry and I decided to adopt. After looking at our options, we decided on a special needs child. God answered our prayers on our wedding anniversary with a baby! We were finally parents! Motherhood started with only two days to prepare for a developmentally delayed child.

Not until two years later did God stop me in my tracks and get my attention. I was going to a Bible study for moms with preschool kids. The first day, one of the teachers stood up and gave her testimony, saying, "When I was 16 years old, I had an abortion." I was glued to my chair for the next 30 minutes. I could relate to all the pain, guilt, and shame.

Then she mentioned a free pregnancy counseling center that offered post-abortion support. I wrote down the number and called.

I went to the support group meeting, not knowing a soul, sat and listened. I cried all the way home afterward. God had led me to a place where people understood and where I could get help and healing.

CHAPTER 9

Fury and Forgiveness

"The Lord is gracious and full of compassion, slow to anger and great in mercy." (Psalm 145:8)

"And whenever you stand praying, if you have anything against anyone, forgive him, that your Father in heaven may also forgive you your trespasses." (Mark 11:25)

Pure, unbridled anger is such an unlovely thing...in other people. When it describes our own feelings, however, we often excuse it. Especially when we're right, which is most of the time, right?

Take this problem with infertility, for example. Like any form of grief, the feelings surrounding our inability to have children will move through stages. Anger is part of the natural progression. We "deserve" to be angry!

We are angry at ourselves for our complete helplessness. We are angry at our husbands when they don't understand. We are angry at our parents for pestering us about having children.

We get really angry every time we see a pregnant woman or someone else holding a baby. We lash out when someone asks why we haven't started a family yet. We are just angry, angry, angry...especially at God.

Hell hath no fury like a woman's scorn, and that fury can be equaled in a woman whose desire for children goes unfulfilled.

Anger that is never addressed, however, leads to two stages that are even uglier—an unforgiving heart and bitterness. These sister emotions claw at each other like cats in a never-ending brawl. Unchecked anger fuels this fight until you and others around you are left in shreds.

The Bible has frank words to say about the consequences of unresolved anger. Wrathful people stir up strife *(Proverbs 15:18a)*. Wrath is cruel and anger is a torrent, partnered in crime with jealousy *(Proverbs 27:4)*. Anger rests in the bosom of fools *(Ecclesiastes 7:9b)*. Ouch.

King David's wife Michal is a good example of how haughty anger can bring unwanted consequences. This royal daughter of Saul once was madly in love with the young David, but the years of turmoil and wars had embittered her toward her husband. When Michal saw David dancing in the grand parade as the ark of the covenant was brought back to the people of Israel, she despised him and didn't miss the chance to tell him *(2 Samuel 6:20)*.

David's response puts her in her place...God has chosen him, not Saul, to rule as king. The following verse metes out the justice against her: "And Michal daughter of Saul had no children to the day of her death." She bears no children to David—either because he refuses to have further relations with her or because God closes her womb. Whichever the case was, Michal spends her life childless...the result of an unchecked anger.

How do we deal with our anger then? How do we calm the flow of rage that wells up in our soul, seeking an outlet, like volcanic magma pressing toward a mountainous explosion?

First, recognize that anger is a natural emotion that arises from an encounter with injustice. We should be furious when we see others who are being mistreated or wronged. Anger drives us to attack poverty, human trafficking, terrorism, cancer, and all other societal ills foisted upon us by Satan.

It is the ideal alternative to fear when we ourselves come under attack. It enables us to engage in full defense mode to counter whatever siege we are undergoing.

In its purest, ideal form, our anger reflects God's own emotion when His righteousness is undermined, ignored, or twisted by His children or the forces of darkness. He seems to be most angry when we set up idols in our hearts and worship them instead of Him.

But like all of our God-given attributes, anger can be used for good or bad. It goes to bad when Satan encourages us to harbor it for our own selfish interests, tracking us off God's course and into Satan's evil purposes.

Take your gaze off your circumstances and lift it instead toward God. Our Heavenly Father owns exclusive rights to revenge. God's righteous fury is a dreadful thing—a rain of fire and destruction upon His enemies. His kind of anger is not something we want for ourselves.

Even so, He is slow to anger *(Psalm 145:8)*, and His anger is short-lived *(Psalm 30:5a)*. Because He is full of compassion, He forgives iniquity, many times turns His anger away, and does not stir up all His wrath *(Psalm 78:38)*.

To quell anger in ourselves, follow God's example and slow down. Take a deep breath. Consider the destructive consequences when wrath is unleashed. God so loved His children in the Bible that He didn't completely destroy them even when they fully deserved it...over and over again. He exercised supreme patience.

Do we love others enough, too, to withhold our destructive words? Can you envision how your anger will play out against the sensitivities of others? Have you already seen the crippling effects of simmering resentment in your marriage?

With infertility, the polar opposite of wrath isn't just love or joy, although those are infinitely preferable states. The real antidotes for anger are a deep trust in God and thanksgiving to Him.

We can withhold our anger, we can bite our tongues to keep from saying harmful words. We can go exercise to work out our anger against a treadmill, or we could just avoid it by engaging in other distractions and entertainment.

Our hearts, however, must be changed for long-term peace and release from anger. We need to focus our attention on God and give Him our complete trust. His purposes and plans for our life are good, even when we can't see the full picture.

When you shift your concerns toward thanksgiving, actively seeking reasons to be thankful for the blessings God has bestowed upon you, you begin beating your own sword into a plowshare. You cultivate a garden of growth and fruitfulness in your heart. You find yourself reaping the sweet fruits of forgiveness and joy, with a surprising absence of bitterness. You forgive those who have hurt you. God will pave the way to forgiveness for you.

This rarely happens instantaneously...it requires faithful, hard work on your part. It means actively putting your hand to the shovel and digging out the weeds.

One of the best contemporary stories about forgiveness is told by Corrie ten Boom, who was imprisoned along with her family in a World War II concentration camp after giving safe haven to Jews in their home. Corrie experienced unspeakable horrors at the hands of cold-hearted guards; she watched her sister Betsie die a slow, painful death under Nazi brutality.

Not long after Corrie's release from the camp and the end of the war, Corrie began a speaking tour in Germany to tell about God's love and the need for forgiveness. At the close of one such speech, she was dismayed to see a familiar face making his way through the crowd to greet her—one of her ruthless captors.

"It came back with a rush: the huge room with its harsh overhead lights, the pathetic pile of dresses and shoes in the center of the floor, the shame of walking naked past this man," Corrie recalled. "...Now he was in front of me, hand thrust out: 'A fine message, *fräulein*! How good it is to know that, as you say, all our sins are at the bottom of the sea!'

"And I, who had spoken so glibly of forgiveness, fumbled in my pocketbook rather than take that hand. ...It was the first time since my release that I had been face to face with one of my captors and my blood seemed to freeze.

"'You mentioned Ravensbrück in your talk,' he was saying. 'I was a guard in there.' No, he did not remember me. 'But since that time,' he went on, 'I have become a Christian. I know that God has forgiven me for the cruel things I did there, but I would like to hear it from your lips as well. *Fräulein*'—again the hand came out— 'will you forgive me?'

"And I stood there—I whose sins had every day to be forgiven—and could not. Betsie had died in that place—could he erase her slow terrible death simply for the asking?

"It could not have been many seconds that he stood there, hand held out, but to me it seemed hours as I wrestled with the most difficult thing I had ever had to do.

"For I had to do it—I knew that. The message that God forgives has a prior condition: that we forgive those who have injured us. 'If you do not forgive men their trespasses,' Jesus says, 'neither will your Father in heaven forgive your trespasses.'"

Corrie knew that those who were able to forgive their former enemies were able also to return to the outside world and rebuild their lives, no matter what the physical scars. Those who nursed their bitterness remained invalids.

"And still I stood there with the coldness clutching my heart. But forgiveness is not an emotion—I knew that too. Forgiveness is an act of the will, and the will can function regardless of the temperature of the heart.

"'Jesus, help me!' I prayed silently. 'I can lift my hand. I can do that much. You supply the feeling.'

"And so woodenly, mechanically, I thrust my hand into the one stretched out to me. And as I did, an incredible thing took place. The current started in my shoulder, raced down my arm, sprang into our joined hands. And then this healing warmth seemed to flood my whole being, bringing tears to my eyes.

"'I forgive you, brother!' I cried. 'With all my heart!'"[1]

Can you exercise that same kind of forgiveness? As Corrie said, it requires an act of the will, just as God has commanded us. And like so many paradoxical aspects of the Christian walk, it changes our hearts as it changed Corrie's emotions. Just as forgiveness wells up out of a grateful heart, the practice of forgiveness reprograms our hearts to become more loving.

The ultimate example of unconditional love and forgiveness is in Jesus Christ's sacrifice on the cross. Among His final words for us here on earth were, *"Father, forgive them, for they do not know what they do"* (Luke 23:34).

Praise God for His beautiful compassion for us. May He bring us to the point where anger dissolves into trust and thanksgiving. May we grow more and more like Him in our own forgiveness.

PRAYER:

O God, You Yourself have declared that You are compassionate and gracious, slow to anger, abounding in love and faithfulness. You abound in love and forgive sin and rebellion against You.

At the same time, I praise You, O God, that You are a just and righteous God who hates sin and burns with anger when You see how sinful and wicked we have become. You cannot tolerate evil, and yet Your love for us and Your mercy is so great that while we were still sinners, Christ died for us...O Father, how can we thank You enough for saving us from our sins through the death of Your only Son?

I confess to You now that I have been angry...at infertility, at others, at You. While my wrath might have been justified at times, I admit that I have often sinned in anger, with selfish attitudes and thoughts. Cleanse me, O God, from anger that injures others. You have warned me that my anger with others may make me subject to Your judgment—that if I have called someone a fool, I will be in danger of the fire of hell. Oh, what a miserable, unbearable thought!

Instead, Father, cool the out-of-control blazes in my heart. Wash me clean with Your living water, quenching the flames of fury. Forgive me when I have shaken my fist at You, Lord, my loving Creator. Teach me to forgive others and myself.

Remove any idols in my heart that I have set up to worship instead of loving You. Help me to recognize when my anger belongs to a favorite idol...tear down anything that prevents me from focusing only on You. Do not let me allow the sun to go down on my anger.

I thank You that vengeance belongs to You and that You (not I) will bring justice on the unrighteous. Inspire my heart with Your sweet contentment, with Your infinite patience, as I wait upon You.

May the words of my mouth and the meditations of my heart be acceptable in Your sight, O Lord, my strength and my Redeemer. In Jesus' name, Amen.

(Exodus 34:6; Numbers 14:18a; Romans 5:8; Matthew 5:21-22; Ephesians 4:26; Romans 12:19; Psalm 19:14)

❦ ❦ ❦

FOR REFLECTION:

❖ Read Proverbs 15. What do you learn about God in this passage? What do you learn about yourself? Can you think of any situations in your past where a soft answer would have turned away wrath?

_____

_____

_____

_____

❖ List three situations that cause you to become angry. Identify the source of your anger for each—is it because you have a deep concern for others or a sense that the situation has been unfair to you? How would you resolve your anger for each of these situations in light of God's love for you?

_____

_____

_____

_____

❖ Consider a person who has made you angry in recent days. Resolve to forgive the person and apologize if your anger caused you to sin against him/her...take your petition before God and ask for His help because it's not often easy! If appropriate, write a letter, make a call, or speak to the person who needs your apology. Make it a "soft answer" without justification.

_____

_____

🍎 🍎 🍎
DARCI'S STORY (CONTINUED FROM CHAPTER 4):

The most difficult thing for me was to be content—to act out what I said I believed—that whatever God gave me was for my good and His glory. I struggled most when around my husband Cody's family who were not comfortable talking about our difficulty with infertility.

I would never have chosen this "gift," but knowing what I have learned—I would choose it again. My security in God's providence and sovereignty has grown and deepened greatly through this, and He used this to bring me to grips with my faith.

Someone dear to me shared, "Given a choice, we would all choose to be shallow." Pain brings depth—without it, we could not minister to others.

Karen, my dearest friend, was always quick to ask how I felt about certain things—talking about her children, coming to her children's events, etc. She would frequently ask how I was dealing with it all—what was helpful, what was not. She was faithful all the way through, communicating, never offering advice, caring, sharing her struggles (even though she could get pregnant anytime she wanted). I never struggled being with her.

It still grieves me, though, to hear Christians have such a nonbiblical view of children. So many make comments about those who have more than three children. Children are a blessing, and we should encourage others—even if it is the sixth or 10th child, even if the mother is 40 years old or older.

Remember, we all share the same struggle, no matter what God gives—the question is, will we obey and trust? I pray we will.

CHAPTER 10

From Fear Into Faith

"The Lord is my light and my salvation; whom shall I fear? The Lord is the strength of my life; of whom shall I be afraid?" (Psalm 27:1)

"Fear not, for I am with you; be not dismayed, for I am your God. I will strengthen you, yes, I will help you, I will uphold you with My righteous right hand." (Isaiah 41:10)

"But we have this treasure in earthen vessels, that the excellence of the power may be of God and not of us. We are hard-pressed on every side, yet not crushed; we are perplexed, but not in despair; persecuted, but not forsaken; struck down, but not destroyed....For all things are for your sakes, that grace, having spread through the many, may cause thanksgiving to abound to the glory of God." (2 Corinthians 4:7-9,15)

It's midnight. Those anxieties you swept under the rug this morning are back. You're wide-eyed and your heart pounds. Your mind bounces around inside your head like a beach ball at a pool party. Sleep becomes restless or impossible.

What keeps you up at night? Is it anger? Is it worry over your job or finances? Is it an impulsive sin from earlier in the day? Is it something careless your husband said to you? All of the above?

Or is it fear? Are you afraid you'll never have children? We women are sometimes harassed by illogical fears, but the fear of remaining childless is a rational one. It is very real, very important, and very concerning.

What if you're never going to get pregnant? What if you'll never be able to adopt? What if you're past 45 and many of your options have vanished? What if God never answers your prayers?

When fears creep in like roaches, they climb through the cracks made by an insufficient faith and trust in God. You aren't looking to Christ to provide for you. Your faith is too weak.

Now before you begin to feel completely useless, remember that faith is easy when there's nothing to fear. Our faith in God is quite confident when the sun is shining and birds are singing. Throw even the sturdiest of us into the darkness of an emotional morass, however, and faith tends to evaporate.

In a faithless vacuum, our fears can lead us to panic and paralysis. They can drive us into sinful thoughts, words, and actions. We have no anchor, no peace, no rest in the tossing waves of turbulent imaginings.

But take heart...you are not left alone. Real faith begins in the midst of real fears, when we have no other option but to put our trust in God. Real faith rests in Him alone and not on our circumstances or our own abilities.

Go to the book of Esther and read the entire story. It's a remarkable account of one woman's courage in the face of death in order to save her people, the Israelites.

Esther is a beautiful young woman—a Jew exiled in the Persian empire, bereft of her parents but guarded by her wise cousin, Mordecai. Because the Jews were under constant threat, her real name, Hadassah, is hidden in exchange for a Persian name that means "star."

King Ahasuerus reigns over the vast Persian empire at the time. But in spite of his powerful position, he tends to heed the advice of crafty underlings. After discarding his queen Vashti, Ahasuerus agrees to hold a "beauty contest" to choose a new queen.

But this is no pageant. Esther is swept up into the king's court with a bevy of other fearful young girls, their fate sealed by the king's decree—only one chance at becoming the next queen or else being relegated to harem life forever. This was a prison...no longer would any of them have freedom.

By the grace of God, Esther meets with the king's favor and is instantly thrust into royal standing. This didn't give her automatic access to the king, however. She had to be invited...and showing up without an appointment meant instant death.

When one of the king's chief advisors, Haman, makes plans to murder all the Jews, Mordecai gets notice of the plot. He sends word to Esther: she must go before the king and beg him to spare her people.

Esther hesitates. She knows she will meet a certain death if she appears at the throne room without being asked. Mordecai urges her to go anyway: *"Do not think in your heart that you will escape...any more than all the other Jews,"* he says. *"Yet who knows whether you have come to the kingdom for such a time as this?" (Esther 4:13-14)*

Esther, with all the courage she can muster, calls upon the local Jews to fast and pray. She fasts, too. And so, she decides to go to the king, which is against his law, uttering this resolute statement: *"If I perish, I perish" (Esther 4:16b).*

God blesses Esther in return for her faith. The king accepts her, hears her petition, and eventually allows the Jews to live. In an ironic twist, the evil Haman is hanged on gallows he had prepared for Mordecai.

What do we learn from Queen Esther? She does not have any authority in this situation. It's completely out of her control. But what she can control is her response to it. Instead of shrinking in fear and pulling away from everyone, she takes charge of what she can accomplish. She approaches her life with complete trust in the God who placed her in this spot. She chooses faith instead of fear.

One of the most frustrating aspects of infertility is our complete powerlessness. Even with medical advances, this is not something we can just fix by ourselves. The creation of life is entirely God's doing. It is His miracle, not ours.

When you reach the point where all of your own strength is gone...all of your efforts have failed...all of your hopes are dashed...and there is nothing left you can do...you are at the point where God can use you best.

His results for you may not look like what you had planned. You may have to wait longer. You may have to consider foster care. You may have to realize that helping teach children in an after-school tutoring program is the closest you will ever get to parenthood. You may have to accept that your dream may not be His dream for you.

But if children do arrive in your life—through birth, adoption, or ministry—you will look back and see His powerful hand at work in answer to your prayers. You will wonder why you ever doubted Him. You will see just how small your faith was and just how big His love is.

Among Jesus' most radical commands to His disciples is the admonition to "fear not." He issues this mandate when the disciples are in the middle of a cataclysmic storm on the Sea of Galilee. He says, "Don't be afraid," when He is walking on the water...when His disciples see Him transfigured into a shining vision on the mountain...when they wonder if they will be saved. They have real reasons to be afraid! These are not imaginary problems!

Over and over, Jesus promises He will always be with them. He tells them that having faith the size of a mustard seed is enough for Him to produce fruit and growth in them. He reminds them again and again that *with God, all things are possible.*

Walk today, therefore, in faith and trust that God is who He says He is. Work, knowing He has good plans for you. Rest, knowing Jesus will be with you. Sleep, comforted by the peace of His Holy Spirit that surpasses all understanding.

"The peace of God is internal, not external," wrote pastor Neil T. Anderson. "The peace of God is something you need to appropriate daily in your inner world in the midst of the storms that rage in the external world....Chaos may be occurring all around you, but God is bigger than any storm."[1]

Complete trust is the only way you will harness God's power to serve His kingdom. Ask Him to help you turn your fear into faith. Take His hand on this journey, and you will be fearless!

PRAYER:

Great and powerful God, I praise You for choosing to live among us. You are our mighty Savior. O, how marvelous to know that You take delight in us with gladness. With Your love, You will calm all my fears. How I yearn to hear You rejoice over me with joyful songs!

Yet I come to You helpless...unable to face my fears...unable to move...unable to make this situation right. Teach me again about Your power and strength in the midst of my weakness. Fill me again with the empowerment of Your Holy Spirit. Forgive me for my fearfulness.

When I have a spirit of fear and timidity, remind me that this is not from You—it is orchestrated by Satan. Instead, You give me Your spirit of power, love, and self-discipline. Help me to trust in You. Reassure me that Your angel will encamp around those who fear You and that You will deliver us.

When I feel worthless, help me to remember that I am worthwhile in Your eyes. When I can't sleep, remind me that Your Son Jesus Christ left me with a huge gift—peace of mind and heart, something the world cannot give. You have admonished me to not be troubled or afraid. You have commanded me to be strong and courageous, unafraid, not discouraged, because You go with me wherever I go.

Your love invokes no fear, because perfect love expels all fear. When I am afraid, prompt me to immediately put my trust in You. You will shelter me under Your wings. Your faithful promises are my armor and protection. I do not have to be afraid of the terrors of the night, nor the arrow that flies in the day. Help me not to dread the disease that stalks in darkness nor the disaster that strikes at midday. You are the One who comforts me, a tender and compassionate Father. You watch over those who fear You, those who rely on Your unfailing love and hope in Your mercy.

You alone, O Lord, are the One who can answer my prayers and free me from all my fears. You are the first and the last, the One who has admonished me over and over again not to fear. How many times have I recited the 23rd Psalm without really believing it? You are the One who walks with me through the valley of the shadow of death, comforting me with Your rod and staff...I will fear no evil.

In accepting all this, I lay one of my greatest fears before You—the possibility that I may never have children—and I turn it completely over to You. I call upon Your mercy to answer my prayers with peace and thanksgiving to You. Help me to look for Your good purposes for my life, and help me to trust in Your good and perfect plans. In Jesus' name, Amen.

(Zephaniah 3:17; 2 Timothy 1:7; Psalm 34:7; John 14:27; Joshua 1:9; 1 John 4:18; Psalm 56:3; Psalm 91:4-8; Psalm 33:18; Psalm 34:4; Revelation 1:17; Psalm 23:4)

FOR REFLECTION:

❖ What inspires you about Queen Esther's story? What did you learn about her approach to an insurmountable problem?

_____

_____

_____

❖ What are some of the fears that frequently haunt you? List them here, then draw a line through the ones you can easily dismiss. For the remaining ones, face them with a head-on attack—commit them to prayer, laying them before the throne of God…even if you have to do this repeatedly. Eventually, you will be able to lay them to rest or resolve them with God's help.

_____

_____

_____

- ❖ Memorize these three things to do when you're afraid:
    1. *Remember* that you belong to Jesus Christ—Your salvation is through Him alone, and heaven is His free gift.
    2. *Prepare to act*—Get out of bed...do not give in to the paralysis of fear.
    3. *Pray*—Ask God to do the impossible for you.

🍎🍎🍎

JADE'S STORY (CONTINUED FROM CHAPTER 6):

Where do I begin? Seven years without a live birth, five years seeing an infertility specialist. Tests to determine if tubes were open (they were), if sperm alive (very!), if hormones were normal (they were). Lots of tests, repeated. One pregnancy spontaneously miscarried at the end of the first trimester. Otherwise, no conceptions and five years of "charting"—such a "joyful" activity!

Decisions together? Not at first! I didn't want to "go exploring" about infertility, so my husband made the first appointment with the specialist, told me we were "going shopping," and got me en route to the doctor's office before he confessed where we were heading. I went ballistic...but we did begin the process.

Expenses were tough, costly. Our insurance did not cover infertility treatments. At the time, we were living at poverty level, working as support staff with a Christian organization...taking on extra jobs to pay for the tests...scheduling tests according to when we had the time for extra work.

The hardest problem was the "weepies" when my cycle hit that time of super sensitive emotions. I had to be so careful as we were in constant "people" and ministry activities, and weeping publicly didn't jive with talking about the abundant life!

We decided humor was the best way to keep from crying as well as trying to not embarrass the other person yet. We had several one-liners to reply to, "Why don't y'all have kids yet?"

"It's just not in the water we're drinking." "Kids? You mean those little pink things with a diaper at one end and a scream at the other?" "Oh. We have alarm clocks."

Or, to answer the question, "Is there something wrong with one of you?"—"Well, I have freckles." Or, "Yes, I voted for the loser in the last election."

Note—*women* asked these questions. Never once did a *man* ask about my personal life or lack of children!

I had to deal with restrictions, too, from the infertility specialist. I hated that I could no longer run or jog. I had run 10k races and such for 15 years, and my doctor felt this might be affecting fertility in some way.

I stopped running for five years, gained weight, and didn't have a way to deal with stress…until the week I turned 30, lost a baby, and decided to take my life back from the constant thought of conception. I went out for a two-mile run and have been running ever since. My first baby/pregnancy (that went full-term) was conceived the day before a 10K!

CHAPTER 11

For the Man of the House

"Wives, submit to your own husbands, as to the Lord. For the husband is head of the wife as also Christ is head of the church; and He is the Savior of the body. Therefore, just as the church is subject to Christ, let the wives be to their own husbands in everything." (Ephesians 5:22-24)

For those of you who have grown up in the age of gender equality, the old biblical model for marriage seems archaic and unfair. According to Scriptures, the husband is to be the head of the household. That means he's number one, and you are number two. Doesn't sound very appealing, does it?

In a "liberated" culture, God's design for marriage is either extremely unpopular or downright abomination. Those verses in Ephesians 5:22-24 rankle a lot of contemporary women.

But the reality is that the husband has a God-given role as the leader in marriage. It's his responsibility to take care of you and his children. In His great plan, God wired men and women differently—we are distinct creatures, each with a specific role to fulfill His commandments for creation.

Before we examine our role as wives, let's look at God's plan for husbands.

If God posted a job description for "husband" on a career website, here's what it might say:

Wanted: Family chief executive officer (FCEO). Must be a man (biologically male from birth). Must be old enough to take care of himself and additional persons. Reports to God through personal relationship with Jesus Christ; will be held accountable by local church. Needs to be visionary, able to lead himself and others into new territories. Has to be willing to negotiate terms with second-in-command. Must contribute to family budget in a significant way, through income earned and careful expenditures, with personal self-sacrifice essential. Responsible for developing a healthy home environment that provides shelter, guards safety, and encourages co-workers. Other job responsibilities include Bible reading, consistent prayer, caring for second-in-command, babysitting, performing household tasks, and future planning. No vacations or holidays, except as approved by second-in-command. Recreational time with children essential. No experience necessary; must be willing to learn on the job. No salary as FCEO, but fringe benefits available with second-in-command, based on good behavior. Must sign contract for lifetime career with no resignation.

That's a pretty tall order for our husbands. I am sure that many grooms waiting at the altar might think twice if they had to read the fine print of this contract!

Our husbands have probably found out by now that marriage is not a 50-50 proposition...it takes 100 percent from both partners to make it work efficiently. Chances are your husband has probably sacrificed much in marrying you and working through the infertility process with you. And unless he is already a father, he will have to sacrifice much in the future for your children.

Consider your husband's response to infertility in the marriage. How are his experiences different from your grief?

There is greater pressure on our husbands in marriage than we often realize as women. If he is the primary provider or co-provider, it's up to him to go to work every day to bring home a paycheck. He knows he is also supposed to help with housework (whether he is consistent or not).

But even if he knows he needs to get tasks done when he gets home, he can be exhausted from the 21st-century demands on his energy and time at work, just like you. It takes a lot of effort to be a husband. If he cares about you, he is concerned about doing his best at all times.

Infertility adds an extra layer of obligation and worry on him. His job performance in the bedroom can be under a whole new level of stress. If you are going through infertility treatments together, his health can be affected by medications. If your bedtime activity is now regimented, he has to step up to the plate, whether he feels like it or not! That's a lot of stress that he might not have expected in marriage.

Also, men do not communicate in the same way as women. They are much more direct, they use fewer words, and they don't often speak at the same emotional level. For example, a woman may express her emotions by saying "I *feel* such-and-such way" in conversations with her husband. It's a language he may have difficulty understanding. He rarely wants to engage in communication at that depth. Instead, he will frequently use the expression "I *think* such-and-such about the situation." He believes it's his job to fix things, not necessarily listen to how you feel. That can be frustrating on both sides.

And, as a result, our husbands may clam up when it comes to sharing how they feel during this process. While their level of grief may not be as intense as yours, it is still grief—either for your inability to conceive or possibly their inability to provide. They, too, may feel anger, confusion, guilt, jealousy, an unforgiving attitude, resentment, or sorrow.

Our men may not be able to identify these emotions in themselves. That doesn't make their feelings any less genuine. We wives need to be sensitive to their infertility experience and recognize that our men may not be able to express their emotions verbally. Like the pressure of an overheated water tank, their anger could explode, burning us in wrath. Our guys might not see that their anger is displaced. We have to forgive them just as they forgive us.

Men also have a greater tendency to become withdrawn in complicated situations. That's very frustrating for wives who need their husbands' cooperation in making infertility doctors' appointments, scheduling treatments, or seeing counseling. In general, men really hate going to the doctor. They think they can take of themselves without assistance.

But the reality is that married men live longer than single men. In fact, "the longer a man stays married, the greater his survival advantage over his unmarried peers."[1] If it weren't for our prodding about our husbands' health, they wouldn't live as long! Remind him of this from time to time.

Men also have a different viewpoint about children. They don't have the same maternal hardwiring; they don't have the intense craving we have to hold children in our arms. Don't get me wrong...their desire for children can be very strong. But it's going to be from a different mindset and emotional background. Talk with him about his desires, which may change over time.

His desire may be based on a wish to please you, a little bit of ego (who doesn't want to hand out the cigars?), a longing to be in charge of a family, and especially a desire to serve God by raising children to follow Him. He sees himself as the family provider and wants a family he can nourish. If he's a Christian, he wants to leave a legacy of faith.

Because of your differing approaches to infertility, it will be easy for both of you to be in conflict over the number of children to have, whether or not to adopt, which doctors to see, how much to spend on treatment or adoption, and so forth.

When you are in the middle of a heated argument, stop for a moment to consider his side of the equation. Where is he coming from? Does he have bottled-up anger that needs to be defused, even if it's not really directed at you? Does he need to be comforted, just as you need comfort from him? What are his expectations, and shouldn't they be considered at least equally with yours?

Listen to me carefully here. When we women put all our emphasis on a child—wanting to have one, or having a child with a serious illness, injury, or disability—in many cases, husbands leave. Why? When it takes so much of their mental and emotional energies, focused on what they have to do, some husbands feel left behind. They go to work, they come home, and they help out, but they may feel squeezed in all directions and finally can't handle it.

If this is the way your husband feels, he may be too scared to say anything or bring it up. Men have a fight-or-flight response if a woman digs in. If he sees no chance of changing the situation, he gives up.

That's why it's so important that you both put this issue on the altar of God. And look to your husband for his needs as well as yours. Here are some simple steps:

- Look for evidence of how he feels. You need to be aware of how this situation is affecting him, even if he doesn't talk or say a lot about it.
- Pray every day, multiple times a day, for him.
- Do things together that he likes to do, with or without other friends, so that he knows you are vitally interested in his life as well as what you wish.
- Find common ground—dancing, hiking, skiing, going to museums, taking a boat ride, etc. Look for a non-stressful, casual way to relate together. This is not to diminish the issues but simply put them aside for a while to focus on your relationship.

Ultimately, you have to go back to the original premise God planned for marriage. Your husband is number one, and you are number two. If we expect to receive God's blessing upon our families, we must submit to the God-given authority placed upon our husbands to make the best decisions possible for our marriages...even when we are in violent disagreement.

That's because our husbands must one day answer to God for their leadership over us and over their household. They are the ones expected by Him to be Jesus Christ Himself in the home—self-sacrificial, loving, and faithful to God. They are to be the warrior leaders in our life battles together.

Our husbands have a big job. Sometimes we need to just get out the way and let them do it.

PRAYER:

Oh, how I praise You, Lord! Help my husband today to draw closer to You than ever before. Teach him to fear You and delight greatly in Your commandments.

Bless my husband and our home with a wealth of Your wisdom, and bestow the riches of Your heavenly realm upon us. Clothe my husband with Your righteousness forever. Help him to live uprightly, in integrity and character, so that Your light will shine on him when he is caught in the darkness of despair.

Make my husband generous, full of compassion, and just...a man who deals graciously and lends, guiding his affairs with discretion. Keep him firmly planted, unshaken by the problems of life. Let him be remembered in the future as a godly man, unafraid of evil or bad news. Give him a steadfast heart, one that trusts in You alone.

Give him a heart for loving others and serving You, reaching out to the poor and growing in faith. Exalt him in the eyes of others, and clothe him in Your honor, even as he humbles himself before You.

Help us both to grow closer together in our marriage, our pattern of communication, patience with each other, and understanding each other's point of view. Grant us the blessing of Your presence with us, even when we fail. Help me to love him more every day. In Your Son Jesus Christ's name, Amen.

(Psalm 112:1-9)

FOR REFLECTION:

❖ Pray for your husband every day this week. Using your own words, pray for him through Psalm 18:25-36, echoing a few verses each day from the words of David.

❖ Make a list of the qualities that you find appealing in your husband...even if you are mad at him at the moment! Make an effort to praise him verbally for one of them today...even better if you can do it in front of someone else. He needs your affirmation.

❖ Do three things to please him, such as making his favorite dessert, giving him a backrub, washing his car windshield and leaving a love note, or watching a movie together that he likes. Think carefully about what would make him happy. Make this a sacrifice of love, one that does not expect a reward. Write down your choices and his response.

🍎 🍎 🍎

JOSHUA'S STORY:

In the process of making decisions about parenthood, men and women tend to have different feelings. Men don't have the same emotions or feel the monthly physiological changes that women do. As believers, we men want to be the spiritual leaders. And most men want to fix things. But the reality for us is that we can't step in and fix it. So the burden weighs heavy on us, too, because we don't know what to do.

When Kristen and I had to make the decision, however, whether to proceed with in-vitro fertilization or adopt, God brought us to the same conclusion: He had called us to parent. That much was clear, it was one of those rocks we continued to cling to as we went to the Lord on our knees in prayer. If God needed our DNA to further His kingdom, He would provide it. In the meantime, we believed He was calling us to pursue adoption.

Men can compartmentalize decisions and not second-guess them. Once the decision to adopt was made, it was sealed and finished in my mind. I have never questioned that I was called to adopt my child and that I am my little girl's father.

My faith has strengthened a lot during this time, knowing I have to trust the Lord for what my family looks like. Adoption is not for the weak of heart, not the thing to do because it's trendy. It will test you in ways you haven't been tested before. But if we really understand what Christ has done for His Church, we know that once we are saved we are adopted into His family permanently. When the judge told us our adoption was final, it was just like our salvation—sealed in Christ.

It's extremely important that you have a support team going into any type of adoption, especially with infertility. Your supporters need to understand what language will be offensive, understand enough about the conversations to speak the truth. Surround yourself with people who know the adoption process and helpful language, especially what it means to be adopted by Christ. The people who understand these matters have meant the most to us. They were there for us, were willing to learn and listen, not judging when we needed to talk or get our feelings out.

We have seen families struggle after adoption, not realizing it would be hard. I don't try to scare them away, but they do need to understand that it's a commitment and covenant that will rock your world if you're not prepared for it. They need to make sure they're ready for it, grounded as believers, grounded as a couple.

We men can be a little clueless to the language that other men and women are using, but our wives are not. There are triggers that will take place in conversation, and you can't prepare for all of them with your wife. Someone will say something off-hand, or a baby shower invitation will arrive, or it's that time of the month for your wife. We husbands become "on guard" for rest of our lives, needing to be ready to protect our wives. It will always be that way because the pain of infertility doesn't always go away for them. We will have to deal with challenging emotions for the rest of our marriage.

As the protector, there have been moments when I should have jumped in to rescue Kristen, but I didn't have time to process the situation. I have asked her to be quiet at times and let me catch up with her thinking and emotions. In the process, God has shown me how to lead my family and lead it well. He is refining my character, calling me to step up and have conversations with my wife and others, communicating clearly so I will know how to lead appropriately.

One unfortunate part of adoption is that it's costly; in particular, it can be a financial burden. To fulfill the requirements of the adoption agency, we invited some of the folks closest to us to share in how God was providing adoption for us. For us, this was no different from sending letters in advance of a mission trip. We never questioned the cost, though. For us, the Lord provided the resources we needed and grew our trust in Him to provide for our family's needs. Adoption will grow you to trust God for the finances, whether you have money or don't, as well as in every other area of your life!

As husbands of strong women of faith, we can sometimes have a sense of feeling inferior. While our wives want us to be the spiritual leaders, we can sometimes feel challenged by their God-given abilities. We need to find boldness, though, trusting that God has placed us as the husbands and fathers in our families for a reason and receive our wives' encouragement.

Kristen and I continue to come back to the understanding that God has a plan for our lives—He has provided us with a wonderful marriage, He has a plan for what our family looks like, and He still loves us. He will give us the grace to get us through the difficult parts of our journey.

CHAPTER 12

Is He Ready for "Dadhood"?

"Behold, children are a heritage from the Lord, the fruit of the womb is a reward. Like arrows in the hand of a warrior, so are the children of one's youth. Happy is the man who has his quiver full of them...." (Psalm 127:3-5a)

"Therefore you shall lay up these words of mine in your heart and in your soul, and bind them as a sign on your hand, and they shall be as frontlets between your eyes. You shall teach them to your children, speaking of them when you sit in your house, when you walk by the way, when you lie down, and when you rise up." (Deuteronomy 11:18-19)

As you pray for your husband's role in marriage, pray also for his preparation to be the father of your children. Even if he is already serving in some kind of fatherhood role, he needs your prayers to be an even better father.

What does it take to be a godly father? How can you help him now, before children arrive in your lives?

Pray for his heart. Pray that the eyes of his heart will be opened, that the Holy Spirit will inspire him to grow into this role. He hasn't grown up playing with baby dolls and doesn't really know all the ins and outs of fatherhood, unless he has already done some babysitting! Ask God to soften his heart to be ready for any little ones that He gives him.

Pray for common ground for the both of you. A man desires to be a strong leader. Sometimes that will make him a little too stubborn or hard-headed to accept advice from you. Also, he may have different ideas about discipline, indulgence, what jobs you'll share as parents, and what jobs he expects for himself only or for you to handle.

Take some time now to talk through a few these issues now. If he is reluctant to get started down this road yet, thinking it's too premature, be patient and wait.

But if you have started in an adoption process, it is not too early to work on those fatherhood issues—adoption can drag out for a long time, but it can also happen almost overnight. He needs to be ready.

Pray for his handling of the finances. Pray for his work and for his ability to provide. Pray especially for his health, if you plan together for him to carry the weight of the family earnings if one of you were to take time off.

Read through some Christian books together, especially those that focus on the roles of both spouses. Read them aloud together: assign one night a week as your "reading night," taking turns in reading study books and discussing them afterward. Decide where you agree and disagree on your roles—praise God for the agreements, and ask Him together to help you work through the disagreements.

Take notes now, though, for a time in the future when you could be closer to either bringing a child into your home or engaging in children's ministry, to remind you to include him in your personal preparations. Give him jobs to do, as he wishes, in preparing your home—painting a room, shopping for a stroller (especially one with handles that would fit his height), child-proofing cabinets or electrical outlets. Or work with him on his role in co-teaching a Sunday School class, tutoring children in an inner-city mission, etc.

Remember that being a father figure will be an exciting, challenging time in his life, too. He needs your prayers for this.

Pray that he will seek to serve His Lord first. If he is not a Christian, pray that God will lead him into a new relationship with Jesus Christ. God can bring us to our knees and at the same time show us His incredible love for us as our Eternal Father.

Ask His Holy Spirit to be a Guide to your husband and to fill him with His fruits of love, joy, peace, patience, kindness, goodness, faithfulness, gentleness, and self-control...especially patience.

Pray for growth in his knowledge of the Bible and his future role as teacher/mentor to children. He needs to be studying up now for the times when he will need to teach the precepts of a Christian life, both through his words and his actions.

Pray for him to be "long-suffering," through this process and beyond. He will need a giant capacity for patience with children, especially teenagers! It is a quality so rarely developed in our hurry-up, workaday world. Pray that God will reveal to your husband His own patience in putting up with our sinful nature.

As Christ loved His children and called them to be His own, ask Him to teach your husband how to reach out to children of all ages. Your husband may not be the best communicator, so pray that he will make the effort to move out of his comfort zone to express his love for children...verbally and in his daily living.

Pray that your husband will grow to love you more and more each day, as Christ loved His church. One of the most important things a father can do for his children is to love their mother and be faithful to her, demonstrating his love for her daily. It's a tall order to fill, and he won't do it perfectly. Pray for God to work in him and through him in your marriage.

Pray for his growth as a Christian servant. Pray that he will grow more mature in loving others, especially his own parents or your parents. Ask God to remove negative thoughts and any critical spirit in him toward others, so that he can lead children to be loving as well.

Pray for your husband to live soberly. He needs an alert mind, to protect children from any danger. Excessive use of alcohol, drugs, or any other debilitating habit will prevent him from doing his job at work and fulfilling his responsibilities at home.

Likewise, playing video games incessantly, gambling, viewing pornography, or any other similar addiction is not compatible with being a good male role model. Please pray for him, and seek professional counseling for both of you if your husband has problems beyond his control.

Finally, pray that your husband will be hopeful for the future. Even if you are going through a meltdown right now in the hopelessness of infertility, pray that God will fill your husband with a capacity to comfort you. Ask God to give him a positive attitude about the future, whether children arrive or not.

Our eternal hope comes only through Christ and His great promise of heaven for us. Pray that your husband will commit himself now to seeking God's kingdom here, for the life to come.

Your man will never be the perfect husband or dad. But you can rest assured that God will shape him as you pray for him. And He will shape your heart in the process, too.

🍎 🍎 🍎

PRAYER:

O gracious and loving Father, Creator of my husband, Father to him—please bless my husband and prepare him to be a godly father.

I pray that the eyes of his heart will be opened, that Your Holy Spirit will inspire him to grow into this role. Make him a strong leader, and give me wisdom and strength to work with him over issues of job-sharing.

Help him to get ready for new roles in his life. Please give him good work that will help support our family, and give him good health so that he will be able to tackle his job. I pray You will show him how to be a good steward of our finances so that we will not be stressed by the expenses in the future.

Let Your Holy Spirit to be a Guide to my husband and fill him with Your fruits of love, joy, peace, patience, kindness, goodness, faithfulness, gentleness, and self-control. Inspire him to grow in his knowledge of the Bible and his future role as teacher/mentor to children. Give my husband a new depth of patience and long-suffering to prepare him for the needs of little ones.

Please make me a thoughtful, loving wife, so that it will be easier for my husband to love me more and more every day. Please touch his heart so that he will have a tenderness for me.

Help my husband to grow more mature in loving others, especially our parents and other family members. Please remove any negative thoughts and any critical spirit in him toward others, so that he can lead children to be loving as well. Please help him to live soberly.

As Abraham looked to You for all of his needs, ready to sacrifice everything to follow You, please give my husband a sacrificial heart. Help him to see that what he may give up in terms of worldly prizes will be rewarded by God in the intangibles of heaven. Help my husband to see that You will provide for him as he continues to trust more and more in You.

Please instill a spirit of hope in my husband, for our future and our marriage. Give us both a sense of Your presence with us, that we may move forward in confidence that Your plans are good for us.

In the loving name of Jesus Christ, Amen.

(Psalm 119:18; Galatians 5:22-23; Colossians 3:19; Genesis 22:1-18; Proverbs 19:21)

FOR REFLECTION:

❖ Pray for your husband every day this week through a few of the suggestions listed above in the Scriptures and prayer. Write your prayers here, and commit the answers to Him. You cannot change your husband, but God can. Seek God's will for this aspect of your husband's character and life.

❖ Make a list of possible jobs that would make your husband feel a part of a child-rearing or child-ministry activity. Set this list aside until the time comes that you may have children in your lives, so that you can invite him to join you in preparation.

❖ Write three things that your husband and you could do together to work with children in your church, community Christian organizations that benefit at-risk children, or your own extended family. Talk with your husband about opportunities for his input and interest in working together with you. Don't stress him by bringing his own fatherhood preparation into this—simply consider it time that you both could spend together having a positive impact in other children's lives.

🌱 🌱 🌱

RYAN'S AND CANDACE'S STORY:

RYAN: When we started infertility treatments, Candace's reaction was emotional, while I took a more clinical approach...not fun, just something we had to go through. At one point, it was uncomfortable for me to undergo a delicate, exposed procedure with a dozen medical residents observing. The nurse told me to "relax"—ha!

For all we went through, we never found any conclusive, definitive reason we couldn't conceive. So I started praying for our child, almost every night, for 10 years until our daughter was born.

I don't ever remember thinking that it wasn't going to happen. I wasn't discouraged. I questioned "why" but never wavered in my faith that we would be parents. And it didn't matter to me one way or the other how God would provide.

I had to protect Candace through some emotional situations, though. Once, when she attended a church gathering, one of the elders commented that Candace and I needed to "hurry up and get pregnant and have a child." Unbeknownst to him, Candace was very fragile emotionally, having already begun infertility testing. When she arrived home in tears, I called him on the phone and explained our situation. He, of course, was stunned and would never have knowingly said anything to hurt her.

And I think it's neat that, years later, God had us sitting in the hospital on our wedding anniversary, waiting for our precious daughter, Isabella, to be born. When it was time to bring her home, friends came over from our church, put banners up at our house, and left food in the refrigerator for us.

We see God's sovereign hand on every step of our journey to becoming parents. Had any of our treatments or attempts to conceive been successful, we never would have adopted Isabella, who is the perfect child for us and the child God planned for us all along.

CANDACE: I've heard it said that childbirth is an excruciating pain soon forgotten when the new mother holds her baby in her arms. In much the same way, infertility was excruciatingly painful for me, but today my pain, too, is long gone.

I prayed diligently for a pregnancy, filled with hope, then was disappointed time and again. Before marrying, my hope was to have six children. Year after year, I saw the possibility of having even one child slipping away.

One of the hardest things was guarding myself against envy and learning to be happy for friends who were all having children. At times, it was agonizing to sit through baby showers and listen to all the talk of babies. On one occasion, I hosted a shower and one of the older guests said, "Candace, everyone here has a child but you." I had a hard time keeping my composure. Now I realize that well-meaning people often misspoke simply because they had no idea what we were going through. I should have been more forthcoming with fellow believers and, instead of being hurt by wayward comments, responded by asking them to join us in prayer for a child.

While going through the adoption waiting process, several of our friends "shared" their children with us by having them come to our house when they needed childcare, and we were designated in the wills of several sets of parents as guardians of their children. This act of trust encouraged us as it showed that our friends would choose to entrust their children with us. Three of our pastors wrote letters of reference for us, all of them so gracious and willing to talk with us whenever we needed it.

Three years into the adoption process, when Ryan's job was transferred to another state, we heard that our paperwork wouldn't transfer. Devastated, I gave up on adoption and prayed that if God was not going to give me a child, He would just take away my desire to be a mom.

But Ryan didn't give up. He contacted our agency in our new location and explained what had happened. They put us on a fast track, and one of the steps was to meet with a pastor of their choice for an interview. As it turns out, within the year, a young girl in this pastor's congregation became pregnant and sought his counsel about adoption—she had seen an ultrasound of her baby and knew she couldn't go through with an abortion, despite her initial intent to do so.

The pastor remembered us and suggested us to her. She reviewed our profile, along with a number of other profiles, and settled on us. We met with her and were invited to the hospital for the birth. We named our child after her birth mother as a means of honoring her and the decision she made to have the child whom she did not plan, but whom God did before the foundation of the world. We never think of Isabella as our "adopted" daughter, just as our daughter.

Through all of this painful journey, I have learned that God is faithful, and while I may not see what He is doing in all situations, I can trust that He is working things together for my good. One of my favorite verses is Philippians 4:13...encouraging me that I can do all things through Christ who strengthens me. With infertility, my "all things" included learning to be patient, facing medical procedures, finding joy in sorrow, and learning to be truly happy for others who had children.

I have also learned from my husband to be persistent in prayer. Ryan never quit praying or believing that his prayer would be answered.

And, as far as wanting six children, one child has filled our hearts as much as six ever could. And we have been blessed to share in the lives of many other children through the years. It has been our joy to serve in a variety of children and youth ministries. Our home has been graced by an endless array of neighborhood children, friends, and classmates, leaving us with treasured memories. We hope that we blessed them as much as they blessed us.

One of my greatest joys was when Isabella picked up a baby bottle at church, filled it with her own money, and hand-delivered it to the local Christian crisis pregnancy center, in hopes that another young woman would choose life!

CHAPTER 13

Keeping the Love Flame Burning

"Let him kiss me with the kisses of his mouth—for your love is better than wine....He brought me to the banqueting house, and his banner over me was love." (Song of Solomon 1:2; 2:4)

"Let the husband render to his wife the affection due her, and likewise also the wife to her husband. The wife does not have authority over her own body, but the husband does. And likewise the husband does not have authority over his own body, but the wife does. Do not deprive one another except with consent for a time, that you may give yourselves to fasting and prayer; and come together again so that Satan does not tempt you because of your lack of self-control." (1 Corinthians 7:3-5)

In the battle against infertility, one of the first casualties is a carefree enjoyment of sexuality. Gone are the days of unbridled passion without worries or distraction. Sex might still be somewhat enjoyable, but now it's entwined with a driven purpose that can stifle enjoyment.

The stress of infertility takes its toll on both partners. You become a slave to the calendar and your cycle. Sex can become a planned, programmed event that's more mechanical than romantic.

And what happened to the joy of sex? Fertility drugs might be messing with your libido. Worries cloud your thought life, the real seat of arousal in women. While you're making love, you're wondering if this is "the moment" when you'll get pregnant. Tends to ruin the mood, doesn't it?

While sex tends to be more casual for your husband, he can feel the burden of producing an heir. If he's the source of the infertility problems, he can experience loss of confidence in the pressure of getting everything to work right. Infertility attacks his concept of manhood and his confidence.

Age may play a role in adding pressure on your man. If you're both in your thirties and beyond, you may begin to switch roles with your husband in terms of sexual interest. His sex drive probably peaked in his twenties, and he may be starting to slow down a bit. Yours may be just now revving up.

What if your biological clock calls for a mid-day tryst? Are both of you really able to shut off the workday to hop into bed? Timed sex is really a problem if you work miles apart, especially for days on end. Your husband starts to feel like a stud horse, not in a good way.

If you're going through infertility treatments, the clinical management by your physician can destroy intimacy. What used to be private and cloistered in your marriage is now exposed and put under the microscope in examination rooms.

So, how do you restore real affection and intimacy in your marriage? What does it take to bring back the thrilling moments of loving, passionate sex?

Go back to your Bible to see what role sex plays in God's design for your marriage. Again, in Genesis Chapter 1, God commands people to "be fruitful and multiply." Sexual intercourse is fundamentally intended for procreation.

In His seventh commandment (*Exodus 20:14*), He prohibits adultery. God makes it very clear throughout the Bible that sexual activity is to reserved exclusively for marriage and is to be conducted solely between a man and woman. Anything outside of these parameters can produce children outside of wedlock and/or destroy His design for marriage.

Okay, okay, you say, but what about the fun? Do Christians think sex is only supposed to be a robotic act to make babies?

To quote the apostle Paul (completely out of context) as he is frequently fond of saying, "Certainly not!"

Dr. Ed Wheat and his wife Gaye make the argument in their book *Intended for Pleasure* that God created the incredible physiology of our bodies and the physical act of sex for more than just ensuring the continuation of the human race.

"It may surprise some of you to learn that the Bible speaks so openly, so joyously of sex in marriage. Almost every book of the Bible has something to say about sex, and Song of Solomon exquisitely depicts the love relationship in marriage....God's plan for our pleasure has never changed, and we realize this even more as we consider how we are 'fearfully and wonderfully made' *(Psalm 139:14)*. When we discover the many intricate details of our bodies that provide so many intense, wonderful physical sensations for husbands and wives to enjoy together, we can be sure that He intended us to experience full satisfaction in the marriage relationship....Intended for pleasure—yes, in the fullest meaning of the word."[1]

See? God really has created sex to be a fantastic, rollercoaster ride of sheer pleasure! It's His wonderful gift that can be opened and enjoyed over and over!

If you've never read through Song of Solomon, pull your Bible out and read the entire book. Some scholars say that the book is an allegory of the loving relationship between God and His people. That's true. But it's also the love story of a man and woman who are committed to each other for marriage.

God gave us sex, too, as the most personally bonding occupation between you and your husband. Because of its intense intimacy and (literally) the "laying bare" of your bodies and souls, sex finds its ultimate purpose in uniting you with your husband as one flesh, one heartbeat. The vulnerability of being exposed in this way is only safe when cocooned in lifelong vows for commitment to the sanctity of the marriage bed.

If infertility has robbed you of your passion and true oneness in your marriage, you will have to work a little harder now to bring the fun and excitement back into your home. Don't let Satan steal your joy!

Does your hormonal calendar rule your sex life? Then make sure you also plan fun date times as your "foreplay" for the requisite act of sex. Spend some quality time with your husband in taking a walk, playing a board game, going to a movie, or some other calm, fun activity you enjoy together. Just don't wear him out before he has to perform! Save the excitement for the bedroom!

Find ways to give your husband his favorite pleasures or some new ones. Give him a long backrub—that's a no-brainer way to make him happy. Get a warm bath or shower ready for the two of you. And don't forget...the way to a man's heart is typically through his stomach. Fix his favorite dish or order a pizza delivery!

Commit with your husband to never discuss your sexual activity with anyone other than your physician. Ask him to keep his lips zipped when hanging out with the guys. If you're having problems, conversations around the water cooler or with your girlfriends are not the best places for sex counseling. And even if your mom is your best friend, don't go confiding in her either!

Your bedroom is the last bastion of your privacy. If you need counseling, bring it up first with your physician and then take it as necessary to a qualified Christian counselor or therapist. Otherwise, let your bedroom activities remain an intimate secret that only you and your husband share.

Pray with your husband specifically about your sex life together. Praise God for bringing you together and for giving you His magnificent gift of sex.

After a short time of praise and thanksgiving, lift up your worries, your needs, your issues before the Lord. Listen to your husband's prayers; learn from his out-loud thoughts about what is bugging him. Silently perhaps, both of you should ask God for wisdom and peace in how to spend your bedroom time together.

But talk with your husband first about prayer timing. For some couples, prayer is a way to end their conversation time together before jumping into canoodling. But prayer together can also be a mood-killer.

Get your husband on board with praying together, maybe on one specific night each week as your "prayer night" when it won't infringe on lovemaking time.

Finally, always remember that all men like to *play*. Down deep, they are still little boys who like to throw rocks in the water, play hide-and-seek, go exploring, or jump up and down at a football game. Learn what "play" means to your mate, and find ways to foster togetherness in what he considers to be fun.

The more you can play together outside the bedroom, the more exciting things will be when you get down to the serious business of sex. Have fun!

Recognize that pursuing intimacy is important not only for you and your husband but for you and Jesus Christ as well. Teaching pastor Kyle Idleman likens apathy in marriage to spiritual apathy:

"When a husband and wife have been married for a while, it's natural to find that some of the feelings have started to fade. The commitment might be strong, but the passion got lost along the way. The best thing they can do to rekindle that love is to start pursuing each other the way that they used to. He begins to buy her flowers....She writes him love letters....She dresses up for him....He takes her out on dates. As they *come after* each other with extravagant and sacrificial acts of love and devotion, the feelings and the passion will start to return.

"That's a great place to start in your relationship with Christ....Get on your knees next to your bed and talk to God about your day. Turn on some worship music in your car and sing along....start reading and meditating on God's word....it will begin to stir the fire that has grown dim."[2]

Just as you need to keep your intimacy alive with your spouse, rekindle your love for Jesus by dedicating time to Him. He has promised you will find Him when you seek Him!

PRAYER:

Great and wonderful Creator, how I bless You for creating us, for choosing marriage for us, and for inventing sexual activity! Your plans are awesome and amazing, indeed! I praise You for the wonder of sexual attraction and the fulfillment it brings. I honor You and submit to You my wishes, my husband's needs, and our marriage bed, all laid upon Your altar.

I confess, Father, that too often I have sought my own desires and wishes, with a lack of interest in seeking what is best for my husband. I confess my own impatience when his wishes get in the way of what I want. Forgive me for the times I have failed to recognize that this is a gift from You; teach me gratitude.

Thank You, my Provider, for granting me a husband. Thank You for making his body in a perfect way to complement mine. Thank You for giving us a growing love for each other; do not let time and stresses diminish our feelings for each other, even as we may fall into a comfortable routine.

Please help me to use my life, my time, and my body to glorify You. Help me to be submissive to my husband, so that even if he doesn't always obey Your word, he might be silently won over by my sweet conduct. Show me how to adorn my heart with the incorruptible beauty of a gentle and quiet spirit, something that is very precious in Your sight and pleasing to my husband. Make me more like the "holy women" of the Bible who trusted in You and adorned themselves this way.

I ask that You will provide for my husband the joy of sharing the marriage bed with me. Help him to remember that sexual activity is designed to meet needs for both of us. Teach him the joy and pleasure of making our together time a selfless gift of himself. Give me discernment to know and be sensitive to my husband's energy levels as well.

If there are any of my activities (or his) that are distracting us from spending quality time together, I pray that You will show us so that we may withdraw from them for a time. Help us to focus on each other, even as the demands of our commitments outside home may keep us apart. Show us how to balance our work in such a way that we do not neglect each other. Show us both the things that will make each other happy.

Bless us tonight, this week, this month, this year with a renewed love and a greater sense of Your presence in our marriage. Give us a marriage bed that celebrates all the good gifts You have given us. Teach me how to pursue Your love anew as well. In Jesus' name, Amen.

(1 Peter 3:1-5; Deuteronomy 24:5)

FOR REFLECTION:

❖ Read Song of Solomon; decide which passage appeals most to you. Write a paragraph or two in your own words as a love letter to your husband. Leave it under his pillow.

_____
_____
_____

❖ Think of ways you can restore some of the charm in your love life. Fix his favorite meal or a pie, add a fragrance he likes to your pillows, light a candle in your bedroom, or do whatever makes you both feel intimate. Decide ahead of time to squelch any disappointment if he doesn't respond or if you're suddenly not in the mood.

_____
_____
_____

❖ Communicate with your husband, out loud, about any possible hindrances to bedroom fun. For example, he might wish for you to get to bed sooner at night. Commit to making at least one change in your routine to accommodate him.

_____
_____
_____

❦ ❦ ❦

MARIA'S STORY:

We tried for three years to conceive our first child, went through all the infertility testing and oral medications with no problems found or favorable results. We had been accepted to an infertility drug study and were to start it the month after our child was conceived. This incredible sign of God's grace showed us that each child is indeed a gift from God—in accordance with His timing. We have been trying for baby number two for more than a year...nothing yet.

Infertility certainly puts a strain on one aspect of the marriage relationship that should be fun and spontaneous (my husband would say, "I feel like a stud sometimes," or "Oh, is it that time again?"), but my husband and I have tried to keep the issue in perspective—that the marriage relationship is complete without children, and that even if we aren't blessed with more children, we are complete as a family with just husband and wife. I think of all my single friends and realize I am so blessed to have a husband as wonderful as he is. This puts children into perspective.

Probably the most difficult aspect of wanting children is to be around families with lots of children, to hear about people getting pregnant at the drop of a hat, and to hear of all the abortions that go on. Even though our first experience showed us that God opens the womb (and closes it) in His perfect time, the envy and desire for more children is still there. I often feel guilty for feeling that way, having been blessed with a beautiful daughter, but I also feel that God is compassionate and understanding of our human nature.

The whole experience has given me a real sense of how specifically God chooses to bless with children. Every child is a gift from above, chosen for a specific time and place—whether the parent is expecting a child or not, whether they are using birth control or not.

MEGAN'S STORY (CONTINUED FROM CHAPTER 8):

With communication and intimacy, infertility is where the walls go up in our marriage. There are times of depression for me, and I shut my family out. I want to be alone with no pressures. My husband, Larry, still doesn't understand that I would like to experience being pregnant full-term, having a baby, and nursing. For a long time, I felt like half a woman because I couldn't produce children. I also felt guilty because I couldn't give Larry a child of his own. He is so wonderful with kids, especially babies. The nursery is always where he wants to help at church!

Larry assures me from time to time that his life is "fulfilled," and it doesn't matter that there is not a "little Larry" of his own in this world. He and I love our adopted Andrew as though he were born to us. We know he was an answer to prayer and a gift from God.

CHAPTER 14

Coping with Conflicts

"It is honorable for a man to stop striving, since any fool can start a quarrel." (Proverbs 20:3)

"Hatred stirs up strife, but love covers all sins." (Proverbs 10:12)

"But avoid foolish and ignorant disputes, knowing that they generate strife." (2 Timothy 2:23)

So, what did you and your husband fight about today? You didn't fight? Okay, then what did you and your husband quibble over today?

Conflicts arise at all levels, even in the best of marriages—from tossing out a slightly irritable snippet to arguing over the empty ketchup bottle to engaging in full-blown, drag-out, throwing-stuff fights. It just comes with the territory. I am sure that the first argument in the Garden of Eden was over who was at fault for eating the apple...or which one would sew the fig leaves together!

When two completely different people are thrown into the same household together for any length of time, differences of opinion are going to surface. Did he have to insult your cooking in front of your mom? Why didn't he pay that bill on time? Was he irritated with the dent you put on his car? Did he replace the toilet paper on the roller turning the right direction? (Actually, I would be happy if *anyone* in my family simply replaced the paper on the roller!)

If you've been through counseling either before or after marriage, you know that the major emphasis is on conflict resolution. And if you think figuring out finances, in-law visits, housing choices, or movie night decisions is tough, just wait until children are around!!

While several of the Bible marriages display harmony, one marriage—actually, a polygamous marriage—is fraught with fighting. Rachel and Leah are Jacob's wives, and the pattern of their patched-together marriage is bitterness, strife, and jealousy.

You probably know the story in Genesis of how Jacob marries two sisters; he gets duped into marrying the less lovely one (Leah) and has to work-pay for the other (Rachel). It's an arrangement born out of deception, where Jacob receives ironic retribution for his own treatment of his brother, Esau.

Now Jacob is saddled with two wives: he's crazy about one and barely tolerates the other. Childbearing becomes a one-upmanship game for these sisters, each vying for their husband's attention and even donating their handmaidens to be two additional wives for Jacob. What a mess.

Leah enjoys a fruitful womb and lack of affection from Jacob, while Rachel endures a season of barrenness but is blessed by Jacob's attention. Even though Rachel eventually bears him two sons, the whole family is marked by cunning, chaos, and conflict. There's an undercurrent of drama, and while it's not stated in the Bible, one can imagine Jacob often throwing up his hands and leaving the whole scene to go for long walks in the desert.

God fulfills His covenant promise to Abraham by making Jacob the father of many sons. But Jacob's desires, combined with the selfishness of Rachel and Leah, create an acid environment that poisons everyone. The sons of these four women eventually become the founding families of the nation of Israel but not before a majority of them send their brother Joseph into Egyptian slavery.

Jacob's household is the prime example of why God's plan from the beginning for monogamy—one husband, one wife—has endured the millennia as the ideal, God-blessed arrangement. And yet, because of our continuing sinfulness, we often fail to handle marital strife any better than our spiritual ancestors did.

How well you manage the conflicts in your marriage now will set up your communication patterns for making important decisions in dealing with infertility, deciding about treatment or adoption, handling child-rearing together, or choosing ministries. You and your husband are in this marriage together, for better or worse. Make sure the "worse" is not the result of your own selfishness.

Discussing your infertility woes together can actually be a good bonding time, if you approach it from the right point of view.

Consider timing. Right after you both get home from an exhausting day at work isn't the best time to bring up life-changing subjects. Be patient. Plan ahead for these heart-to-heart talks. Turn off the TV, set your phones on silent, and talk over a favorite meal together. Go for a long walk on your favorite path. Minimize distractions.

Make sure your husband knows what you're going to discuss, so he's not blind-sided. Remind him, and yourself, that this is a subject where emotions are going to be running on high. Ask him to be patient with you.

Start with prayer and end with prayer, whether aloud or silently. Let all of your conversations be bathed in the light of the Holy Spirit. Invite Him to be with you at all times in your discussions. Ask Him to search your hearts, guide your thoughts, comfort you in your pain, and help you to be prudent with your words.

Listen carefully to your husband's thoughts...typically, husbands are not as forthcoming in expressing feelings as much as wives are. Take note of his expectations. Ask him to be patient about hearing you out as well.

Take a deep breath whenever his interests and wishes are in conflict with yours. Dig deeper with him, without accusing, to find out exactly why he feels a certain way. Did he grow up with a large or small family? Does he have fears about holding tiny babies in a gentle way? Is something holding him back? Understand his point of view before jumping to conclusions.

Author Heather Holleman, a Penn State English instructor involved in Faculty Commons (part of the Cru Christian ministry on college campuses), gives practical advice for how to be gracious and charitable in disagreement...in this case, with a department head:

"Instead of storming into my boss's office with a list of grievances, each time, I said, 'I'm confused. Can you help me?' This gracious, charitable question diffused conflict and moved him from a reactive, defensive state to a responsive one. I learned to believe the best, begin with a gracious question, and state what I believe kindly."[1]

Consider your own needs and desires. Narrow your battlefields to only one or two of your top priorities...no matter what you might think, you don't get everything you want in a marriage! Come into the conversation ready to compromise where necessary. Give up what's not essential.

You'll find lots of other books that deal with ongoing conflicts between husband and wife. Typical rules of engagement require certain tactics for success. Stick to one issue—avoid rabbit-trail subjects. Be clear and precise in expressing how you are feeling or thinking—your husband is not clairvoyant (he can't read your mind). Don't let "the sun go down on your anger"—settle all disputes, if possible, before you turn the lights out, or sleep will be impossible.

One interesting approach to addressing marital problems is found in *The Love Dare*, a companion book to the movie *Fireproof*. The 40-day "dare" to love your spouse unconditionally takes you through the qualities of true love, with the toughest one being forgiveness:

"Imagine you find yourself in a prison-like setting. As you look around, you see a number of cells visible from where you're standing. You see people from your past incarcerated there—people who wounded you.... Even your spouse is locked in nearby, trapped with all the others in this jail of your own making.

"This prison, you see, is a room within your own heart. This dark, drafty, depressing chamber exists inside you every day. But not far away, Jesus is standing there, extending to you a key that will release every inmate.... Your freedom is now dependent on your forgiveness."[2]

Seek to forgive your husband whenever possible. Make it a point to dwell on his positive attributes and dismiss his shortcomings when they are not significant. Try to see the conflict from his point of view.

However, when conflicts are long-term...resulting in angry outbursts, verbal abuse, or physical violence...seek help from your pastor or another Christian counselor. Any conflict that puts you in a position of bodily or psychological damage is poisonous to your marriage and very dangerous for you. Don't be afraid to ask for outside help.

Remember that you both are in this together. There is nothing else in your marriage that will require being on the same hymnbook page in the way child-rearing does. Get yourself and your husband ready to sing the same words, in the same key, at the same time! Your goal is to praise and worship Jesus Christ in harmony!

PRAYER:

Gracious God, You are so wise and good—through Your perfect plan for marriage, You have given me a husband to serve as my friend and leader. I praise You for fulfilling my needs for companionship and an opportunity to become a mother.

I thank You in the midst of the trials in our marriage. I will not cease to praise You and give glory to You, even when the conflicts erode my happiness. O God, forgive me for my selfishness. Forgive my husband when he thinks only of himself.

Help us to start by imitating You, walking in love as Your Son, Christ, also loved us and gave Himself for us. Let us sacrifice our selfish ambitions on the altar of our marriage, as a sweet-smelling aroma to You.

Lead us to walk out of the darkness and instead walk as children of light, reaping the fruit of Your Holy Spirit—goodness, righteousness, truth—and discovering what is acceptable to You. Let us redeem our time together.

Fill us with Your Spirit of harmony, speaking to one another in psalms and hymns and spiritual songs, making a melodious marriage that gives thanks always for all things to You, Our God and Father, submitting to each other in a holy fear.

Teach me anew how to submit to my husband as to You and respect my husband's headship. Help my husband to love me even more, in the same way

Jesus loved the church with sacrifice, cleansing, and nourishing. For we two are members of Christ's body, just as we have joined together as one flesh in marriage.

Open our hearts to wisely understand and accept Your will for our lives, and teach us how to love each other the same way You love us. In Your Son's beautiful, loving name, Amen.

(Ephesians 5)

🍎 🍎 🍎

FOR REFLECTION:

❖ Recall the last time you and your husband fought, argued, or quibbled over an issue. How would you describe your attitude toward him in the middle of your conflict? Did your attitude reflect God's love or not? If you have any regrets, how could you approach the same problem from a different point of view?

_____
_____
_____
_____

❖ What emotions does your husband express in a conflict? Does he communicate well or not? Can you think of language that you can use in the middle of an argument that would help defuse the tension between you?

_____
_____
_____
_____

❖ Make a point this week to go through one entire day without challenging, fussing at, arguing, or acting superior to your husband, no matter what he says. If you can keep this pattern for several days, write down the results—in your own heart and the attitude of your husband. Pray, too, about your conflicts and having a marriage that glorifies God.

LAUREN'S STORY (CONTINUED FROM CHAPTER 3):

How has infertility affected our marriage? Financially, it has been an extreme burden. We are in debt to the physicians because the medication is so expensive. And yet, our communication and intimacy in our marriage has overwhelmingly increased for the better as well as my spiritual life; his spiritual walk is now being strongly tested.

Family members do not know we have undergone treatments, nor co-workers, because I don't want to give anyone a chance to distract us from our walk by words. Our families do encourage us to relax and it will happen; they do not know the full extent of our problems. Because it's an intimate problem that we feel is ours alone to share, we spend time talking together and being close all the time now.

ERIN'S STORY:

We dealt with infertility for about eight years. My physical problems involved endometriosis. I had one tubal pregnancy and two surgeries to remove the endometriosis.

The hardest problem with infertility for me was feeling broken. I can remember waking up one morning crying and crying, thinking I couldn't go to work or even face the day. My husband called his office, canceled his patients, and held me all day and let me cry. That day changed my heart, and I was content after that to be patient with God's plan for us.

Our prayers for a baby were finally answered through adoption. After they placed our son in my arms, my frustration with infertility melted away. These days, I always stop by our church nursery every Sunday for a baby fix. Nothing is more precious!

CHAPTER 15

Becoming a "Jewel" Wife

"Who can find a virtuous wife? For her worth is far above rubies. The heart of her husband safely trusts her; so he will have no lack of gain....

"Charm is deceitful and beauty is passing, but a woman who fears the Lord, she shall be praised. Give her of the fruit of her hands, and let her own works praise her in the gates." (Proverbs 31:10-11,30-31)

When you walked away from your wedding ceremony holding hands with your new husband, life looked pretty good. You had a general idea about how to be a good wife.

You'd probably agree, though, that your expectations and identification in your role as the "Mrs." have evolved in the intervening time. You gave up some of your advantages but gained more in the bargain. Life has certainly changed since you were a "Miss"!

How do you see yourself now? As the "better half"? Do you cringe at the idea of being a "weaker vessel"? Do you still dislike your assigned moniker as "helpmeet"?

First, the Scriptures never refer to a wife as the better half of a marriage...that's a cultural idiom. The Creation story in Genesis makes it pretty clear that man and woman were created by God with *equal value*, yet with *different roles*.

Nowhere in Scripture does it ever say that men are more highly prized by God than women, or vice versa...we are on equal footing before our righteous, holy, just, and merciful Lord. We are just as sinful as men, yet we are just as much loved by our great Creator. Men and women who trust in Christ Jesus as their Savior will share equal joy in heaven!

That, however, doesn't change the fact that we have different earthly roles to fulfill. Throughout Scripture, God's order maintains that men have the responsibility of being the primary leader of the family, with women as second in command.

This reality doesn't make us women any less spiritual, any less esteemed, any less distinguished in our service to God. It does, however, establish a hierarchy of authority.

It's true that both husbands and wives are commanded to submit to each other in marriage. You have to surrender your autonomy to your husband, just as he has to submit his freedom to you. And you both have to submit to God.

But, your husband is going to answer directly to God for how well he fulfilled his leadership role in marriage. God requires our husbands to be even more responsible than we should be in our roles! That's a tall order.

Remember, too, that our husbands can only be effective in their role when we are effective in ours. Are you making an earnest effort to respect him? Have you learned to accept your role as his helper? Here's the hidden treasure: It's a fantastic gift from God!

There is huge joy and huge freedom in relinquishing most of the control to your husband. It doesn't mean you're some kind of slave. You're still the advisor, equally half of the stewardship team, responsible for making lots and lots of decisions, and all-around queen of the household. You have plenty of God-given responsibilities to do.

Being a "jewel" wife is serious business. Although author Jane Austen never married, she highly esteemed the role of wifehood and wrote often of its virtues. She also admonished her readers to be women of good character. "Men of sense," Austen wrote in her 1815 novel *Emma*, "whatever you may choose to say, do not want silly wives."[1]

I encourage you to study the "Wonder Woman" of the Bible. Yes, it's that lady in Proverbs 31:10-31. For three decades, I have been trying to live up to her impossible standards. That's because my loving husband read this passage aloud when he proposed to me. It was very sweet of him, but I fell off that pedestal pretty quickly!

Still, we can learn a lot from this nameless paragon of womanhood. It's an acrostic poem, which means that the first letter of each stanza begins with a letter of the alphabet in the original Hebrew text. No doubt young Israelite girls were expected to learn this poem by heart so that they could model their lives after this exemplary lady.

In just 22 verses, we find that this woman is rarer than costly jewels. She is an astute financial manager at home. She engages in commerce, gets up early in the morning, and works hard to make sure everyone in her household has plenty to eat.

She is prudent in business and investments. She strengthens her body with exercise and work. She seeks to perform quality work, and she perseveres in it. At the same time, she volunteers to help the poor.

She dresses herself and her family in fine quality clothing...she must have been a good shopper or made all their clothes! Her husband is free to pursue his responsibilities in public life because she is skillful in running the home.

She is wise, prepares for the future, and reaps the rewards of her diligence. She is kind in her speech and teaching. The praise and honor from her husband and children are her greatest reward.

The basis of her strength, wisdom, diligence, and character stems from her relationship with God and His providence. Her Lord is sovereign in her life, and she is obedient to Him.

Mercy! I'm sure all of our husbands would love to be married to that woman! But they married us, so we need to own up to our need to be godly wives. We'll never be perfect, but with God's help, we can store up treasures in heaven in our earthly work here below.

While you struggle with infertility, don't forget your vow to be a faithful wife. That's your first responsibility, and it remains your primary role (after your identity as a follower of Christ), whether or not you ever become a mom. Motherhood will always rank second.

Every effort you make to strengthen your marriage and your home is a gift to God...lifted up in obedience to Him and in thanksgiving for all He has already done for you. When you seek His purpose as a godly wife, you will find the inexpressible joy of experiencing His pleasure in you.

You will LOVE every minute of being His woman!

PRAYER:

Holy Spirit, guide me into becoming the woman and wife You created me to be. Please show me, in my relationship with my husband, how to tackle the role You have prepared for me.

O God, sometimes being a submitting wife is so difficult. I need Your strength, wisdom, character, faith, and hope to be the very best helpmeet my husband needs. Help me to rejoice in my own role, develop it to my very best abilities, and honor You by honoring my husband. As I serve him, help me remember that I will be serving You.

First and foremost, help me to earn my husband's trust, doing him good always and avoiding selfish attitudes. Make me a diligent worker, not slacking but staying focused on the job at hand—and I will need lots of energy, Lord, to do this.

God, please help me to be a good cook! I want to seek out healthy foods and meals for my husband, myself, and eventually my family. Help me to make this a priority for our well-being.

Make me a good steward, too, of the finances and resources You have given us. Make me a wise money-manager, and help me contribute to the family income. Give me ideas for being thrifty and ways to stretch our budget.

Likewise, show me how to extend generosity toward others who are less fortunate. Make me unafraid of the future, so that I can give generously when possible.

Help me to encourage my husband to take a leadership role outside of our home, where he can learn to serve others. Make me so skillful in running the home that he will be free to pursue responsibilities in his public life.

Clothe me, O God, in Your strength and honor. Make me a modest dresser who does not call inappropriate attention to myself; instead, help me to dress so that I will look attractive for sharing Your good news and appealing for my husband.

Help me to stay physically fit, as much as possible with the demands on me. I pray You will give me the energy, time, and desire to exercise. Make me strong to serve You and my husband.

Help me to never "eat the bread of idleness" but stay watchful for the ways of our household. When I open my mouth to say something, let my words come from a forgiving heart. Give me the fruits of Your Holy Spirit, especially kindness, and teach me Your wisdom from Your word.

Let me not seek my husband's praise, but keep my eyes on You as I "run for the prize" in following You. You are sovereign...You are loving...You are my Provider. Give me the daily grace I need to become a wife after Your own heart. In the blessed name of Jesus, Amen.

(Proverbs 31:10-31)

❦ ❦ ❦

FOR REFLECTION:

❖ Read Proverbs 31:10-31. Decide which characteristics of this "wonder wife" you share with her, and list them below. Give praise to God that He has given you these gifts.

_____

_____

_____

❖ Now determine two or three traits or accomplishments from this description that you would like to develop in your own life. Ask God to help you make these a reality.

_____

_____

❖ Whether cooking is your "thing" or not, try out at least two new recipes this week. Even if what you make is not completely successful with your husband, keep trying until you find something healthy you can both enjoy. Write your results below.

_____

_____

_____

_____

🌹 🌹 🌹

KATIE'S STORY:

We were married three years when we decided to start trying to get pregnant. About one-and-a-half years later, my ob/gyn suggested that my husband be checked because there seemed to be no medical reason why I wasn't getting pregnant. A testicular biopsy revealed immature, deformed sperm as well as an extremely low sperm count. There was no medical history to account for this. So we *knew God allowed it for our good.* And as much as it hurt, we were thankful that we were spared from more years of trying futilely to get pregnant. We knew and we could go on with life. (This problem is not correctable, so further treatment was not available.)

The hardest adjustment initially was to realize that our dreams of having *many* children would probably not be a reality—that having *any* children would be a miracle—by adoption even.

The second hardest adjustment was the realization that we had to cope with well-meaning comments and questions—"When are you going to start your family?" etc.—and we watched *every one* of our best friends find out they were expecting their first. Again, God was good. He enabled us *by His grace* to *truly* rejoice with our friends and to be there when their little ones were born. We enjoyed their children in place of our own.

Thirdly, we had to accept that we would not experience or understand fully the pregnancy/nursing experience, etc.

God's faithfulness is the character trait I have learned the most about. The Holy Spirit continually reassured me that He is capable of miracles, and I have no doubt!! God's sovereignty has been evident through every detail. And He has made His lovingkindness so real to me. Where I am weak, He has been strong and His will is best.

CHAPTER 16

The Privilege of Prayer Time

"Therefore I exhort first of all that supplications, prayers, intercessions, and giving of thanks be made for all men, for kings and all who are in authority, that we may lead a quiet and peaceable life in all godliness and reverence. For this is good and acceptable in the sight of God our Savior...." (1 Timothy 2:1-3a)

"...Listen to the cry and the prayer which Your servant is praying before You: that Your eyes may be open...that You may hear the prayer which Your servant makes toward this place. And may You hear the supplications of Your servant and of Your people Israel, when they pray toward this place. Hear from heaven Your dwelling place, and when You hear, forgive." (2 Chronicles 6:19-21)

"Continue earnestly in prayer, being vigilant in it with thanksgiving." (Colossians 4:2)

All the videos and self-help books in the world can't really prepare you for infertility, motherhood, adoption, or teaching little ones. While our thought life may be focused on (or dare I say it, obsessed with) children at the moment, the eventual reality is often different from our dreams.

Case in point: When I was younger and single, I volunteered to help in the toddler nursery at church, thinking this would be a lot of fun. On my first Sunday morning, I was left alone in charge of seven rambunctious two-year-olds. As the situation quickly deteriorated into chaos, I found myself completely overwhelmed and befuddled. I had no training to deal with this. But I quickly learned that the universal language isn't love—it's food. The only way I was able to gain some semblance of order was when I bribed them with animal crackers and juice!

In the same way, abrupt changes in our seasons of life can be like your car getting T-boned at a red light...motherhood (or finding out that motherhood will be impossible) becomes a broadside assault, leaving us dazed and wondering what happened. The unexpected emotions, the reality of baby care, the heartbreak, or the potential isolation can knock us down and make us wonder what happened.

The best preparation for steering through future storms begins not in medical treatments, exploring adoption possibilities, or dealing with realistic expectations. It begins with your own spiritual maturity and training.

To begin, do a personal check-up on your prayer life and Bible study time. Are you satisfied with it? Are you spending as much time as you'd like each day quietly talking with the Lord? Are you able to read and reflect on your Bible daily, even if it's only a few verses? Have you engaged with a group Bible study in the past year?

Becoming more spiritually-minded usually means devoting time to devotion, disciplining yourself to be still and quiet. If you're a 24/7 "Martha," it's very hard to make yourself sit at Jesus' feet as His "Mary" (*Luke 10:38-42*).

One solution is to get your husband on board with your need for down time, away from everything and in solitude with God. Asking him to give you 15 minutes of quiet time for your spiritual health isn't unreasonable. Demonstrate to him that devotion to your spiritual input is good for your soul and good for being a wife.

Carving out a consistent quiet time means you have to give it priority in the midst of all the other demands on you. Remind yourself that you can't keep emptying your tank without refilling it...you will eventually run out of gas.

Work hard now to make your spiritual reflection time sacrosanct. Get away from your computer, turn off your phone, close the door, put in earplugs, grab a cup of coffee...whatever it takes for you to focus your mind solely on your conversation with God. Meditate on His words and what they mean to you for the moment and the future.

Use your "empty nest" to let your roots go deep into His truth. Author Heather Holleman learned in her first attempts at growing berry plants that she had to pluck off all the blossoms for two years in order to grow healthy berries...she wouldn't have fruit until the third summer after planting. "Maybe God knows that we need seasons of total emptiness, no fruit, not even blossoms, in order to get our roots deep and strong," Holleman said.[1]

Later, if you wind up with children in your home, make sure they understand your need for your very own "alone time" with God. Your example will set the stage for them to understand their need of a quiet time as well.

Susanna Wesley, who lived from 1669 to 1742, bore 19 children into this world. Nine of them died as infants. With her pastor husband absent for long periods of time and often in debt, she also bore the responsibilities of running the home and educating her children.

Susanna was a committed Christian and Bible student in her own right—she fastidiously maintained daily devotions and tried to commit nearly *two hours* every day to prayer. The story goes that she would pull her apron over her head as a warning to her children that she was entering a time of meditation with her Lord. One can imagine the children tiptoeing around the house when Susanna was apron-hooded! Two of them, John and Charles, grew into the men who founded the Methodist Church.[2]

Susanna's example is an inspiration to all of us, reminding us that we have little excuse in our "time-saving" world to ignore our prayer life.

As you commit yourself deeply into prayer time, ask God to give you direction and opportunities to serve Him. He may lead you to do some baby-sitting for a friend, work in a church nursery, or volunteer in a school. He may provide you with an unexpected mission.

Also, ask God to help you find a mentor, an older Christian woman you respect, in your church, family, or community. Ask this woman to come alongside you, perhaps meet you for coffee once a month, and pray for you as you go through this season. Find someone who will commit to hanging with you through the long haul.

As you devote more time to personal prayer life and enjoying prayer conversations with God and your mentor, you will find yourself more and more engaged in "Mary" moments and fewer times in a "Martha" frenzy. Then you will discover the richness of what Jesus called the "good part" that you will never have taken away from you. It's a wonderful privilege that God calls us to enjoy every day!

PRAYER:

O God, please begin preparing me now to become the woman You have planned for me to be. Let me look to You as my great Father, and look to Christ as my loving Brother.

Help me, first of all, to have realistic expectations of what my life should look like from Your perspective. Help me to recognize that I will have to answer to You for the way that I spend my days.

Help me, too, to work on my relationship with You. Please help me carve time out of my busy schedule to spend time in prayer with You. Let me hear Your voice speaking to me from Your word as I study it, meditate on it, and follow it.

Show me ways and open doors for me to do some baby-sitting, fostering, children's work at church, teaching, volunteering, and even godparenting for other people's children. Show me in this service how to relate to little ones up to teenagers, that I may learn from these experiences for the future You are preparing.

O Lord, please place in my path an older Christian woman who will meet with me. Make her a prayer warrior who will come alongside me to pray for me and my struggles with infertility.

Show me, O Christ, how to feed Your little sheep. Show me what it takes to become a godly mother or mentor myself...in provision, healthy living, spiritual growth, and discipline in love.

Finally, O Lord Jesus, make me a "Mary" who loves to come sit at Your feet to learn from You. Let me not get so caught up in the frenzy of life or motherhood that I fail to see You as my first priority. Fill my heart with the love of Your Holy Spirit to pass along to others.

In the abundant love of Christ, Amen.

(Romans 15:30; John 21:17; Luke 10:39)

FOR REFLECTION:

❖ Read Daniel 6. Ponder how this story of Daniel's faithfulness to prayer compares to your own prayer/devotional time. Set a time today or this week to spend 30 minutes in steadfast prayer...and set a timer to keep yourself accountable!

❖ There are many verses in Bible about bringing our lives into submission to God's laws and will. Review 1 Corinthians 9:26-27 and Romans 12:1-2. How can you begin working on training yourself right now in spiritual matters?

❖ Pray right now for a Christian mentor/mom. This could be someone in your family, your church, or circle of friends. Pray for God to show you someone you could approach to ask for prayers and sharing time together in conversations about infertility or motherhood. Write down some possibilities.

🍎🍎🍎
LAUREN'S STORY (CONTINUED FROM CHAPTER 14):

In the past, the careless words of others cut deeply. "What are you waiting on?" "Don't you like children?" "Don't you know it's God's command to have children?" "We are to mirror God's image and further the Christian race with many kids...do you believe God's word?"

My reply has sometimes been simply, "I can't have any!" Or sometimes I've just stood there and cried, staring at their children.

Now, I just respond with God's truth, which is, "God is never late and not usually early—our baby will be here at the appointed time to be, at the calling God has placed on his/her life. We are waiting on God's perfect timing."

My prayer partner as well as our pastor and his wife have always encouraged me and loved me and continue to give me hope. Listening and loving and sharing the word of God...that's all anyone can do. You do all you can in the natural world and pray, and God does the rest.

We have worked with our youth at church. We are constantly taking nieces and nephews and loving them. Also, I've been called to pray over and love other women through their pregnancies, which is hard at first but rewarding. I have come into contact with a couple of women I encourage with positive words, praying and giving them Scriptures I have stood on and continue to do.

CHAPTER 17

Dealing with In-Laws, Outside Pressures

"Honor your father and your mother, as the Lord your God has commanded you, that your days may be long, and that it may be well with you in the land which the Lord your God is giving you." (Deuteronomy 5:16)

"For in the time of trouble He shall hide me in His pavilion; in the secret place of His tabernacle He shall hide me; He shall set me high upon a rock. And now my head shall be lifted up above my enemies all around me; therefore I will offer sacrifices of joy in His tabernacle; I will sing, yes, I will sing praises to the Lord." (Psalm 27:5-6)

"So, what are you waiting for?"
"You guys having some kind of bedroom problems?"
"I'm not getting any younger, you know...when are you going to give me a grandchild?"

Your parents. They've birthed you, raised you, still love you, and keep on being worried about you.

After you and your doctor, the people most concerned about your inability to have children are your parents, your siblings, and in-laws.

Your friends will be sympathetic, but your close family members typically have a vested interest in seeing you and your husband become parents. They want to see the family grow!

Some will be pushy and start prodding you with annoying questions from the get-go. Others may be thinking about you and wondering what's going on but not saying anything. The most obnoxious ones will make embarrassing comments about you in public!!

However it comes, the pressure from family members can be upsetting, intense, and maddening. It's bad enough that you feel disappointed in yourself, and their expectations can leave you with the distinct impression that they are disappointed in you, too. It can be even worse in large families where everyone has lots of kids and the unspoken expectation is for you to follow suit.

It's not easy dealing with the pressures from family, in-laws, friends, and fellow church members—how do you answer their questions with grace?

You and your husband first need to spend time talking with each other privately about how to handle specific family members and groups. You two need to be together in all of your decisions and thought processes before breaking any news to your family. Don't wait until the subject comes up at the extended family dinner table to know how both of you will answer.

Confiding with your close family is important and respectful to them. If you don't begin this conversation with them at some point, the elephant in the room will go on a rampage.

But communicating information about your infertility is touchy. Decide with your husband whether one or both of you will discuss it with your respective families. Anticipate their questions, and be ready with answers that you have agreed on.

Plan your announcements carefully ahead of time, deciding how much information to share. This is not happy news to broadcast willy-nilly like a pregnancy. Instead, think of your conversations about infertility as a call for support from your family. Choose a time when you can meet in person or make a joint phone call. Telling each set of parents separately is probably a good idea.

Consider also the dynamics between parents and other family members when you are sharing any sensitive news. Whatever you tell to one will likely be shared with the rest of the family, so decide in advance just how much you want the whole group to know.

Keep your personal information to a minimum. What's between you and your husband and your doctor should stay there. Your bedroom secrets belong in your bedroom. Be intentional in telling your family members to avoid bringing up the subject with you; comfort them by telling them that you are "working on things" and that they will be the first to know if you have any good news.

Listen quietly and nod if they want to help you "fix" the situation. But be firm if you do not wish to receive unwanted advice. If you have a physician working with you, tell them so. You are better off listening to your physician than old wives' remedies. Of course, you could always politely nod and pretend as if their home remedy has merit!

If your family members are Christian, ask them to pray for you. You really do need their prayers. Give them your specific prayer requests.

Ask them to keep your situation as private as possible. Unless you're open to have an entire church praying for you, ask them to keep your requests off the typical prayer chains. A lot depends on your comfort level.

If you are considering adoption, think about keeping your intentions under wraps until you have investigated it and are starting the process. There may be some, particularly in older generations, who will think you are "giving up" or that adoption is only second best or that it's just too risky...as if birthing biological children isn't risky enough! Tell them when you are confident enough to explain the process and why you have chosen that route.

When it comes to answering nosy questions and rude comments, prepare yourself in advance for how you will respond. Most of the time, we simply react by lashing out in anger, recoiling in stony silence, or fleeing the situation.

Recognize, though, that people who haven't gone through infertility don't really understand. It's the same with cancer or chemotherapy...if you haven't had it, it's hard to imagine all the fears and hardships of those who endure it.

Most people are simply interested in you and want the best for you. We are all naturally curious people, and we all make mistakes in our conversations with others. Be sympathetic to their lack of understanding. They have no idea of the cauldron of emotions that are boiling just below the surface of your smile. No need to unleash it all on them!

In a conversation that threatens your personal space about your infertility, resolve to stay calm. Smile, answer briefly, and change the subject. To friends, explain that you would rather not discuss your situation outside of the family. To family members, say that it's something you'd rather discuss at a later date.

Need help in setting boundaries? Talk with your pastor or another Christian counselor to explore solutions that guard your marriage and privacy.

Of course, you can always tell the truth—that you are praying about it! Then ask your friends and family to pray for you...for wisdom, faith, and the blessing of children in your family. Even atheists will at least agree to wish you well.

In the midst of these difficult situations, remember that you have an advocate in Jesus Christ. He is there beside you, and you will never be alone even in a crowd of fertile women. Ask Him to prepare your heart for dealing with your family. Ask Him to give you peace when the storm clouds gather. Ask Him to fill you with His love for those who rub you the wrong way.

Don't let bitterness or unforgiveness take root in your heart toward family and friends. "We all must be reminded that unforgiveness can creep into and lurk around the secret corners of our hearts, and we can give place to it without even recognizing what it is," said author Stormie Omartian. "That's why we must periodically ask God to reveal any unforgiveness in us—especially toward our family members. Forgiveness has to flow in us before the power of the Holy Spirit flows through us when we pray."[1] Good advice!

Someday, you'll be the older one talking with a younger infertile woman. This experience now will teach you how to be loving, respectful, and not-so-nosy yourself!

🍎 🍎 🍎

PRAYER:

O Lord God, my Father, when I am having trouble communicating with my parents and in-laws, please be right by my side...please give me words to approach them in wisdom, kindness, and respect.

Please help me to honor my parents and my parents-in-law as my elders, as You have ordained and commanded. Please help me to ignore any callous remarks, any manipulation, any attacks that I might perceive they are making upon me. Instead of responding in defense, help me to choose my words carefully that I may turn away any wrath with a soft answer.

Father, help me to reach out to those members of my extended family who will be sympathetic to our needs for prayer and privacy. Give me patience with everyone in my family, and give me opportunities to share information as needed.

My husband and I need Your harmony and unity of spirit...please help us as we discuss when/where/how to communicate with our parents and other family members. Help us to walk worthy of Your calling, with all lowliness and gentleness, with longsuffering, bearing with one another in love, endeavoring to keep the unity of Your Spirit in the bond of peace. For You are our one and only God and Father—let us lean upon You.

Give us prudence and discretion as well, that we may keep our home and bedroom sacrosanct for Your glory and not our own. You are our great Physician...help us to turn to You for guidance as we venture into unknown waters. Help us to love those who address us unlovingly; help us to bless those who use careless words. Inspire us to do good for them and pray for them, even if they try to use us or manipulate us.

I pray even now that You will change or encourage the hearts of our parents and in-laws, preparing them ahead of time for news of our situation. Teach them how to be an encouragement to us, supporting us, and backing off when tensions become too much. Show them how to love us, even as You love us and provide for us. In the meek and gentle nature of Christ, Amen.

(Proverbs 15:1; Ephesians 4:1-6; Proverbs 5:1-2; Mark 2:17; Matthew 5:43-48)

FOR REFLECTION:

❖ Identify sources of tension between you and your extended family members. Pray for these particular people, and write down your prayers for God to prepare them and you for positive communication.

_____

_____

_____

_____

❖ Who are your allies? Write their names, and make a point to meet with them in person, if possible, to talk about your situation, ask for prayer, and ask for discretion in sharing your information with others. Keep an on-going line of communication with them.

_____

_____

_____

_____

❖ Pray with and for your husband this evening. Pray here now, in writing, for a sweetness of spirit that accepts his family (and yours) together; pray for unity and harmony between the two of you, so that family members will see your hope, determination, and focus for the future.

_____

_____

_____

_____

MEGAN'S STORY (CONTINUED FROM CHAPTER 13):

Family comments can hurt...badly. "You were the first to marry but the last to start a family." "Look at Emmie (a sibling). Maybe you could talk to them and see what their secret to having kids is." Or, "Looks like the only things we'll get from you are grandpuppies." This was said right after we got our new dog. And, "We have six grandchildren, and looks like that will be all since Megan and Larry aren't trying that hard to have any of their own."

Neither my mother nor my mother-in-law had any trouble getting pregnant, and neither had miscarriages or problems carrying their babies full term. All their babies were healthy and normal. To talk about infertility with either one was like talking a foreign language!

On one occasion when all of the extended family were gathered together, one of my pregnant siblings saw a magazine and commented, "Oh look at that cute dress...I wish I could order that, but I can't because I'm pregnant." I ignored it until the third time the subject came up. Then I said, "I would give my right arm to be in maternity clothes instead of the regular clothes you want so badly. I guess that's one thing I'll never ask to borrow of yours." Not very nice, but the comments stopped!

Another, on her second pregnancy, said, "Even if it's a monkey, this is our last one." I said, "At least you're having something," and walked out.

One said, "I'm saving all my maternity clothes for you." I said, "Don't hold your breath...give them to the local pregnancy clinic."

I have been in rooms where people talk non-stop about their birthing experiences. I either walk out to "powder my nose" or sit there, smiling sweetly, not saying a word. But nowadays, if someone says something hurtful, I just smile and walk away with no comment.

I really feel that people are so consumed in their stories they just don't think about who they're talking to or what the other people may be thinking. Sometimes it may be ignorance and sometimes conceit. It's the bragging that burns at me.

Though God has forgiven me, that doesn't mean I still don't have "bad baby days." I do. However, now, I have a friend to call, or I talk with my husband, or I find a project to do—healthy things.

Another family member has always wanted to be a mom. Shortly after she married, she had trouble conceiving and was diagnosed with endometriosis. After long years, she and her husband finally applied for adoption. Through my experiences, different but no less painful, we can talk to one another about what we are feeling and going through. Many a night we have talked and cried over the phone and prayed for one another. I now have a soul mate who understands.

At this point, I don't know if I'll ever feel comfortable around infants—that's okay, too. I just work with three-year-olds and up. I do enjoy baby showers. I've even felt the baby kick inside my sister's tummy! That's something I never thought I could or would do! See, God can heal and help you to dance again!

CHAPTER 18

Getting Your Financial House in Order

"*His lord said to him, 'Well done, good and faithful servant; you were faithful over a few things, I will make you ruler over many things. Enter into the joy of your lord.'*" (Matthew 25:21)

"*Honor the Lord with your possessions, and with the firstfruits of all your increase; so your barns will be filled with plenty, and your vats will overflow with new wine.*" (Proverbs 3:9-10)

"*Better is a little with the fear of the Lord, than great treasure with trouble.*" (Proverbs 15:16)

"You can't be in debt and win. It doesn't work.... You've got to tell your money what to do or it will leave."–Dave Ramsey[1]

Financial advisor Dave Ramsey has helped millions of couples, families, and individuals gain control of their personal/home finances, get out of debt, and prepare for the future. His common-sense solutions and advice get right down to the nitty-gritty of the temptations and pressures we face in making daily financial decisions.

How are you doing in this area of your marriage and your personal life? Are you and your husband able to freely discuss and agree on budgeting? Have you made it your mission to stay out of debt and achieve financial peace through responsible earning, saving, and spending?

Infertility treatments can be extremely expensive. Rearing children is even more expensive. Are you working now on your finances to prepare for those possibilities?

Some of the great scourges of the American lifestyle in the late 20th and early 21st centuries have been obsession with materialism, impulsive spending, and keeping up with the ever-expanding advances in technical gadgetry. Too many people have become slaves to their credit cards.

We face difficulties, too, with securing the basic necessities of food, clothing, shelter, and transportation. The steady advance of inflation outruns salaries that haven't kept the same pace. Limited earning power and underemployment combine to create soaring debt.

So, what does God say about all this in the Scripture? Believe it or not, money (or the love of it) represents a significant portion of the Bible's subject matter; some say the Bible has more than 2,000 verses about wealth, contentment, greed, and financial planning![2]

The key word is stewardship. This single word encompasses the Christian obligation (and joy) to follow God's commandments, admonishments, and examples in managing our earthly goods wisely.

Here are some of the typical lessons you'll find as you rove through Ecclesiastes, Proverbs, and the New Testament: Work hard, and don't fall into lazy patterns. Give your "firstfruits," the first 10 percent of your earnings, to the Lord's work...it's called a tithe, and it's only a tenth of all that belongs to God anyway. Pay your taxes. Take care of your family and aging parents. Plan wisely and save for the future. Use your wealth to give generously to others. Don't go into debt, and especially don't let yourself become obligated to someone else's debt. Love God, serve others, and put yourself last. Be a good "steward" of whatever God has given you, little or lots.

It all sounds so simple...and yet trying to follow God's path is so hard when all the bills are thrown at you. Oftentimes, there's too little left over or not even enough to make ends meet.

If you and your husband can agree on a budget or who handles the bill paying, you are among an elite few. Differences in how to manage money are fodder for marital arguments and sometimes even result in divorce.

If you and your husband tend to disagree, look for a household money management course to take together, preferably at a church in your community, where you can learn about wise ways to handle the family finances.

It's particularly imperative to nail down your finances right now, in case you're in the work force and decide to stay at home at some point if your family grows. Budget and save now for daycare or other babysitting services if you decide to remain employed. Make sure you and your husband are on the same page financially regarding your role as homemaker or wage earner. Find ways to adequately finance infertility treatments, if recommended, so that you won't go into debt.

It's equally important to work on conservation of resources. Carefully consider how you are spending money as well as making it. Are you buying coffee at expensive coffeehouses, when you could spend a few minutes at home to make your own carry-out mugful? Review your spending habits to see where you could hold back from overspending. As my grandfather was fond of saying, "Money talks...it says good-bye!"

Pray, pray, pray...for sufficient income now to balance your budget and start saving for kids...for your husband to be ready for the role of sole breadwinner if you decide to become a stay-at-home mom...for your financial stewardship to be God-honoring...to be ready for any financial sacrifices you may have to make.

Rather than go into debt to buy something, wait and pray...give God the opportunity to provide, giving you a double blessing!

God hears even your most mundane prayers. This is not pie-in-the-sky, health-and-wealth, God-is-your-personal-genie prayer. Instead, it means praying in humility and faith for God to meet your *needs* (not your *wants*), especially for financial stability. He is faithful to provide, and you will find His gifts to be above and beyond what you ask or desire.

Even Jesus, when He taught His disciples how to pray, included that humble cry for God to "give us this day our daily bread." Not tomorrow's bread, not a castle, not a Ferrari, but our daily bread. The Heavenly

Father who listened to Jesus still hears your prayers today. Go ask Him right now.

🕊 🕊 🕊

PRAYER:

Gracious God, our Jehovah-Jireh Provider, I cry out for discernment in this area of our marriage and life. I lift up my voice for understanding of our financial obligations to You; I seek this as much as I seek out silver and hidden treasures! Let me understand how to fear You and find Your wisdom and knowledge, for You give it freely, storing it up for those who love You and seek to walk in Your ways. Be a shield to us; guard our paths and preserve our resources.

Let me look to those who are diligent in work and devotion to You; let me consider their ways and be wise. Help us to gather our finances together during this time, before we are in dire need, that we may be prepared. Let us not "fall asleep at the wheel" so that poverty would come upon us and our monies become plundered.

Help my husband and myself to seek honest work and income, working hard so that we will have sufficient means to receive and rear children. But keep us from trusting only in our wealth, thinking that it will protect us. Lift our eyes to trust You. Do not let the pleasures and luxuries of life make us poor, but neither let us overwork to be rich...for riches certainly make themselves wings and fly away like an eagle to heaven!

As we review our debt level, remind us that we can become slaves to credit cards and lenders...do not let them rule over us, for You are our God and Guide. Help us to avoid falling into greater debt, and help us to pay off any obligations that do not make sense in our budget. Keep us from frivolous spending, that we may have enough to eat, a roof over our heads, clothing, and transportation—before we consider adding children to our household.

Finally, O Lord, help us to provide for those who need us now and in the future, and give us the power to do so. We trust in Your good plans for us, to give us adequate financial provisions, as we bow in humility and fear to You. You hold the riches and honor and life that we desire. Make us godly servants who rely totally on You. In the providing grace of Jesus Christ, Amen.

(Proverbs 2:3-8; 6:6-11; 13:11; 18:11; 21:17; 23:4-5; 22:7, 26-27; 28:19; 3:27; 10:22; 22:4)

FOR REFLECTION:

❖ Take a good, long look at your budget before you sit down with your husband to talk about it. Where are your sources of income? What kind of savings do you have or need for family planning? Consider putting a budgeting program on your computer or creating one manually, to show categories and the status of your available resources and spending.

_____
_____
_____
_____

❖ Identify areas where you could reduce some of your spending, and write three of those expenses below. Commit to reducing these areas for one month, and pocket the savings in a separate account or envelope. After a month, review your spending again to see if there are further ways you cut back to prepare for the expenses of infertility and having children.

_____
_____
_____
_____

❖ Pray with and for your husband today, before making a "finance date" to talk with him. Look for a local church program on finances that you could attend together, or seek a godly financial counselor who can help you make a budget. Pray that your husband will be receptive to looking carefully together at how to prepare for children.

_____
_____
_____
_____

KATIE'S STORY (CONTINUED FROM CHAPTER 15):

God has provided the financial means to pay for the three adoptions we've had. They are very expensive as a rule. The first was *free*! The second was tough, but we paid it. And the third was paid by a family member...$9,000! God does provide!

We were probably more communicative and closer when working through an adoption process. It requires much prayer, decision-making, and time (meetings, interviews, answering questions biological parents don't have to consider).

The only problem we've had with family and in-laws is that one set of parents did not understand why we wanted a third child—and the other set wished we would not accept a special needs child.

God doesn't always give us what we want. But He does give us what we need. As difficult as infertility was, the blessings far exceed it. The verses I claimed for the unknown future regarding children were in Jeremiah 29:11-13. After receiving our first child, we felt God leading us to adopt a second, and I claimed 1 Samuel 1:27-28.

I have to cling to my God and His character or else I could not know so assuredly that His ways are perfect. The realization that He saw fit to entrust the upbringing of three precious—and very different—children to my husband and me is overwhelming and humbling. The adjustments adoption brings and the issues it raises (birthparents, etc.) stretch us. There are always constant reminders that our children are adopted. But we have always thought of the process as a positive one—even in the difficult times. And there is no resentment.

CHAPTER 19

The Church and You

"And let us consider one another in order to stir up love and good works, not forsaking the assembling of ourselves together, as is the manner of some, but exhorting one another, and so much the more as you see the Day approaching." (Hebrews 10:24-25)

"For as the body is one and has many members, but all the members of that one body, being many, are one body, so also is Christ. For by one Spirit we were all baptized into one body–whether Jews or Greeks, whether slaves or free–and have all been made to drink into one Spirit. For in fact the body is not one member but many....Now you are the body of Christ, and members individually." (1 Corinthians 12:12-14, 27)

"Then we who are alive and remain shall be caught up together with them in the clouds to meet the Lord in the air. And thus we shall always be with the Lord." (1 Thessalonians 4:17)

Do you attend church regularly? Not just Easter and Christmas, not just whenever you feel like it, not just for weddings and funerals...but actually standing, sitting, or kneeling on Sunday mornings alongside other Christians in worship?

Sure, it's quite wonderful to worship God when you are all alone, especially walking through woods or along a beach. Yes, it's comforting and peaceful to have quiet moments at home or at work to pause and bow your head in devotion and prayer. You don't have to walk into a church to be in the presence of God, to worship and praise Him. He is always with you, always ready to listen.

But it's essential to frequently join hands with other believers and share their physical presence in a joint time of prayer, singing hymns, repentance, learning, and praise. Why?

Worship with other believers isn't an option for Christ-followers—it's a strong admonition for all of us, as it was among the early church members. During the first century, the new Christian Hebrews scattered abroad outside of Israel were wavering in their faith. The writer of the book of Hebrews in the New Testament recognized their need for joint assembly.

In the verse above, he cites several key reasons. First, there is a tender reminder for us to consider other people, to get out of ourselves for a moment and recognize the value and needs of others. For too many people, going to a church service is no different from attending a concert—sitting in the audience, enjoying the music and lectures, and walking away with a "feel good" attitude. This kind of worship is self-fulfillment at its finest, without the irritation of having others' problems rub off on us.

But that's not the purpose of assembling together. In church, we find others of like faith. We share their joys, sorrows, successes, failures. We link arms to fight spiritual battles together. We greet others in the love of Jesus Christ, offer encouragement to them, stand alongside them, serve with them, pray with them and for them, and eventually part with them, with the assurance we will see them again in heaven.

Church founder Timothy Keller wrote a very condemning—and at the same time very encouraging—book about "recovering the heart of the Christian faith" in his book, *The Prodigal God*. Keller knew well the sentiments of those who find churches unpleasant to so many young people, especially those who have encountered legalistic "elder brothers" within the body of believers.

"Many people who are spiritually searching have had bad experiences with churches," Keller said. "So they want nothing further to do with them. They are interested in a relationship with God, but not if they have to be part of an organization."

But, he said, "feasting" is essentially communal by nature...as it will be when we share the feast with the Lamb (Jesus) in heaven. "Besides that, there is no way you will be able to grow spiritually apart from a deep involvement in a community of other believers. You can't live the Christian life without a band of Christian friends, without a family of believers in which you find a place.... Only if you are part of a community of believers seeking to resemble, serve, and love Jesus will you ever get to know Him and grow into His likeness."[1]

As Christians, we are individuals joined together in the body of Christ. We cannot operate separately from each other. We do not lose our uniqueness—rather, the opposite is true, that we find our unique purpose in serving other believers, in the same way a hand or foot serves the entire human body.

We are called to stir one another up to love and good works. Where does that start? With ourselves. You know how good it feels when you do something nice for another person, even something as little as giving up your place in line for another. The joy-giver always gets more joy than the receiver! How much more, then, is your joy when you reach out in service to your fellow soldiers in the faith.

There's an urgency, too, in the author's voice in the above verse as he asks the Hebrews to "exhort" each other—a strong word that signifies earnest warning, advice, pressing forward, goading. Rather than negative nagging, Christians are called to put the spurs to each other to stay in the race, to fight the good fight, to persevere. We need each other to keep going.

Jesus Christ is our ultimate example for Sabbath worship—teaching and healing in the temple and going to synagogues every week, even when He was on the road. We stand in His presence when we lift our arms together in praise to Him. What a great reason to go!

So, what does all this have to do with our battle with infertility? It means we will find hope, comfort, and reassurance in the assembly of other Christians, especially when we reach out in fellowship with other Christian women.

Consider the story of Elizabeth in the early chapters of the book of Luke. Here's a woman of God, faithfully serving alongside her husband, but they are well into post-childbearing years and burdened by the reproach that childlessness holds for them in their society. She and her husband, Zacharias, are both of the house of Aaron—which means they together are descendants of the very first priests.

They both walk blamelessly before God in all of His commandments and ordinances. So what is God waiting for? Why hasn't He rewarded them with children for all of their obedience to Him? God has very definite plans in making them wait...He is preparing them to become parents of John the Baptist, the one who will herald the arrival of the Messiah Christ.

Gabriel, God's special messenger angel who stands in His presence, is sent to bring the good news to Zacharias. This poor father-to-be, who can't bear to comprehend and believe such incredible news, expresses his disbelief and is chastised with muteness. He won't be able to tell anyone now.

Elizabeth responds in similar fashion to discovering her pregnancy...she hides for five months. This precious gift of a yet-to-be-born son, this scary but amazing news is so overwhelming that she can't bring herself to tell anyone. Even though she recognizes that this is God's doing, maybe she is fearful that either she will lose the child or that others will mock her for being an old mother.

But God sends Mary to her. When Mary arrives, Elizabeth is thrilled to feel her baby joyfully "leap" inside her. Elizabeth, suddenly filled with Holy Spirit, bursts into loud praise to God. It's time to rejoice at her impending birth and the good news that Mary will bear the Savior of the world!

Elizabeth's reaction is based on the shared pregnancy and joy of being with Mary, her cousin. She blesses Mary, blesses the Child Savior to be born, and recognizes that He will be her Lord. Ironically, she blesses Mary for believing that God will fulfill those things that He has told Mary by the angel Gabriel. Mary, in response, launches into her own song of praise.

The two cousins stay together three more months, just long enough for Mary to perhaps start "showing" she is pregnant and have to tell Joseph about it. One imagines that these two women encouraged each other during that time. Shortly afterward, Elizabeth gives birth to John.

The next verse is very telling: "When her neighbors and relatives heard how the Lord had shown great mercy to her, they rejoiced with her." Did Elizabeth continue to hide herself until the birth? We don't know. But we do know this, that those who were with her in community fellowship were willing and ready to rejoice with her. There is no hint of the things that Elizabeth might have feared.

When the mouth of Zacharias is opened, he prophesies about the missions of John and Jesus in the future. Fear comes upon those who dwell around this little family in the hill country of Judea, and they discuss all of his sayings. All those who hear about these events keep them in their hearts, perhaps to relate them later to those who would write about Christ. They wonder what kind of child John will be.

Elizabeth and Zacharias are not alone, even if they feel isolated. They are part of a greater family (Levites) and local neighborhood who are eagerly watching what God is performing here. A multitude of people are praying for Zacharias as he performs his job as priest and the angel Gabriel appears to him.

You could say that the people around this couple are their "church," their body of believers. These are people who care about them, love them, rejoice with them, honor them, and pray for them. They are important in this story.

How actively involved are you and your husband in your church? Is the body of Christ joining hands to help you? How can you find support through fellow Christians?

It takes getting involved, more than just running in and out of church, more than just shaking hands and leaving. Your fellow believers won't get to know you until you get to know them. You cannot remain isolated.

Find a Bible-believing church and dive in. Go to Sunday School if your church offers it. Join a Bible study with other women at your church or in your community...or start a group study yourself under the guidance of a church leader. Volunteer for service at Christian events, like serving at a soup kitchen or going on a weekend mission trip. Seek the presence of other strong Christians. Get a solid mentor.

Did you have an abortion in the past? Do you feel as if the guilt and shame will be obvious to those around you? Do you stay away from church because you believe that these "holy" church-goers will condemn and reject you?

Give them a little more credit for understanding you—one in every four women sitting around you may also have had an abortion. They may sit in shame and silence about their own past, but they will embrace you with forgiveness and love. The church is supposed to be a hospital for sinners, not a country club of perfect people. Find a body of believers with open arms for you.

Another big deterrent for you may be the envy you experience when seeing others in the church with their children...especially if you attend a church with an incredible birth rate!

As you observe the young families around you, it's so easy to slip into despair. The dull, throbbing pain surfaces immediately as you silently bewail your empty arms. You miss the child who would have been yours without the abortion or miscarriage. You wish for the pain to go away and melt into the bliss of motherhood.

Hurting is not a sin. The knife-sharp sting of infertility is a crime against you, a token from the devil himself.

Don't let envy, however, eat you up. It can grow into a consuming fire that devours you and all others who cross your path. It robs you of your relationship with Christ. It destroys all good things, marriages, and friendships.

It will disappear when you stop feeling sorry for yourself and seek to enter the joy of others who have children. If you see a young mom trying to herd her string of toddlers, ask her if you can grab one of the tiny hands and walk alongside her. Enter her world for a moment, give her the joy of friendship, share her smiles, relish the encounter with a little one.

Dispensing of envy is a constant practice, another fight in the spiritual battles we face daily. You cannot do this alone. You need the help, support, care, and love of other Christians. Boldly share with others your need for prayer. Ask them to help you in your struggles.

You know what happens? You suddenly discover that lots of other couples sitting beside you have been through the exact same battle. You get their sympathy, their encouragement, their cheerleading. You get spurred on in your faith. You persevere with their help.

You find Christ in the face of others who love Him. What better way to experience His love right now here on earth? And what joy you will share with them someday in His heaven!

PRAYER:

O Jesus, the Brother and Head of Your church, please bless me with a good, strong fellowship with other believers. Help me to find kindred spirits in the church I attend now, or help me to find a church with people whom I may embrace and who will embrace me, flaws and all.

Help me not to fall into a pattern of isolation, regret, and hiding. Open my eyes and heart to the needs and gifts of others around me in the pews. Let me join them with gladness and simplicity of heart, praising You and finding favor.

Please help me to find a Bible study with other women, somewhere I can open up Your Word and find Your truths through a solid teacher. Make me circumspect and cautious to seek only a place where Your Word is treated with respect as infallible, unchanging, and holy. Give us a church where we can worship You in spirit and in truth.

Find friends for me in Your church. Place godly women, and men for my husband, in our path so that we may come to know them better and share prayer needs with each other. Let us be part of a church that is growing, walking in fear of You and in the comfort of Your Holy Spirit.

Incorporate us both now in a place of service, where we can find areas to express the spiritual gifts You have provided for us. Help us to seek and find open doors for getting involved in the mission of Your church.

As my husband and I observe other families around us with children, do not let us slip into a state of despair, envy, grief, or despondency. Help us in this spiritual battle, where Satan loves to come in and destroy the body of faith.

Give me boldness and action to reach out my hands to others, to serve alongside women who have small children. Help me in my struggle to be gracious and loving.

Remind me that being in Your church, Your fellowship of believers, Your body of Christ, is where I belong. Meet me there in Your house. In the fulfilling name of Jesus Christ, Amen.

(Acts 2:46-47; John 4:24; Acts 9:31; Matthew 16:18)

FOR REFLECTION:

❖ Are you involved at a local church? Do you participate in the church's worship and other activities? If not, look now at your church's offerings for serving beyond just attending church. Write down one way you could get more involved.

_____
_____
_____

❖ Are you currently attending a women's Bible study? If not, look for one in your area (doesn't have to be at your home church) where you can be "well fed" on God's word and participate without fear or hesitation. If you are already in a study, write down two ways that this fellowship blesses you.

_____
_____
_____

❖ Pray with and for your husband today about your joint growth in faith through church membership and involvement. Ask God to show you both how to become more involved in the life of the church. Or, if you're too involved, ask Him to show you where you should concentrate your efforts and where to let go of responsibilities. If your husband does not attend with you, pray for a softened heart for him to join you.

___

___

___

___

🍎🍎🍎

MEGAN'S STORY (CONTINUED FROM CHAPTER 17):

It seemed when we started the process of getting pregnant, *everyone but me* was getting pregnant—friends, sister-in-law, church members. One of the hardest situations was that we went to one of the most fertile churches I've ever seen...not just couples having their first child, but families having twins or their third, fourth, or fifth child with little or no effort in getting pregnant. Instead of feeling happy for them, I was eaten up with jealousy.

Another hard thing was going to baby showers. For a while, especially after my miscarriage, I couldn't go. I'd just send a gift. My stomach would turn at maternity shops or the infant departments at stores. I'd cringe every time I'd see a pregnant woman—anywhere—at the mall, in restaurants, and especially at church. Then I'd feel guilty for not having a "Christian" attitude toward them.

The hardest of all was walking into the church nursery. Holding those babies, hearing them cry, feeding them was too much. My initial intent was to fill the need for a child. But I discovered I do love children and enjoy teaching, whether kids at school or in a Sunday School class. I really don't feel any "void" now.

JADE'S STORY (CONTINUED FROM CHAPTER 10):

The only Christian who really comforted me had lost her only two kids (each at 18 months) to a genetic degenerative disease. She never adopted. She continued in ministry for a full lifetime. At the time she comforted me, she was 50-plus. With her usual sense of humor, she told me to "shape up" and accept what God brings with "no whining"! I respected her because I knew her tragic circumstances. She drew people like June bugs to a porch light....

MARIA'S STORY (CONTINUED FROM CHAPTER 13):

One thing I found comforting to me was not to hear the results of another's experience but just that they had dealt with the issue. Every person's experience and outcome are so different that I don't think it is beneficial to hear about their babies (or none). God blessed us with a child, but it would have been crushing to have heard nothing but positive results from others, only to not ever be able to conceive ourselves. Basically, just be a listening and empathetic ear to others, which is what I was blessed to experience from others.

CHAPTER 20

The Sisterhood of Friendships

"A [woman] who has friends must [herself] be friendly, but there is a friend who sticks closer than a [sister]." (Proverbs 18:24)

"Two are better than one, because they have a good reward for their labor. For if they fall, one will lift up [her] companion. But woe to [her] who is alone when [she] falls, for [she] has no one to help [her] up. Again, if two lie down together, they will keep warm; but how can one be warm alone?" (Ecclesiastes 4:9-11)

Making and keeping friends gets a lot harder as you grow older. School "BFFs" get married, move away, have kids. Other women you've known get jobs and move up in their careers. We stay constantly busy in the chaotic frenzy of daily life.

Yet friendship for women isn't just a nicety. It's a necessity. To stay sane in an increasingly crazier world, we need good friends...true friends.

We need the kind of friends described in The Four Loves by C. S. Lewis as the ones who meet us and surprise us with kinship: "The typical expression of opening Friendship would be something like, 'What? You too? I thought I was the only one....' When two such persons discover one another, when whether with immense difficulties and semi-articulate fumbling or with what would seem to us amazing and elliptical speed, they share their vision—it is then that Friendship is born. And instantly they stand together in an immense solitude."[1]

God has programmed us to reach out to other women when we need help or simply want companionship. Our female friends offer a deeper level of friendship than what men are typically able to fulfill. Other women understand what we're going through because they identify with it all the way down to their cellular level—it's in our DNA.

Anne Shirley, the main character in *Anne of Green Gables*, longs for a "bosom friend"... "an intimate friend, you know—a really kindred spirit to whom I can confide my innermost soul. I've dreamed of meeting her all my life."[2]

Anne eventually finds her friend in Diana Barry. When Diana marries early, the two young women remain extraordinarily devoted to each other, and Anne shares in the wonder and miracle of motherhood when Diana has her first son.

Biblical friendships were close-knit, too, like those between daughter-in-law Ruth with her mother-in-law Naomi, between King David and Jonathan, and between cousins Mary and Elizabeth. These relationships were marked by intense loyalty, sacrifice, and long-term commitment. They were bound together for life.

Such friendships seem archaic today. We don't have time to pick up the phone and call, much less run out to lunch or meet at the park—without making a very serious effort. It's much easier to just pull up your friends in online social media and visit each other's "perfect lives" over an Internet satellite. We rarely meet face-to-face even with friends who live within a mile of us.

But when you hit the wall of infertility...when you can't talk with your husband or even your mom about it...when some acquaintance throws out a careless comment about kids or a thoughtless word about Mother's Day...where do you run for help?

Certainly, we go first to Jesus in prayer. The Proverbs verse at the beginning of this chapter is often said to describe our Savior, the One who would come as the "Friend" who sticks with us. He is always ready to listen, and His Holy Spirit comforts us.

As our heavenly Friend, He is also the one who provides us with friends. But as with other good gifts from our Heavenly Father, we have to open our hearts to receive them.

Stay in touch with your friends. If you haven't developed a close circle of Christian friends—women you can trust—it's time to reach out. Your best bet is to start at your church home or in a group of Christian women in your area, such as a community Bible study.

Open your schedule to invite someone into your home or to have a sandwich together in the park. Take the first step. Do not be discouraged by calendar conflicts or rebuffs. Pray for opportunities.

If you have Christian friends who live miles away or in another country, communicate by email or video time. Set appointments to talk together that work for both of your calendars, to meet online for conversations.

Look for mature believers, too—especially older women you respect, who have the potential to pour their lives into yours. Listen to their advice, and look for ways to offer friendship to them in return. It's a wonderful blessing to have friends of all ages.

Persevere in finding friends and keeping them. It will take a great deal of effort on your part, but the rewards are so worth it. When two men are friends, it's usually pretty uncomplicated...they meet for a game of golf or go hunting together, with conversations that rarely go beyond the activity of the moment.

If you're married and childless, make an extra effort to hang out with your single childless girlfriends—they'll have time for you, and you won't be bothered by "mom" stories of the latest cute thing that some other friend's child has done. If you're single, seek out your married childless girlfriends—you can minister to each other. You can be great allies together as women coping with lack of motherhood.

Friendships between women, though, can get messy and complicated; our feelings are closer to the surface and more readily expressed verbally, which means that our feelings are quickly bruised. It's easier to retreat from a situation than develop the good listening skills and acceptance that are essential to female relationships.

How, for example, do you cope with a close friend who becomes pregnant when you aren't, or a friend who goes on to have a baby around the time you would have (if you hadn't miscarried)?

In situations involving personal grief, remember what it is like to be on the outside looking in. "It may help you forgive a friend's insensitive comment if you consider that the friend is also stunned by your devastation," said Elizabeth B. Brown, author and teacher.

"He or she is unsure of what is best to say or do and wants to be there for you in your difficult time. Without a doubt, your friend would also wonder how he or she could possibly handle such a tragedy. Sure, the friend who holds your hand and says the wrong thing is made of dearer stuff than the one who shies away."[3]

Your first tactic is to refocus your priority—to *love* your friend, no matter what. She has an unplanned pregnancy and complains about it? Remind yourself, before you lash out, that this might be an unexpected hardship for her—like you, she's having to deal with an unwanted situation.

Your second tactic is to recognize that pregnant friends probably feel very awkward around you, not knowing what to say, not knowing whether it's more painful to ignore you than to hang out with you. Be honest with them. Tell them that your head is saying, "Don't be jealous...rejoice with your friend" at the same time your heart is raging with envy. Ask them for patience, forgiveness, and transparency. Ask them to pray for you.

Your third resource is to actively embrace joy. This means releasing any deeply held resentment and steeling yourself to jump into a true joy for your friend. You will find such relief when you do.

When my late sister-in-law became pregnant (while I was still in the throes of post-surgery recovery and cancer-reducing hormones), she feared telling me. When she finally revealed it and told me how afraid she was of hurting me, I reached out in love and reassurance to her—I knew she cared for me, and that made the difference.

You keep your buddies when you keep their secrets, keep listening, keep your own feelings in check, and keep working at the friendship. True friends, rooted in their common faith in Jesus Christ, are the ones who help each other—when one falls, the other is there to pick up the pieces (*Ecclesiastes 4:10*).

Scriptures also teach that real friends challenge each other in their walk: "*As iron sharpens iron, so a [woman] sharpens the countenance of [her] friend (Proverbs 27:17).*" A Christian friend walks beside you, won't leave you to flounder in despair, gently shares the truth, and encourages you to seek God's will for your life. Thank Him for these friends.

Your friends need you to be a godly friend, too. Like Anne and Diana in the Green Gables series, or Woody and Buzz Lightyear in the movie *Toy Story*, you'll have your ups and downs—but you'll still find that good friends are one of God's greatest blessings here on earth.

Pray to the Friend above all friends, the One who carries our loads faithfully, the One from whom all good gifts come, including friends. He is the Third Cord in the strands of our friendship ropes. Ask Him to give you the kind of "bosom friends" you need and to make you the very best friend you can be.

"What a friend we have in Jesus, all our sins and griefs to bear! What a privilege to carry everything to God in prayer!...

"Can we find a friend so faithful, who will all our sorrows share? Jesus knows our every weakness; take it to the Lord in prayer.

"Are we weak and heavy-laden, cumbered with a load of care? Precious Savior, still our refuge—take it to the Lord in prayer.

"Do thy friends despise, forsake thee? Take it to the Lord in prayer! In His arms He'll take and shield thee, thou wilt find a solace there."

By Joseph M. Scriven, 1855

PRAYER:

Jesus Christ, our Friend in joy and sorrow—bless me with friends who will walk beside me on this road of infertility. Help me to cultivate friendships, old and new, among women who will enrich my life and whose lives I can bless.

Help me to choose my friends carefully, recognizing that they have influence to lead me astray. Let me find Christian friends who are wise, prudent, sincere, and uplifting.

To that end, please fill my heart and soul with the wonderful fruits of Your Holy Spirit—give me love, joy, peace, patience, kindness, goodness, faithfulness, gentleness, and self-control, all to share with my friends. As I listen to the promptings of Your Holy Spirit, give me words of sweetness that will speak comfort over my friends and build them up. Make me a "friendly friend"!

Savior and Friend, please speak to me face to face, as Someone who is my heavenly Friend. When I feel as if my friends have forgotten me, remind me that You will never leave me or abandon Your friendship with me.

Remind me to pray for my friends and their needs—remind me to lift them up to You, and call me to rejoice whenever I see You answer those prayers. Do not let me forsake my friends.

If my friends, speaking the truth in love, give me advice or offer constructive criticism, do not let me become disheartened or angry. Help me to remember that "faithful are the wounds of a friend" who seeks only my best interests, unlike the flattery of the wicked.

When I am tempted to backbite or take up a reproach against my friends, perhaps for some indiscretion, remind me that I am a sinner, too, and fill my heart with forgiveness. Shape me into the kind of friend who attracts other friends through fragrant words and heartfelt deeds.

Someday, Lord, if You provide children or opportunities to pour my life into children, give me friends I can call—just as You shared in the parable about the woman who had lost her prized coin, saying, "Rejoice with me, for I have found the piece which I lost!"

I praise You, O Jesus Christ, because You have called me to be Your friend, telling me all things You heard from Your Father God. Thank You for Your friendship and love! In Your sacrificial name, Amen.

(Proverbs 12:26; Galatians 5:22-23; Exodus 33:11; Proverbs 18:24; Job 42:10; Proverbs 27:6; Psalm 15:3; Proverbs 27:9-10; Luke 15:8-10; John 15:15)

🍎 🍎 🍎

FOR REFLECTION:

❖ Make a list of three good friends who are Christian women. If you don't have three, look for new friends to make at church or among your family and acquaintances. Contact one or more of them to meet for coffee, lunch, or a snack in the park. List your appointments below:

❖ When you meet with friends, make a point of asking them first about their struggles and trials before you share yours with infertility. Use this time (or wait until later) to pray together for your friend and to ask your friend to pray for you.

❖ Pray for a godly mentor, an older Christian woman who is willing to come alongside you in prayer, advice, encouragement, and fellowship. Consider asking a fellow church member to commit to prayer and meeting once a month for a year. Ask your pastor for help in finding that person, if necessary.

🍎 🍎 🍎

CAROLINE'S STORY (CONTINUED FROM CHAPTER 2):

After a miscarriage, I called someone I know who has had eight miscarriages. She said that our goal as Christian women is to have our children in heaven...and ours are there already. I have learned I can talk okay to women in "my boat" (miscarriages or with the death of a child).

I also learned through the experience of my daughter Bethany's death and two miscarriages that it is not the situation that matters but how you deal with it—choosing to glorify God or to muddle in self-pity. Look to Christ because He's been through the same emotions at some point in His time here.

MEGAN'S STORY (CONTINUED FROM CHAPTER 19):

When I find out about a friend who's had a miscarriage, I either call or usually write a note. I tell her that *it's okay* to grieve this loss, no matter if she "wasn't very far along" in her pregnancy. I also encourage her to pray for comfort and that she can call me if she's having a "bad baby day" and wants someone to talk to.

If it is someone who just found out she is infertile, I tell her that it's okay to grieve for this, too. But I encourage her by reminding her that there are all kinds of "mommies," not just birth moms—for example, foster mom, adoptive mom, grand-mom, helping neighbor moms or someone in a nursing home or hospital, etc.

I also tell her she is still very much a woman—though she may be unable to reproduce at this time. Then I encourage her to call or write me if she needs someone to talk to from time to time.

I also encourage people to join a support group, even if they feel that they can't share their feelings. Just being with others who are going through similar situations can help.

CHAPTER 21

Motherhood in Your Workplace/Career

"And whatever you do, do it heartily, as to the Lord and not to men, knowing that from the Lord you will receive the reward of the inheritance; for you serve the Lord Christ." (Colossians 3:23-24)

Heigh ho, heigh ho, it's off to work we go!

Whether full-time or part-time—at a home, office, school, hospital, store, restaurant, college, construction site, whatever—your work is a huge part of your life. It may be rewarding or intolerably grueling, but you identify with your career. Your identity becomes wrapped up in your occupation. After all, it's often the first question someone asks upon meeting you—"What do you do?"

As much as you may try to avoid it, your infertility problems can affect your job—and vice versa. The stress of work is compounded by your private stress over inability to have children.

It's also possible that work-related anxiety can affect your hormone levels. And if you're on fertility drugs, you know how they can affect your attitude and anxiety levels on the job.

Something as simple as different work shifts between you and your husband can conflict with those times for lovemaking when fertility is highest. Maybe you both come home too tired for the necessary sex. Some marital bliss!

If you and your husband still wish to have children, you will have to make some important decisions about work. Little babies cannot take care of themselves...someone has to be the keeper, whether it's you, your husband, your family, or a daycare.

So if a child comes along in your life, it will mean dramatic changes for both of you. Do you need to go back to work full-time? Do you convert to part-time? Do you quit altogether? Can you do outside work at home via the Internet? Does your husband change his work so that he can stay at home as Mr. Mom? Do you need to get childcare in your home or away from home?

These are issues you will not be able to decide by yourself. You and your husband must compromise and agree to meet the realities of parenthood, finances, career options, and childcare. Both of you will have to make sacrifices.

One of the greatest myths of feminist bravado is the concept that you can have it all—bring home the bacon, fry it up in the pan. You can have a fabulous, exotic career and keep a perfect house. You can work all day at a high-profile, wildly rewarding job and come home to perfect children with a happy husband.

Well, wake up and smell the coffee burning on the stove. It takes huge amounts of energy to be a mother, whether you have a full-time job outside of the house or stay at home. Even if you are at home all the time, keeping a perfectly tidy house with little children is completely impossible. Comedienne Phyllis Diller said, "Cleaning your house while your kids are still growing up is like shoveling the walk before it stops snowing."[1]

Try to be a godly mother, and the effort is staggering. Here are some of the realities:

Balancing full-time work and motherhood is a daily dance. Snow days? Sick days? It's really difficult to bring the kids with you and hide them in your office or under the boardroom table. You need someone to be the "mom" or "dad" who can pick them up from school or stay with them—a family member or paid assistant to help.

You will spend less time with your child if you are at work longer hours than you are at home. It will take a lot of effort, after you are tired from the day's demands, to make sure that you give as much time as possible to your child.

If you keep working after children arrive, you face disdain by some who think that the only full-time career for a woman is being a homemaker. (This can be a big issue in some churches.) Conversely, if you leave your career to be at home full-time, you face the shock and disbelief by some professional women, the loss of workplace camaraderie, the loss of self-esteem in building your own profession, the loss of experiencing what you were educated to perform, and of course, the loss of income.

There are no easy solutions. It's essential, then, that you and your husband make decisions now to balance work and family. He will have to adjust his own workload, too, to become a good father.

If you exit the public workplace, even for just a few years while children are small, there are sacrifices to your career trajectory—look ahead and be prepared to start over, as needed, in building up your work experience, knowledge, and skills that become rusty away from work.

What a great opportunity for prayer! When you cover this situation in prayer together, you will be surprised at how God will provide—whether it's a raise for one of you, a different work opportunity, an unexpected caregiver, or an out-of-the-blue financial provision.

After you have bathed your finances and careers in prayer before God together, sit down together with paper and pencil in hand. Ask God to show you how to adjust your family budget should it become necessary.

If either of you wishes to stay home, try to shift all of your living expenses now to one spouse's income and begin socking the other's paycheck into a savings account, teaching you to live on one salary. It will also mean sacrificing some of your restaurant dinners, non-essential services, giving fewer or less extravagant gifts, and looking for ways every day to reduce spending or increase income. Look for additional education or training that could lead to a promotion or change of career.

As difficult as it might be, consider moving to less expensive housing. Getting out of debt is utterly critical. But do not neglect giving back to God—He has promised to help you through this time and provide for you.

Whatever decision you make about your career, think in terms of your *calling*...not the career title you adopt.

"...Our calling does not necessarily have to be our occupation," wrote LeAnne Blackmore in *Obscure No More*, a study about overlooked characters in the Bible.

"Calling reaches beyond that...the bigger purpose of my life is to know God. He guarantees that when we pursue Him, great things will be accomplished through us for His kingdom. This guarantee comes regardless of our station in life and regardless of the circumstances of the world around us. That's exciting!"[2]

If motherhood never materializes for you, can you find personal fulfillment then in your work? The answer is yes, if you're seeking to serve Christ in whatever circumstances He has placed you...in an office, at a store, on a farm, at a school, on a hospital floor, in a home, or on the road. Look for those divine opportunities to reach out to others with your hands, words, mind, heart, and skills.

Pray right now and every day for God to teach you in this process. Ask Him to open your eyes to new possibilities. Ask Him to open the right doors and close the wrong ones. Ask Him to help you re-orient your personal identity, from *what you do* at work to *who you are* in Jesus Christ—your true identity as the child of a loving King.

Most of all, ask Him to give you *great joy* in placing your finances and career decisions on the altar as a sacrifice to Him. You will find an incredible freedom and peace when you do.

PRAYER:

O Gracious God, You have seen my affliction and the toil of my hands in work. You know my efforts—You are with me wherever I go, and Your presence follows me in the workplace. Let me see Your hands at work with me.

I know, though, that all of my work and efforts will be in vain unless You build "the house" of my life. Unless You are watching over me, my watchful attention is useless. In vain will I rise up early and stay up late working, toiling for food to eat—You will give me the strength and sleep that I need because You love me. Help me to follow Your will.

Your blessing upon me—that I might become the woman You intended me to be—is the wealth I crave. You are my Provider. Therefore, keep me from chasing after material, meaningless things that will vanish with the wind. Instead, teach me satisfaction with having enough to eat and drink, a roof over my head, sufficient clothing—Your presence is all I really need, the best gift to treasure.

Teach me how to rest in You, too, especially on Your Sabbath day. Help me to work well all week so that I may look back at my work and see that it was good. Make me a skilled worker who plies my craft with energy, a cheerful spirit, and a desire to please You. Help me to live a life worthy of You, bearing fruit in my work and growing in knowledge of You. You are my example—I will consider all of Your works and meditate on Your mighty deeds.

As I work, help me to prepare for the possibility of motherhood or ministry, financially and spiritually. Let me reap the rewards of hard work, not indulge in idle fantasies. Keep me actively working that I may be ready for whatever decision my husband and I make about work; do not let me act sluggardly.

Finally, help me to remember that wisdom is so much better to receive than gold and receiving understanding is better than silver. I praise You that You are willing to give generously of Your wisdom to those who ask for it. Please help my husband and me to make wise decisions for parenthood, as You provide it, in the future.

In the unfailing name of Jesus Christ, Amen.

(Genesis 31:42; Psalm 127:1-2; Proverbs 10:22; Ecclesiastes 2:11, 3:13; Genesis 2:2; Exodus 31:6; Colossians 1:10; Psalm 77:12; Proverbs 12:11-14, 6:6, 16:16)

FOR REFLECTION:

❖ Today or on your next day at work, take a few minutes to evaluate your situation. How would your work change if you suddenly had a baby to care for? Write down some potential issues that would come up.

_____
_____
_____
_____

❖ Pray about your job/career and ask God for wisdom, for both you and your husband. Ask God to show you clearly which doors are open and which ones are closed.

_____
_____
_____
_____

❖ Look at options now for childcare and begin to get estimates on costs. Review your budget to see how you will afford working or not working to cover the care. Write down three alternatives to working in your current position that would allow you to receive adequate income.

_____
_____
_____
_____

❦ ❦ ❦

GRACE'S STORY:

I had a uniquely challenging experience with infertility in my work life. As a women's ministry director at our church, I spent a lot of time with women who were mothers or becoming mothers. In fact, the majority of my work involved motherhood: welcoming new young moms, supporting women expecting with meal trains, overseeing a group ministry mentoring young moms, and so forth. The role of motherhood was very central to my daily work.

So how did I feel? Completely disqualified from motherhood. One of the biggest lies Satan kept repeating to me was, "You have nothing to offer." Every time I thought I was healing from the pain, I would work on a project that eventually would cut my heart, as if I was ripping off a scab that couldn't catch a break! I felt raw all the time. I was in a season of my life when everyone else around me had kids or were having kids. I was surrounded by baby bump photos, diaper bags, baby showers, Mommy-and-me playdates, everything geared toward motherhood. I tried to celebrate the wonder of new life—it is a miracle and beautiful– but to the grieving woman, it is salt in a wound.

I had a few supports, but I felt pressure as a Christian woman to speak only positive things. It didn't serve me well, but it helped me survive in that environment. If I had started the process of expressing the pain then, I might not have gotten the work done. Even so, my first official day on the job coincided with the first day I started taking Pergonal, a strong fertility medication—and I cried all day at work.

After two rounds of intra-uterine insemination with no pregnancy, I got the call from my doctor that he wanted to conduct a laparoscopic surgery to check for and repair any endometriosis. This was right at the same time I was about to host a large women's event. I remember being so scared of surgery and afraid of something being terribly wrong with me. I was tormented by questions like, "Why won't my body work?" After surgery, which confirmed I had endometriosis but no other impediments to pregnancy, still nothing.

Finally, after putting off infertility grief and carrying a lot of emotional weight for so long, it became clear to my husband and me that I needed to step down from my position to focus on God's healing love for me, and to spend time with our beautiful baby girl through adoption. I was a high-functioning "grief-a-holic," getting a lot done in a day but doing it disconnected from my hurting soul. And eventually, payday comes. I wanted to make sure I was safe at home without too many expectations on me when the grief started to release.

When I came across the verses in Proverbs 30 that address four things never satisfied (the "barren womb" is one of them), I realized that infertility is a pain that I had been hiding. In that moment, Jesus said it was okay to cry over this. Before this, I didn't know what to do with all the emotions and feelings I had been bottling up. But He gave me permission to grieve, and grieve deeply. When infertility hits a woman's story, the enemy takes the opportunity to frame every disappointment or closed door in your life as punishment and rejection from God. God was touching not just my infertility pain, but He was going to many hurts I had buried, and He wanted to show me His unconditional love in ALL those spaces.

Interestingly enough, my previous career was as an adoption attorney during my single years. I saw adoption from an outsider's perspective while representing adoptive families. Doing that work lit a passion in me to adopt. During that time, I read *Safely Home* by Randy Alcorn. That book grew a deep affection in me for Asia. "Someday," I told myself, "I want to adopt a daughter from China." God was already using my work life to prepare me for His plans in the future, before I had even met my husband. Little did I know that He would bring us a daughter much closer to home!

CHAPTER 22

New Biotechnology for Infertility

"When Jesus heard it, He said to them, 'Those who are well have no need of a physician, but those who are sick. I did not come to call the righteous, but sinners, to repentance.'" (Mark 2:17)

"For You formed my inward parts; You covered me in my mother's womb. I will praise You, for I am fearfully and wonderfully made; marvelous are Your works." (Psalm 139:13-14a)

What a marvelous era we inhabit! Nearly every day, the news media bring us an announcement of some new medical advancement. Scientists worldwide work feverishly to explore new territories of the human body and its diseases, look for better treatments, and find new methods to preserve health and quality of life.

One of the greatest achievements in recent medical history is the complete mapping of the human genome, something possible only through complicated computer deciphering. Through genetic analysis, scientists can now identify DNA molecules that are culprits for certain disease eruptions. They can also address issues that result in infertility.

Contemporary advances in medical treatment give women (along with their husbands) much wider options for conception. Diagnostic methods using laparoscopic surgery and remote-control cameras are now commonplace in practice. Treatments involving ovulation test strips, fertility drugs, hormone supplements, intra-uterine insemination, in vitro fertilization (IVF), and more are allowing women to overcome impossible conditions and become pregnant.

These innovations, however, come with a price. Skyrocketing medical costs and shrinking insurance coverage may put some treatments completely out of reach. Time away from work, for both of you, reduces pay and job security. Living in a rural area means extensive travel to reach physicians and hospitals specializing in infertility treatment.

You could experience varying levels of pain, discomfort, and recovery associated with some tests and medications. Depending on the treatment, you might have to endure surgery, injections with horse-sized needles, bed rest, nausea, weight gain, and all kinds of poking, prodding, and embarrassment. It's not an entertaining ride, for you or your husband.

Some hormones bring your entire hormonal system to a screeching halt, a crash-landing into menopause—have fun with that. Others hit the accelerator with super doses of ovulation enhancers. Hold on tight; this is no ordinary rollercoaster.

Hanging on to your faith in Jesus Christ and your love for your husband is extremely important during this time. In the midst of your hormonal outbursts of anger, anxiety, or weepiness, you will not be easy to love! As you continue to pray for children, ask God to help you and your husband to have patience with each other, to help you both get through this season in your lives with peace and assurance.

You also need a big measure of God's infinite wisdom. Where do you draw the line? To what lengths of time and treatment will you go, in persevering to have a baby of your own? At what point do you and your husband decide enough is enough?

And where do you decide you have reached your ethical limit? What do Christian physicians have to say about the morality of infertility treatments?

The Christian Medical and Dental Association, a worldwide organization of Christian healthcare professionals, has issued a statement that attempts to provide insight and guidelines. In their analysis of assisted reproductive technology (ART), they include the following principles to guide the development and use of biotechnologies:

• Fertilization resulting from the union of a wife's egg and her husband's sperm is the biblical design.
• Individual human life begins at fertilization.
• God holds us morally responsible for our reproductive choices.
• ART should not result in embryo loss greater than natural occurrence. This can be achieved with current knowledge and technology.[1]

As you can see, your choice of treatment—or even to stop or refrain from treatment—is a matter for discussion between you and your husband in prayer to God before deciding on physician recommendations. While not always possible or feasible, seek the advice of Christian healthcare specialists and the counsel of your pastor before making these life-changing decisions.

Above all, pray for God to provide the right treatments, proper care, discernment, and wise counsel that you need. Pray for wisdom to know when your efforts are finished.

In the meantime, how is your health? Are there some things you could be doing to maintain a healthier lifestyle? Let's look at the big three—nutrition, activity, and sleep—and some of the new technology to help.

In our hurry-up, squeeze-it-all-in lifestyles in the United States, the high-calorie fare we consume at fast food spots and restaurants can pack on the pounds. If you have a struggle with weight gain or even weight loss, consider adjusting your calorie intake, making healthy choices to eat more vegetables, fruits, proteins, and simple fats.

Make your grocery shopping more intentional, increasing fresh foods and reducing the amount of junk food or packaged/processed foods. Read the nutrition information on those specialty coffees or soft drinks, and whew...look at all the calories! Just cutting out some of the sugar you're drinking will help a lot. The Internet has lots of great ways to help—you can download calorie-counter applications and find healthy recipe choices, support groups, and diet programs as well as body mass index measurements.

For exercise, maybe all you have to do is get moving. You don't have to join a gym—just start walking. Keep track of your movement with pedometers and fitness trackers on your smartphone or wrist. Just a few minutes of increased heart rate activity a day can boost your spirits considerably. Use exercise as an anti-depressant!

And, get enough sleep...seven to eight hours is optimum. Are you getting less? In his groundbreaking book on the health benefits of sleeping called *Why We Sleep*, Dr. Matthew Walker contends that lack of sleep or disrupted sleep can affect reproductive systems in both men and women.

Among his recommendations for better sleep, Walker advises a reduction in caffeine; a cool, dark, gadget-free bedroom; a regular sleep schedule (as much as possible); and 30 minutes of natural sunlight in the mornings.[2] Sleep is vitally important for energy, memory, and immunity. Keep a sleep journal or look into sleep applications on fitness trackers and smartphones.

If you have financial barriers to digital gadgets or Internet access, go to your local library and ask about public computers.

Remember always that God alone is the Author of life. No medical treatment or personal health choices or genetic modification can create life—only He can give you a child. As your loving Father, He knows what you need. He is the Great Physician. Rest in His arms and care, and rely on Him to take care of you. You can endure all things through Christ who will strengthen you. Look to Him for your spiritual, emotional, and physical health.

PRAYER:

O Heavenly Father of Lights, Giver of every good and perfect gift from above, there is no variation or shadow of turning with You. Help me to count it all joy as I go through any trials of infertility treatments, knowing that the testing of my faith will produce patience. But let patience have its perfect work in me, that I may be perfect and complete, lacking nothing.

O God, my husband and I need Your wisdom. You have promised that if I ask this of You, that You will give it liberally and without reproach. Let us ask in faith, with no doubting, so that we will know what to do and what Your perfect will is for us in making infertility treatment decisions. Do not let us be like waves of the sea, driven and tossed by the winds of those who do not believe as we do.

Help us to observe Your laws and commandments if we pursue extra measures of medical assistance, just as You have ordained for us, that we may carefully act according to Your judgments and wisdom. Let others see that we are wise and understanding, that we may be a witness to Your glory. For You are near to us—I praise You that we may call upon You for any reason to help us.

As You have established us in this place of childlessness, in my childbearing years, I pray that You will give us mercy and abundant wisdom as You gave to Solomon. Let us have a heart for following You, not asking riches or wealth or honor or long life...just wisdom and knowledge. Grant these to us, that we may serve You.

In all things, O Lord Jesus, let us walk in such a way to please You. Help us to recognize that infertility is part of our sanctification from You. Teach us how to honor You in this, following Your paths of holiness. Give my husband and myself an equal measure of Your Holy Spirit, that we may see and grasp Your hand as we endure this trial together. In Your name, O Jesus Christ, Amen.

(James 1:17, 2-6; Deuteronomy 4:5-7; 2 Chronicles 1:8-12; 1 Thessalonians 4:1-8)

FOR REFLECTION:

❖ As you experience infertility treatments or plan for the future, list three ways that these affect you—physically, spiritually, financially. Lift these issues up to the Lord today and ask Him to see you through any hardships.

_____
_____
_____
_____

❖ How could infertility treatments affect your husband? Pray for him here, to shoulder the responsibility with you and handle the side effects (yours or his) with patience and love.

_____
_____
_____
_____

❖ What decisions do you face in the future regarding the limit of treatment? Commit these to God, asking Him for His infinite wisdom. You may wish to set a timetable for hearing His answers and abiding by them.

_____
_____
_____
_____

❦ ❦ ❦

REBECCA'S STORY:

My husband, Paul, had cancer as a teenager and knew his treatments had the potential to affect his fertility. He was very upfront with me about it, so we went into marriage knowing the likelihood of having a biological child would be slim. But we were okay with adoption.

At first, we did go down the in vitro fertilization track but couldn't get pregnant. It turned out that my "egg quality" was also a problem, not fertilizing properly.

At the time, I was a nurse in an intensive care unit, working 12-hour days, which made it very hard to go to fertility appointments, going in at certain times on certain days for drawing blood, etc. I didn't want to tell the people at work what I was doing...too personal. When we moved, I chose not to apply for a job so I could concentrate on pursuing the treatments. My career-oriented family didn't always understand why I wasn't working, but it turned out to be nice to be at home as I had become a bit burned out with everything.

I was somewhat depressed, feeling something was missing. So I would go to our church's chapel to pray and read. It was a very peaceful place, where no one would bother me. The story of Hannah really touched me, not just her infertility issue but also having Peninah as a thorn in her side. Ultimately, though, I knew that whatever we did, God had the bottom line. If it worked or didn't, it was in God's hands.

After being married eight years and going through treatments at least three years, we decided to adopt and started the process. We expected it would take several years, which is typical. Instead, we received our son Kyle only three months after finishing the paperwork. The birth mother had specifically requested a Catholic family, and we were the only ones in the adoption agency files! I thought, "How much bigger is God than that? He's got our back!"

In general, our family and friends were very supportive of adoption. It was difficult when people sometimes seemed insensitive, but it was probably because I was taking everything too personally. I remember going to a meeting where one of the women very bluntly asked, "Why didn't you have one of your own?" There's no good reply for that! We became regular church-goers, though, and I was able to befriend another woman there who had gone through IVF as well.

Even with Kyle in our lives, I always felt that I would someday get pregnant...this just wasn't over yet. So, we decided to have a frozen embryo transfer from our IVF days and got pregnant right away with Brett, which was miraculous. Now, I felt like everything was finished.

One week after we brought Brett home, the phone rang from an adoption agency offering us a baby girl. I immediately declined the offer, recognizing that this was not the right time for us to adopt again...we already had a four-year-old and a newborn. I never felt guilty afterward, knowing that this baby girl would go to a childless couple.

I eventually chose to homeschool...it was best for Kyle and has worked out well for Brett, too. It was a good decision, and I have never looked back. Homeschooling has allowed us to travel a lot, to Europe and major U.S. cities, and has been a really good experience for the boys.

While we have not gotten pregnant again, this whole process has given Paul and me a stronger marriage. Neither of us desires to have a huge family because we want to pour ourselves into our two boys. And, as difficult as it has been at times when Kyle has struggled with attention deficit, our decision to adopt has never been in question. Both Paul and I feel that our family is complete...both of our boys have blessed us immensely!

CHAPTER 23

Is Adoption an Option?

"*For you did not receive the spirit of bondage again to fear, but you received the Spirit of adoption by whom we cry out, 'Abba, Father.'*" (Romans 8:15)

Is it absolutely essential that your child be genetically related to you? Have you and your husband opened your hearts to consider bringing a child into your family through adoption?

Look at what Scriptures have to say about orphans and adoption:

"*...He chose us in Him before the foundation of the world, that we should be holy and without blame before Him in love, having predestined us to adoption as sons by Jesus Christ to Himself, according to the good pleasure of His will, to the praise of the glory of His grace, by which He made us accepted in the Beloved.*" (Ephesians 1:4-6)

"*Pure and undefiled religion before God and the Father is this: to visit orphans and widows in their trouble, and to keep oneself unspotted from the world.*" (James 1:27)

[Jesus said] "*I will not leave you orphans; I will come to you.*" (John 14:18)

While the Creation mandate calls us to be fruitful and multiply, the Bible never demands that we give birth to our own children. Instead, in multiple Scripture verses, God requires that we act kindly toward those in distress, especially the orphans and widows around us.

One of the obstacles is that newborn babies available for adoption are extremely scarce in today's America. Birth control is widely available and used. And with a declining stigma against out-of-wedlock birth, many single moms-to-be choose to parent their children alone. The results are fewer children available for families desiring to adopt.

Outside of the United States, orphanages are overflowing with young children available for adoption. But if you accept the challenge of adopting from another country, you will need grit, financial sacrifice, flexibility, perseverance, and lots of prayer.

If you are open to adoption, let the Holy Spirit guide you toward making wise decisions. Here are some of the considerations you and your husband should take to the Lord together as you seek His will about adoption:

- Are you willing to parent an older child? Little babies are cuddly and highly desirable, but they are scarce. Most children available for adoption are toddlers all the way up to teens. You need to determine if God is calling you to accept an older child with the liabilities that increased age brings.
- Are you willing to parent a child with special needs? Children with disabilities—blindness, deafness, cerebral palsy, Down Syndrome, AIDS—need parents, too. Do you have the Spirit-given gifts to handle their issues in stride? Do you welcome the challenges of parenting one of these orphans into adulthood? God may be calling you to step far outside of your comfort zone to embrace the difficulties and blessings of this special parenthood.
- Are you willing to parent a child who doesn't look like you? Children who are biracial or come from a different race than your own are no different from any other children when it comes to their need for loving parents. You need to prepare for cultural differences, foreign languages, or travel/paperwork requirements.

- Are you willing to parent a child whose birth parents want an "open adoption"? Some adoptions involve an ongoing communication with birth parents throughout the growing up years of your adopted child. You need to decide from the beginning where to set the boundaries for the benefit of your child.
- Are you willing to delegate a significant amount of your financial resources? Adoption isn't cheap...it can be moderately pricey all the way up to astronomically expensive. If your income is insufficient, pray about asking family members or close friends if they would like to help support your decision with a one-time donation.
- Are you willing to adopt a "snowflake baby"? This term refers to frozen embryos conceived by other couples but left unused and unwanted after in vitro fertilization treatments are done. These children are abandoned to a cryobiological freezer and destined for a slow, deteriorating death. Adopting one of these babies requires certain permissions, capability for carrying a baby to full term, and procedures for implantation. The benefits, though, are the life you can give them and the blessing of experiencing a pregnancy.
- If you already have a child or children, are you willing to bring in others who could potentially disrupt their lives? Having a sibling is a wonderful experience and blessing, but recognize that adoption could throw your existing children's world into a turmoil. Include your children in the decision-making process, even if they are young, so that they understand what is happening and can prepare themselves for it realistically.

Seek the counsel of a reputable Christian adoption agency. Investigate services online to confirm their integrity (even if they profess to being Christians) before you commit to any financial payments. Talk with other adoptive parents about their situations, and get referrals and recommendations.

Warnings: Don't adopt for the praise of others. Don't adopt because it's a fad—celebrities get lots of publicity for it. Don't adopt because other Christians are doing it. There's nothing spiritually superior about adopting children, even special needs children or those born into poverty. Adopt because you want to love that child or children the same as if they were born to you biologically.

As you and your husband talk with God about adoption, remember what God has done for you—if you have accepted His Son, Jesus Christ, as your Savior and Lord, He has adopted you into His family. You are now part of His family, heirs to His kingdom.

But remember, adoption is not easy…parenthood is hard. Eliminate all pie-in-the-sky expectations, and focus on the realities.

Make sure you and your husband are on the same page together concerning adoption, or your marriage will be on a rocky road after a child comes home to live with you.

If you are at odds with each other, don't adopt. Your marriage comes first. Keep it solid. Respect your husband's direction for your family. He is the one who will ultimately answer to God for his leadership. Pray for him.

And if you're a single woman thinking about adoption, as I once contemplated, consider becoming a mentor first. You can make a profound impact in an at-risk child's life, and it's a great opportunity to practice motherhood, observing how you would react as an adoptive mother.

Adoption is a just a step on the journey to parenthood…like childbirth, it's becomes "past tense" in how a child's life becomes intertwined with yours. And just like other important decisions, it needs to be covered in prayer. So go sit at the feet of your Heavenly Father—if you have given Him your heart, He has already adopted you!

🍎 🍎 🍎

PRAYER:

Heavenly Father, the One who in Your great love has adopted me to be Your child…please show me what Your will is for adoption in our lives. You have already blessed us with every spiritual blessing in the heavenly places in Christ, choosing us in Him before the foundation of the world.

Therefore, make my husband and me holy and without blame in Your love, as You have predestined us to adoption as Your son and daughter by Jesus Christ to Himself, according to the good pleasure of Your will. We praise the glory of Your grace, by which You have made us accepted in our Beloved Savior.

Help me, then, to accept the idea of adoption and to overcome any prejudices I might have regarding adoption of a child from another race, ethnic group, or disability. Help me to have the spiritual fortitude to love a child who is somewhat unlovable, either in appearance or behavior.

God, this is a place where I must walk by faith and not by sight. If adoption is for us, show me Your face in the face of an adopted child so that I may serve You as this child's mother. Help me to make it my aim to be well-pleasing to You in this endeavor.

You are my Good Shepherd; I shall not want, even in infertility. Make me to rest in You, in the green pastures and still waters of Your presence, especially if adoption becomes a rollercoaster ride. Please lead me and my husband in the paths of righteousness for Your name's sake, not ours.

If adoption is what You would have us to pursue, please lead us by Your Spirit as Your children. Remove all bondage to fear, that we may receive the Spirit of adoption in You, by Whom we cry out "Abba, Father" to You. Let Your Holy Spirit bear witness with our spirit that we are, indeed, Your children...and if children, then Your heirs, if indeed we suffer through this with Christ. Let us seek Your glory and Your praise, whatever You have planned for us.

If adoption is not according to Your will for us, please show us clearly. Bless my husband with Your wisdom and direction, that he may be a godly, effective leader in our marriage. Help him to make good decisions for both of us.

In the infinite love of Your gracious adoption of us, Amen.

(Ephesians 1:3-5; 2 Corinthians 5:7, 9; Psalm 23:1-3; Romans 8:14-17)

FOR REFLECTION:

❖ Adoption can be considerably more expensive than birthing a child. But so are infertility treatments. Pray and count the costs now, through your own research, to see how God could help you financially through this experience and teach you good stewardship.

❖ List reasons why adoption would be—or would not be—a good option for you and your husband. Commit these to God, and ask Him for His guidance.

_____
_____
_____
_____

❖ Pray now for open doors for adoption, if God is leading you in this direction. It's important to pray for closed doors as well, knowing that God will direct your paths. Pray to bear disappointment as well as life-changing adjustments if you adopt.

_____
_____
_____
_____

🍎🍎🍎

KATIE'S STORY (CONTINUED FROM 18):

I didn't really know anyone who was in our position when we were told we couldn't have children. That was difficult. The advice I was given the most is to wait upon the Lord. Anxious thoughts and taking matters into our own hands often lead to more disappointments. Especially in private adoptions (we've experienced both private and agency), the temptation is to plan and get excited, only to often have the plans fall through—we've had five fall through. My husband was wise enough not to let me do anything until we had the baby for sure. I've seen hearts broken over this.

The encouragement I would give is God's sovereign plan is best and He is faithful to give us the desires of our hearts if we remain faithful. He will change our desires if need be.

Constructive ways to cope:
- Spending time with my nieces who were young, at the time I had no children
- Working in a profession which required that I work daily with preschoolers
- Celebrating birthdays and other occasions with friends' children
- Working with a local adoption agency, volunteering, speaking, being a board member
- Helping our church get involved in the adoption ministry
- Speaking to churches about infertility and adoption

When people would ask when we were going to start a family, we would either say, "We don't know (only God did!)," if the people were mere acquaintances. Or, if we knew them well, we would honestly say we were hoping to adopt. It really didn't "get" to us, at least as far as I can remember.

We still have people frequently ask who our children look like, saying, "They don't look like you." We respond either by saying, "No," and leaving it at that, or they have the same coloring as an aunt or other relative, which is true. Or, more often, we say they are adopted and what a blessing that is!

CHAPTER 24

Branching Out: Fostering and Mentoring

"But Jesus said, 'Let the little children come to Me, and do not forbid them; for of such is the kingdom of heaven.'" (Matthew 19:14)

"If you extend your soul to the hungry and satisfy the afflicted soul, then your light shall dawn in the darkness, and your darkness shall be as the noonday. The Lord will guide you continually, and satisfy your soul in drought, and strengthen your bones; you shall be like a watered garden, and like a spring of water, whose waters do not fail. Those from among you shall build the old waste places; you shall raise up the foundations of many generations; and you shall be called the Repairer of the Breach, The Restorer of Streets to Dwell In." (Isaiah 58:10-12)

One of the basic tenets of Christian parenthood is raising your children in the nurture and admonition of the Lord. When you baptize or dedicate your children before God and His people at church, you are committing your entire life to bring up these little souls in the love of Christ. This is no small job.

So, while you're waiting to get pregnant, or if you've discovered you may never get pregnant, try to look "outside of the box" for ways to fulfill your desire for motherhood. How about foster parenting or mentoring?

If you love little babies, check out your local or state department of children's services to sign up for temporary foster care of an infant. Some states do not allow babies to go directly to their adoptive parents immediately after birth, wherever laws require a waiting period for the birth parents to have the option of changing their minds. Those little babies need short-term care. So, if you're itching to change diapers and push around a stroller, here's your chance.

Most children in foster care are older, however. Consider caring for a toddler or teen. Better still, consider taking on several children from one family so that siblings can stay together. This is a wonderful way for young kids to have a stable, sheltering environment until permanent arrangements can be made for them. Take them with you to church and to Sunday School. They may never have another childhood option to learn about Jesus and His infinite love for them.

Be prepared for extensive questions, background checks, in-home inspections, and other counseling services from the state officials. Fostering is serious business, and you'll need to be transparent in your dealings with officials.

Fostering sometimes leads to adoption. But you must be careful not to let your hopes get away from you...many fostered children go back home to their biological parents. Keep yourself from unhealthy attachment; remind yourself that you are serving God.

What about service to other needy children outside of your home? Christian agencies that minister to at-risk children are always looking for help with after-school care. Often, this means spending an afternoon or two in a one-on-one tutoring program, helping with music or physical fitness, playing games, and helping with summer camps.

How about mentoring? Look for a community program specifically designed to give you one-on-one time with youths or children, to help them with homework, take them to the park, go with them on shopping trips, or take them to church.

Do you enjoy teaching? Churches are always looking for adults to teach children's Sunday School classes and summertime vacation Bible school programs.

An advantage to helping in these kinds of programs is that you discover your spiritual strengths for parenting. And you discover those weaknesses where you aren't ready yet!

While nothing ever prepares you completely for having kids full-time in your home, any time that you spend hanging out with young people is time well spent. Give God a chance to work with you and in you to grow in your walk with Him.

What if none of these options are valid or available for you? You can always "adopt" by sponsoring a needy child overseas. There are several reputable international agencies such as Compassion International and World Vision that can place you with a child sponsorship for a nominal amount of financial support each month.

You usually have the opportunity to pray for that child, send photos and letters, and encourage the child to be successful in spite of limited circumstances. It's a great way to have a long-term impact in helping a child discover a better life.

Want to share Christmas and the good news about Jesus Christ with other children overseas? Check out Samaritan's Purse and its program called Operation Christmas Child. You can fill up a shoebox with toys, school supplies, and personal care items. Samaritan's Purse volunteers will ship it, along with millions of other shoeboxes, across the world to local churches where the love of Jesus Christ is revealed to children who have never heard of Him.

These are options for discussion with your spouse. Make sure he is on the same page with you, because you need to invest your time and resources together. Know his desires about commitment before you volunteer to do anything.

Whatever route you follow, seek God's guidance through prayer. Ask Him to provide the opportunities. Look forward with great expectations to see how He will bring new joy to you and your husband as you work together on furthering His kingdom.

Maybe God is calling you to discover new blessings!

PRAYER:

Holy and loving Father, open the eyes of my heart to see what You might have in store for me, whether parenting our own children or looking in new directions.

Whatever You have planned for my future, grant me a mindset that seeks to serve You, not myself...a love for others that is greater than my selfishness...a sacrificial attitude that mirrors Your sacrifice for me on the cross, O Christ.

When poor little ones cry out, the ones who are fatherless and have no helper, let me hear their pleas and answer. Show me the best place to serve, and give me wisdom and prudence in how to get involved.

Remind me that I, too, am poor and needy...yet You think of me. You are my Help and my Deliverer; do not delay, O my God.

Let me make Your name to be remembered in all generations, so that these children may praise You forever and ever, even after they become adults. I would so love to praise Your works to children, declaring Your mighty acts–please give me those opportunities as You see fit.

If Your Holy Spirit nudges me to become a teacher, please equip me for this role. Help me to teach Your precepts to children, talking only of You, Your truth, Your love, Your grace, and the blessings and rewards of Your commandments. Let me teach about Your glory to children in our home, when we walk with them in the community, and when we become integrally involved in their lives. Give my husband inspiration from Your Holy Spirit, if this is what You wish us to do.

Father, help me to count the cost that sacrificial living incurs. But let me be unafraid to step out in faith, knowing that You will provide the strength and wisdom to perform whatever You demand of me. You will reshape my heart, much as a branch is pruned, that I may bear more fruit. In the discipling spirit of Jesus Christ, Amen.

(Acts 16:14; Job 29:12; Psalm 40:17; Psalm 45:17; Psalm 145:4; Deuteronomy 6:7; Luke 14:28; John 15:2)

FOR REFLECTION:

❖ If you feel called by God to think about fostering, do some research online or at your local library about foster care in your community. Look for articles about pitfalls and expectations. List three benefits and three potential problems you would face.

___

❖ Talk with your pastor and friends, to help you find godly women who have fostered children. Make an appointment for a lunch date or other meeting, to learn about their experience. Write it down here, along with anything you learned.

___

❖ Pray specifically for your own heart and your husband's needs/wishes concerning fostering, mentoring, teaching, sponsorship, or any other relationship with children. Pray for unity and clarity of purpose shared by both of you. Write your prayer here.

___

❦ ❦ ❦

BRITTANY'S STORY:

Our first encounter with fostering was purely accidental. A girl who was going to our church was removed from her home because of abuse. Our pastor asked if there was anyone who would take her so she wouldn't have to go to a stranger's home. We said we would step in, which meant going through foster-parenting training and classes. My husband, Ike, was completely in favor of doing this.

As of today, we've fostered a total of 28 children and youth. For one girl, we were made permanent legal guardians, but the biological mom was not an American citizen and wouldn't give up rights for adoption. This foster child is now an adult and still very much a part of our family...I call her my "daughter."

We didn't face any major issues with learning how to foster, but we met more hurdles and obstacles among people in church who were not supportive. The biggest challenge was in others' reception of foster children...some parents didn't want their kids to be around them, or they automatically blamed foster kids for something bad that happened, even though it wasn't their fault. That hurts. Sadly, some Christians were more judgmental than non-Christians.

When you take in foster kids, you can't expect them to love you...they are hurting and don't want to be in foster care. If a woman wants to take in a foster child as a means to adoption, that's not the best reason to foster; children are not going to receive their foster parents immediately in the same way as they loved their biological parents. No matter how bad the biological parents have been, these children still want a relationship with their mom or dad, and they hold back a little bit from bonding with the foster parents.

Foster kids have to come to grips with that relationship before they can give everything to you, and it can take a long time. Some kids have been abused in horrific ways, but they still want their own mother to show them kindness.

From the fostering side, loving these children isn't instantaneous for you, either. You have to work at loving them. But it's worth it.

So, if you don't have any children of your own and want to adopt, there are many toddlers and older children out there who need families. I currently get up to 10 notifications a week of kids available for adoption. They're not easy cases, usually with emotional problems, abuse, special needs...but we're supposed to care for orphans. These kids are orphans. Why does everyone want a perfect child or baby? Maybe God has something else in mind for your life!

The greatest blessing of fostering? Five of my kids have come to know the Lord! And all have been exposed to His love and gospel truth. We saw a huge transformation in one teen, and it was just unbelievable what happened to him. He was with us for a month before going to a local Christian camp and there accepted Jesus Christ as his Savior. Beforehand, his cursing was awful and disgusting, but afterward, he was a completely different person. Although we had given him a Bible and were doing devotions with him before, it all clicked for him at camp.

Fostering is flexible, too. You can say "no" to any child for fostering or adoption, waiting until you get the child or children who would fit with your family. You need to make sure they are younger than your own children (if you already have one or more) so it doesn't dramatically affect the dynamics of your family. Fostering is usually indefinite in its length and can be a little more than a year. And there is a tremendous need for people who will take sibling groups.

I really feel that the Lord has called me to be a foster mom after making me question my purpose. What was I doing with my time? What was I doing for the kingdom of Christ? I'm fostering now for the Lord and for the kids—I want to make a mark on their lives so they know about the Lord and what "normal" is like. Maybe they will go back and remember this in the future.

CHAPTER 25

When Grief Overwhelms

"Have mercy on me, O Lord, for I am in trouble; My eye wastes away with grief, yes, my soul and my body! For my life is spent with grief, and my years with sighing; My strength fails because of my iniquity, And my bones waste away....But as for me, I trust in You, O Lord; I say, 'You are my God.' ...Be of good courage, and He shall strengthen your heart, all you who hope in the Lord." (Psalm 31:9-10, 14, 24)

"We can't detect a heartbeat."

"I'm sorry, but you've had a miscarriage."

"The birth mom decided to keep her baby."

"You have cancer."

"You will never be able to get pregnant."

Whatever the words, whenever they come, they pierce your heart with rusty-knife violence. Your physical pain and trauma may be alleviated with medicinal treatments, but nothing can quench the agony of your writhing soul or the after-pain dullness of despair. The axe has fallen, granite has sealed the tomb, and all dreams are crushed. You have no strength to lift the weight of your sorrow.

Friends and family, even your husband, are incapable of taking away your pain. Well-meaning loved ones offer phrases like, "It's all for the best," or "The baby wouldn't be normal," or "There's always next time." But their empty attempts fall flat on your ears.

You stumble through the days, months, shrouded in a leaden sheet. Despite your stiff upper lip, you are grieving behind a stony mask.

And that's okay. It's okay to grieve.

Whether you grieve inwardly with a façade of cheer or grieve visibly and audibly, grief is an appropriate response to loss. You have lost your child.

If your baby was stillborn, if you had a miscarriage, or if the baby promised to you in adoption never came home with you, you have just as much right to grieve as a mother who loses a 16-year-old son or a 58-year-old daughter. Your husband has a right to grieve, too, whether or not he feels the pain as intensely as you do.

Those who have never experienced miscarriage or infertility or abortion cannot appreciate your loss—so don't expect them to understand. Resist the temptation to lash out at those who try to comfort you. They are not insensitive. They just don't know how to help.

Following the death of his beloved wife, Joy, C.S. Lewis found grief to be an unnerving experience. "No one ever told me that grief felt so much like fear. I am not afraid, but the sensation is like being afraid....There is a sort of invisible blanket between the world and me. I find it hard to take in what anyone says. Or perhaps, hard to want to take it in....Yet I want the others to be about me. I dread the moments when the house is empty. If only they would talk to one another and not to me."[1]

But accepting the freedom to grieve is not only natural, it's an essential part of the healing process. And, it's an integral part of the Christian life.

The Bible is full of laments. Just read through the Psalms and look at the titles. An entire book is devoted to Jeremiah's "Lamentations" over the desolation of his beloved Israel, captured and taken into exile.

Read through the entire book of Job. You can identify with this godly man, afflicted by Satan precisely because Job is faithful to his God. Job loses everything, including his household possessions, his wealth, and all of his children. He sits in the ash heap, dogged by friends who make snide comments that Job must be guilty of terrible sin.

When Job cries out in his distress, God answers him—reminding Job that He is still in charge, not Job.

Our greatest example, however, is Jesus Christ. We see His grief in its many facets.

Jesus grieved in the face of death. When His good friend Lazarus died and was buried in a tomb, we find those two famous words uttered in John 11:35, the shortest verse in the Bible: "Jesus wept." They speak volumes.

Jesus was grief-stricken and revealed it with tears and mourning. Death was extraordinarily painful for the Author of life.

He wept, too, over the plight of Jerusalem, saying, *"If you had known, even you, especially in this your day, the things that make for your peace! But now they are hidden from your eyes."* (Luke 19:41-42) He hated sin and all its consequences.

Jesus especially shrank back at the anticipation of His own death, sweating drops of blood in the Garden of Gethsemane before humbly taking on the atrocity of the cross.

Jesus knows your pain. Even now, He feels your ache as He sits on the right hand of His Father in heaven, interceding for you. Ask Him to send His Holy Spirit as His Comforter for you.

Even as you grieve privately here on earth, try to reach out to other women among your family and friends. As you do, you'll be surprised to find there are many who have walked this ugly path before you. For example, according to Mayo Clinic, between 10 and 20 percent of all known pregnancies end in miscarriage.[2] That means nearly one in five women has undergone at least one miscarriage. You are not alone if you miscarried! Share your grief with your good friends, and let them help you carry this load. Let them mourn with you in your community of faith.

If you have suffered a miscarriage or stillbirth, recognize also that your body is physically depressed. Just as a woman who bears a child normally goes through some sort of postpartum anxiety or depression, your body needs to recover from this event and the hormonal changes it has induced.

Give yourself time to heal. Take a break from extra activities that might add stress. Indulge in some self-pampering like a manicure/pedicure. Ask your husband to give you a back massage.

Read your Bible daily, especially in the Psalms. Let your heart cry out to the Lord even as the psalmists did. Mark those prayer psalms in your Bible, and take note of the ones that end in a peaceful trust for God's provision and aid. Put your hope and confidence in the Lord, even as they did.

When you are ready, if you feel led by God, spend some time thinking about an appropriate memorial if you lost a child. No matter how far along your pregnancy was at the time, you were carrying a human being, and you may feel the need to name your child. This is a particularly poignant action for those who have lost a child through an abortion—some post-abortion recovery Bible studies encourage naming the lost child, to help continue in the healing process.

Your memorial could be providing a new park bench, planting a tree at a church or in your yard, sponsoring a piece of playground equipment, or buying a new children's book for the library. Look for something that will bring joy to you and others.

For though you may be poor and needy at the moment, God is your ultimate healer. He is your Help and Deliverer *(Psalm 40:17)*.

It's critically important, though, not to linger longer than appropriate in the season of grief. The Preacher in Ecclesiastes 3:4 tells us that there is a time to weep and a time to laugh, a time to mourn and a time to dance. At some point, it's time to move on.

If you are unable to pull yourself up out of depression, seek both medical help and Christian counseling—this could be a symptom of something else going on in your life, either physical or spiritual.

Keep your focus on God. Just as He allows us to grieve, He commands us to rejoice in Him as well. The psalmist in Psalm 118:24 invites us to make God the center of our joy today—"This is the day that the Lord has made; we will rejoice and be glad in it." Let Him turn your mourning into dancing.

PRAYER:

Holy and Sovereign God, Father of our Lord Jesus Christ, I cry out to You in grief. I need Your comforting words, Your everlasting arms beneath me, Your love enfolding me. You, O Lord, are a Shield for me, my Glory and the One who lifts up my head...hear me from Your holy hill.

Help me to acknowledge my need to grieve. Remind me that Your Son, Jesus Christ, has already borne our griefs and carried our sorrows, and that He has been smitten and afflicted for us. Help me to remember that, out of Your great love for us, You have grieved often for Your children in despair on earth and for Your Only Son's great sacrifice.

But You, O God, have defeated death itself. I recognize that while we experience its grim finality in our earthly relationships, death loses its sting in Your presence—with You, the Author of all life, there is only abundant life. Turn my eyes away from the desolation of death and into the fullness of joy and hope that flow from You.

O Lord, do not be far from me; O my Strength, hasten to help me! For You have not despised nor abhorred my affliction, nor have You hidden Your face from me. When I cry to You, I know that I will be heard. And though I walk through the valley of the shadow of death, I will fear no evil, for You are with me and You comfort me.

Turn Yourself to me, and have mercy on me, for I am desolate and afflicted. The troubles of my heart have enlarged; bring me out of my distresses! Look on my affliction and pain, and forgive all my sins. Let me not be ashamed, for I put my trust in You. Let integrity and uprightness preserve me, for I wait for You.

During this season of grief, I will yet praise You according to Your righteousness, and I will sing praise to Your name, O Lord Most High. For You will once again light my lamp of joy; You, the Lord my God, will enlighten my darkness.

Turn my mourning into dancing; clothe me with gladness, to the end that I may sing praise to You and not be silent. O Lord my God, I will give thanks to You forever. In Jesus Christ's name, Amen.

(Psalm 3:3-4; Isaiah 53:4; Psalm 22:19,24; Psalm 23:4; Psalm 25:16-18,21; Psalm 7:17; Psalm 18:28; Psalm 30:11-12)

🍎🍎🍎

FOR REFLECTION:

❖ Read David's lament in Psalm 86. How do David's pains reflect yours? David also turns his pain into praise for God. Write your own lament and praise here.

_____
_____
_____
_____

❖ Now read Psalm 69. David gets very honest with God about his pain and suffering. But he ends with trust in God's mercy and provision. Write your own prayer about your suffering, being honest with where you are right now, but end it with an affirmation of trust in God.

_____
_____
_____
_____

❖ Throughout the lamenting Psalms, David often cites his enemies as the source of his suffering. What or who are your enemies? Write a prayer that asks for healing, of your body and spirit. Ask for forbearance of those whom you may perceive to be adversaries; ask for help in forgiving and loving them, and that God may turn aside any persecution.

_____
_____
_____
_____

🍎🍎🍎

MEGAN'S STORY (CONTINUED FROM CHAPTER 20):

When I enrolled in a Bible study for women going through post-abortion issues,* it was the scariest step of all. Little by little, God was peeling away all these layers of hurt, anger, guilt, and shame from around my heart, like an onion. There were 10 women in my study, ages ranging from 20 to 60. Some were married, divorced, single, with children, or with miscarriages. The one thing in common is that we hurt from our past and wanted help.

We looked at God's character, and many of the truths I learned as a child came back to me. Although I was a Christian at an early age, I found out in high school that I had a learning disability. I turned away from God and tried to do things *my way*. In college, I found a wild crowd, and that's where I got in trouble. I'm not blaming anyone but myself, but I see how easily it led to the destruction of my child.

We looked at all our emotions. I wasn't just angry—I had *rage*. God showed me how to deal with it in a healthy way—not self-destruction through suicide but through writing.

At the end of our study, we had the option of participating in a memorial service for our lost children. I went. So did Larry. I lit a candle in memory of my aborted child and my miscarried child. I named them—Matthew (means God's gift), even though I threw the gift away, and Lane (narrow path) because the miscarriage became a path to lead me to God, to deal with my sin, to ask for forgiveness, and be healed.

The study also helped me to recognize that the miscarriage wasn't just tissue but a child. I could mourn for this one, too, in a healthy way. One of my closest friends from the post-abortion counseling has called or sent a card around the anniversary date of my miscarriage and/or abortion to tell me she loves me but more importantly God loves me, too!

God showed me that all ground is level at the cross. God had forgiven me, and now I needed to forgive myself—which I have done now.

I feel that the infertility was a stepping stone God used to bring me to my knees and bring me to Him.

Though I may never have a "birth child," God has blessed me with an adopted son here on earth, and I have two children in heaven. One day, when the Lord calls me home, I will see and hug my heavenly babies for the first time.

*If you are dealing with post-abortion issues, a great resource for you is Forgiven and Set Free: A Post-Abortion Bible Study for Women, by Linda Cochrane (Grand Rapids: Baker Publishing Group, 2015, Revised and Updated Edition). Many Christian centers/churches throughout the country use this book in their post-abortion studies...look for a study in your local community.

CHAPTER 26

The Crucible of Faith

"He will sit as a refiner and a purifier of silver; He will purify the sons of Levi, and purge them as gold and silver, that they may offer to the Lord an offering in righteousness." (Malachi 3:3)

"Seeing then that we have a great High Priest who has passed through the heavens, Jesus the Son of God, let us hold fast our confession. For we do not have a High Priest who cannot sympathize with our weaknesses, but was in all points tempted as we are, yet without sin." (Hebrews 4:14-15)

"And I will bless her [Sarah] and also give you a son by her; then I will bless her, and she shall be a mother of nations; kings of peoples shall be from her." (Genesis 17:16)

Do you know what a crucible is?

It's the small hollow in a jeweler's oven, fired up to extremely high temperatures. As a silversmith or goldsmith melts precious metals, impurities are carried to the surface of the glimmering liquid. The dross, all the ugly stuff, is skimmed off by the careful craftsman.

What comes out of this process gleams brightly, no longer darkened by pollutants.

The crucible of infertility can bring excruciating pain. God, the master Craftsman, is taking you through a process of purification. As Christ, He has been through it Himself.

After His baptism and before He began His official ministry, Jesus Christ spent 40 days fasting in the desert. At the end of this time, what happened? That crafty devil, Satan, dared to enter the presence of the Almighty God at the point of His fleshly vulnerability—physical hunger and weakness.

When Satan wheedled Jesus with worldly charms, our Lord answered him calmly by speaking His own words from the Scriptures (*Matthew 4, Luke 4*). Finally, Satan threw a ludicrous offer to Christ: all the kingdoms of the world if He will just bow down to him...as if the Lord and Creator of the universe doesn't already own everything.

By then, Jesus had enough. *"Away with you, Satan! For it is written, 'You shall worship the Lord your God, and Him only you shall serve.'"* (*Matthew 4:10*)

Satan departed the stage as God's angels arrived to minister to His Beloved Son. Jesus received blessings and refreshment that signified the end of one season and the beginning of another. Our Holy Lord endured a painful purification process that He didn't need. On the cross, He endured an awful death that He didn't deserve. Why?

In everything, Christ has suffered our own brokenness. He knows our flaws, how we are daily tempted by Satan. He's been there, yet He didn't fall into sin. He intercedes for us in the great throne room of God in heaven, pleading for grace. He tells His Heavenly Father, "Have mercy upon them, for I have walked among them and know their weakness and sorrow." There is no love on earth that can compare with His.

Our Lord took the apostle Paul through a similar desert time. After a stunning encounter with Christ and conversion on the road to Damascus, the formerly ruthless persecutor lived through a short spell of complete blindness and a narrow escape from foes via a basket lowered from a wall. Then he took off for the desert.

Paul disappeared for three years in the desolate Arabian territory (still a hostile environment today for Jews) during which God prepared him for dangerous missions. Much like a soldier trained and equipped for the fight ahead, Paul surfaced stronger and more capable of sharing the good news. He went on to become the greatest missionary of all time, turning the hearts of Gentiles to Jesus Christ.

There are other Bible accounts that tell of desert crucibles. Moses worked as a shepherd for 40 years before God called him from a burning bush. Elijah endured a drought and escaped wicked Jezebel by fleeing to the wilderness. David wandered through the Arabah badlands as an outcast, hotly pursued by King Saul and his troops.

Perhaps a more pertinent application to our situation is the story of Sarah. For years, she endured the role of servant wife to her husband, Abraham, as God led them on a lifelong journey to Canaan.

In the process, Sarah put up with Abraham's lies (her life was endangered twice when he presented her to the local kings as his sister instead of his wife), the constant moving, living in tents instead of a brick-and-mortar home, and the embarrassment of childlessness. This wasn't her journey, it was Abraham's. Yet in submission, she obeyed and followed wherever he led her...for a very long time.

Sarah knew about God's promise, that Abraham and she would have a son of their own together. But why should she believe it? She was decades past child-bearing. It's no wonder she laughed when she heard the promise announced by an angel. Years of bitter disappointment had removed all hope.

In her disgust with God's tardiness, Sarah took matters into her own hands and encouraged Abraham to take her maid Hagar as a second wife and surrogate mother. The outcome, of course, was disastrous. Hagar's ensuing pregnancy and birth of her son, Ishmael, created family strife and generations of hostility.

But God—those two words in the Scriptures carry incredible power—never wavered in His promise. Sarah did become a mother, at a time when she and Abraham were ancient in age. God gave her His reward, the royal privilege of bearing and rearing the young man Isaac who would become an ancestor of the entire Jewish population, an ancestor of Jesus Christ, and the faith ancestor of all Christians today.

Sarah's desert experience was long, tedious, and constantly heartbreaking. God's promises did not fail her, though, in spite of her impatience and impulsiveness. He was faithful even when she was unfaithful. His purposes and plans for her succeeded.

Now, as you withstand the same crucible of desert barrenness, recognize that God may be taking you through a time of purification. Satan's greatest desire right now is to lead you into idolatry—taking your eyes off of Christ and setting them on the idols of the world. In contrast, God desires to rid you of these weighty encumbrances and teach you to love Him fully.

Has a baby become your idol? Do you worship the idea of motherhood more than you worship God Himself? Have you abandoned the Giver in your quest to obtain His gift?

Look for blessings and joys in this desert, in this time of weakness and brokenness. As prophesied in Isaiah 42:3, Christ will neither break the bruised reed nor will He quench a smoking flax.

After the devastating death of her young daughter LeeAnne, Elizabeth B. Brown wrote she "bumbled" through grief's course at first.

"Faith offers no panacea, no quick fix for life's challenges," Brown said, "yet Scripture is the Designer's guide for *what works* and *what doesn't work* when life's problems cause joy's demise....

"No matter the cause of our distress, our pathway back to joy requires the same things: *a choice to be grateful for what was and a decision to appreciate what is*....Character is forged in times of challenge just as a photograph is developed in darkness.

"It was only when I shifted to focus on how blessed we were to share [our daughter's] life for seven years that light began to shine in my darkness....I chose to live with joy, even with a hole in my heart. I found anchors to steady my tilting boat."[1]

If you turn to Him and place your life in His care, the Master Craftsman will reshape your heart and strip away all the ugliness until He sees His reflection in you. His methods may be painful as He plunges you into this crucible, but He is making you more beautiful than ever.

He is turning your life into pure gold. He is making you more like Himself.

🌱 🌱 🌱

PRAYER:

Dear God, I ask You to hold my hand tightly as You take me through this refining process. I know that no temptation has overtaken me except what is common to everyone. But You are faithful, and You will not allow me to be tempted beyond what I am able to bear...You will make a way of escape for me.

Ever since Satan deceived Eve, I face his relentless efforts to derail me. Help me to be sober, vigilant, watching and praying always, because the devil walks about like a roaring lion seeking to devour me. My spirit indeed is willing, but my flesh is weak. Lead me not into temptation, but deliver me from the evil one. For Yours is the kingdom, power, and glory forever.

Instead, teach me to count it all joy and blessing as I persevere in this trial, for when I have been approved, You will give me a "crown of life" promised to those who love You. Let me see that temptation is never from You. Keep me from letting infertility give birth to sin in my heart and actions. Make me swift to hear, slow to speak, slow to wrath.

Continue with me in my trials, just as Your disciples continued with You in Your trials, O Christ—let me enter Your kingdom, just as Your Father bestowed one upon You.

And oh, how I praise You for Your promises! You have promised to "do a new thing" out of nothing—Your Word calls it to spring forth, and I will know it: You will even make a road in the wilderness for me, and rivers in the desert of infertility. Thank You, O God, for blessings that as yet I cannot see. In the abundant name of Jesus Christ, Amen.

(1 Corinthians 10:13; Genesis 3:1; 1 Peter 5:8; Mark 14:38; Matthew 6:13; James 1:2,12-19; Isaiah 43:19)

FOR REFLECTION:

❖ Think about a past or present trial where you endured a difficult situation or painful failure. How is God purifying you? What lessons did God teach you about yourself? List at least two.

❖ Evaluate how you spend your thought time. What "idols" do you worship with your attention? Do they interfere with your worship of God? List the primary things that fit this description. Write a prayer for God to take down those idols. Ask Him to hold your hand in this process.

_____
_____
_____
_____

❖ Consider the story of Sarah in the book of Genesis. How can you identify with her? What did she do rightly, and what mistakes did she make? What can you learn from her experience for following God in the future? What temptations do you need to avoid?

_____
_____
_____
_____

🍎🍎🍎

CATELYN'S STORY (CONTINUED FROM CHAPER 5):

I have a "soul ache" today and a need to share with someone who understands. I miscarried last night.

When we found out we were pregnant, we were so incredibly surprised and excited...not in treatment at the time and pregnant "naturally." It was really early, only seven-and-a-half weeks. I started to spot Saturday night and went to bed for three days. My husband is so broken up.

I feel stupid—stupid for getting so excited and beginning to share our news. But I know God wants to use this. My heart is hurt towards God, but my mouth can praise Him...does that make sense? God's comfort is all around. Last night, our son said (of course, he didn't know anything yet), "I want to fly way up high in the sky and go see God." He had *never* said anything like that before...it was out of the blue.

Thank you for listening. It means more than you'll know.

Another letter some time later:
I want to share our unbelievable news...I'm 17 weeks pregnant! No congratulations...something more akin to "to God be the glory" in a loud voice! This remains a "journey" for us. I know you understand.

I recently went through training in the "Stephen Ministry" (an organization that helps churches provide Christ-centered care to those who are hurting). We had a grief counselor speak to us, pointing out the difference between grieving and mourning—grieving being what we do individually and mourning being a response in community. We realized we had no community earlier to mourn with. We got out our hymnal and sang together, "And Can It Be" [a wonderful hymn of praise that turns our eyes off of ourselves and onto the great hope in Christ.]

CHAPTER 27

Listening to God, Following His Will

"So He said to them, "When you pray, say: Our Father in heaven, hallowed be Your name. Your kingdom come. Your will be done on earth as it is in heaven." (Luke 11:2)

"Trust in the Lord with all your heart, and lean not on your own understanding; in all your ways acknowledge Him, and He shall direct your paths." (Proverbs 3:5-6)

"In Him we have redemption through His blood, the forgiveness of sins, according to the riches of His grace which He made to abound toward us in all wisdom and prudence, having made known to us the mystery of His will, according to His good pleasure which He purposed in Himself, that in the dispensation of the fullness of the times He might gather together in one all things in Christ, both which are in heaven and which are on earth–in Him. In Him also we have obtained an inheritance, being predestined according to the purpose of Him who works all things according to the counsel of His will, that we who first trusted in Christ should be to the praise of His glory." (Ephesians 1:7-12)

"Follow your dreams. Pursue your passion."

Countless speakers at school and college graduations in the past decades have preached these inspiring words to an eager audience of hopeful millennials. Young spirits have absorbed these exhortations and pursued a mishmash of adventures, missions, artistry, and lofty goals...not always, however, with success.

When the realities of life arrive, especially the pragmatic requirements like money and employment, millennials begin to wonder what went wrong. If dreams and passions are the important things in life, why are some young people missing the mark? What happens when hopes and visions are dashed on the rocky trials of day-to-day living?

Obviously, there are no easy answers. The world still needs trained accountants, plumbers, dentists, police officers, nurses, teachers, and farmers, even as some young adults chase after fleeting fame, self-glory, and other self-fulfilling missions. The world still needs women to be wives and mothers, and we still need men to be husbands and fathers, even as young adults delay those goals to follow intangible desires.

You may have had the noble dreams of becoming an astronaut, a Nobel-Prize-winning chemist, or a Christian recording artist. Somewhere along the way, you pursued your passion and may have reached the threshold of success. Children were an afterthought, motherhood the accompanying dessert to the meat and potatoes of a career.

Then, the day comes when you accept the creeping realization that the children you desired aren't arriving on your timetable. You're getting older, your passion for life's daring adventures is growing colder, and your desire to have children increases in desperation.

Our vision grows foggy because we can't see the future. We stumble about, looking for direction, or we plod along in a chosen rut, disillusioned and resentful. How do we find our way?

Can you start over? Can you still find fulfillment in living? Where do you go now? What should your life look like in the future? Where does your path lead? Is childlessness or motherhood His plan for you?

As you examine these questions, start by asking yourself the most important one: What is God's will for my life?

Those who have grown up in the Presbyterian Church have probably heard of the Westminster Confession (belief structure), its catechism (religious instruction), and its first question: "What is the chief end of man?"

The answer is surprising and a bit different from you might expect: "Man's [and woman's] chief end is to glorify God and to enjoy Him forever."

That part about glorifying God seems obvious—if you've invited Christ into your heart as your Savior, you develop a desire to thank Him and bring Him glory in all you do.

But what's that about enjoying Him? It seems a bit presumptuous for us to think about enjoying God. He's the Creator of the universe and the Lord and Master of our lives. But enjoyment? It's not a natural desire when we're tempted to recoil from Him out of guilt and fear or when we believe He is uninterested in our daily lives.

Yet if we strive not only to glorify God but also to enjoy Him, our lives have purpose. What we once thought was paramount in our own plans now pales as we begin to warm up to His directions. The daily battle changes to daily refreshment as we shift gears to serving Him instead of serving ourselves.

Once we accept Jesus Christ (and Him alone) as the Author and Perfecter of our faith and life, our hearts turn toward seeking God's will and not our own, to seeking His friendship and not the material joys of the world.

To quote Frances Schaeffer's book title, "How should we then live?" How can we as Christians know God's will for our lives?

We have four essential areas for study, discernment, and implementation:

First, read your Bible. Nestled in among the stories of wars, kings, prophets, and missionaries, God has laid out all of His plans for you in His words. Just as He spoke in ancient times to a bunch of misfit people, He still speaks to you and me today.

True, He doesn't specifically tell you that your life goal should be seeking a career in fashion design or corporate logistics. His truths, though, apply to our daily lives as much as they guided the people who preceded us by 4,000 years.

Don't get too bogged down by the (seemingly endless) genealogies or priestly duties or heavy prophecies...these have purpose and meaning to your Bible study, but God's vision for you is found in His "still, small voice" of comfort and in His thundering commands.

Persevere in your daily or weekly reading, and you will learn how to align your steps toward godly living. Spend time slowly reading Paul's entire letter to the Romans, especially Chapters 13 and 14 which include practical ways to act out your Christian faith. In every part of the Bible, God speaks of His love for you and His desire for you to do His will.

Next, while you are delving into God's word, *actively seek out the wisdom of godly counselors*. These are people you respect for their faith, their actions, and their advice: your pastors, senior women in your church, mentors, and Christian family counselors.

Make an appointment with one or more of these influence-leaders in your life to talk about your goals. Weigh their recommendations with what you read in the Bible. Ask them to pray for you and hold you accountable to your plans.

Third, review and analyze the circumstances in your life. Has God placed you in a community where you have a lot of options available to you? Has He given you any financial resources to get extra training, or has He made it possible for you to earn the necessary funding?

Has God given you specific talents, skills, and experience? How can you apply those blessings to advancing God's kingdom? If you have training as a financial advisor, you're in a prime position to aid others who are struggling to make a budget. If you have a beautiful voice or have learned to play the guitar, you have the potential to join your church's music team in worship.

If God has placed you as a teacher in an inner-city school, you are already settled in a mission field and may need to recognize divinely given opportunities to serve Him there. If He opens a door for you to go into real estate sales, consider how He might be leading you toward a career change.

Fourth, pray without ceasing. Even if He does not answer your pleas immediately, He hears your prayers. He cares for you, has plans for you, and wants you to ask Him to direct you.

Jesus told the parable *(Luke 18:1-8)* of the unjust judge and the widow who pestered him constantly to give her a ruling against her oppressor. Because of the widow's persistence, the judge relented and attended to her request. Just so, Jesus said that we are to pray with unrelenting fervor, asking God to heed our cries for wisdom. He has promised to be generous in providing it.

As you pray, listen for His voice—in the Bible, in the advice of godly mentors, in the circumstances He provides, in the peace of prayer. Look for ways that all of these come together in harmony. God has a perfect plan for you and desires for you to succeed in it. Have faith in His goals, His mission, His purpose for your life. He will never fail you, even in the difficult moments.

But how do you know you're hearing the truth? Are you listening to God's voice and not some selfish wish? Author LeAnne Blackmore assures us with this: "Is God speaking to you? You can know with certainty if the message you hear lines up with God's character and His word. Whatever battle you are facing,...fear not! The battle belongs to the Lord!"[1]

A strong prayer life renews your mind and gives you a greater vision of God's will. Paul, in his letter to the Romans, gave us this hope: *"And do not be conformed to this world, but be transformed by the renewing of your mind, that you may prove what is that good and acceptable and perfect will of God" (Romans 12:2).*

As you follow, Jesus Christ—through the work of His Holy Spirit—will lead you toward a richer life, abundantly above what you ever asked or imagined, far greater than any grief you bear now. Trust Him and His plans for you.

🙏 🙏 🙏

PRAYER:

O loving and wise God, Your counsel stands forever, the plans of Your heart to all generations. By Your gentle hand upon me, I know that You can make me understand the work of Your plans for me.

While Your vision for me may yet be for an appointed time to come, at the end it will be revealed, and it will not lie. Though it tarries, help me to wait for it; because it will surely come in Your good timing.

You have promised that, in the last days, O God, You will pour out of Your Spirit on all flesh; sons and daughters shall prophesy, young men shall see visions, old men shall dream dreams. Help me to be diligent, patient, not hasty in making decisions—I do not want to fall into poverty of spirit. And while I may think I'm planning my own way, I plead with You to direct my steps, so that I may not turn aside from Your will.

Give me a genuine love and desire for reading Your word on a regular basis. Do not let me ignore this "lamp to my feet" and "light to my path."

You have promised, in Your word, that I can ask You for wisdom—You give to all liberally and without reproach. I also ask for a multitude of wise friends and associates, to help counsel me so that my plans will not go awry.

Father, as the circumstances unfold in my life according to Your good purposes for me, help me not get discouraged or read too much into what is happening around me...let me look squarely at You and trust that the events/people/things You have placed in my life are from Your good plans and for Your glory, not mine. When I encounter closed doors, open my eyes to the open doors You offer.

Help me to pray without ceasing; remind me constantly of Your presence. And in everything, teach me to give thanks, for I know this is Your will in Christ Jesus for me.

Now may You—the God of peace who brought up Jesus from the dead, my great Shepherd through the blood of the everlasting covenant—make me complete in every good work to do Your will, working in me what is well pleasing in Your sight, through Jesus Christ, to Whom be glory forever and ever. Amen.

(Psalm 33:11; 1 Chronicles 28:19; Habakkuk 2:3; Acts 2:17; Proverbs 21:5; Proverbs 16:9; Psalm 119:105; James 1:5; Proverbs 15:22; 1 Thessalonians 5:18; Hebrews 13:20-21)

FOR REFLECTION:

❖ Commit today to a weekly Bible-reading plan—if you can't read every day, commit to at least three days a week, selecting one book each from the Old and New Testaments and reading through one chapter from each. Or search the Internet for Bible-reading plans. Focus on getting the most out of your reading, not just breezing through to check off the daily task!

❖ Can you identify any unusual circumstances in the past when God has directed you concerning His will for your life? Can you see any circumstances now that may be sending you in a new direction to follow Him?

❖ Write a brief prayer here, asking the Holy Spirit to give you clear guidance from the Bible, mentors, and circumstances to help you make decisions in accordance with His will. Follow up later, if applicable, with any answers to your prayer.

🍎 🍎 🍎

GRACE'S STORY (CONTINUED FROM CHAPTER 21):

When my husband, Isaiah, and I began courting (we met on a dating website!), I told him I wanted to adopt, and he was good with it. Adoption was always Plan A for us. It was always God's plan, too. There is no Plan B with God. God saw infertility in my story even before I was an adoption lawyer. He is sovereign. He was always planning for this.

After endometriosis surgery, we waited six months to make a decision between two paths: would we continue to doggedly pursue having a biological child, or would we adopt? We had tried for over two years...it was the focus of our marriage, finances, and energy. For our marriage, we both agreed we needed to take a break. Financially, we couldn't afford to do both at the same time. Emotionally, I knew I'd have to close a door to go through another one. We needed to take some time to pick a path, but we knew we were free to go down either way.

So, we decided not to talk about anything related to our children for two weeks. I had determined that if Isaiah's heart was not overwhelmingly joyful about adoption, I wouldn't press the issue. I had talked with God about moving his heart...I had seen conflict over adoption break other couples. And, I didn't want to make an idol out of having a child.

When we came back together on the discussion, he announced, "I have no doubt whatsoever that God is calling us to adopt." During our two weeks of silence on the subject, God inundated us individually with stories about adoption. God even went to great lengths at times! Isaiah went on a work trip for several days and one day was fishing in a boat between two long-time work friends. There, out in the middle of nowhere, both the man in the front of the boat and the man in the back of the boat began a discussion (unprovoked by my husband) about adoption!

When he shared his confident decision with me, I cried and cried for joy! I felt like I was expecting! God had just given us the news that we were going to have a baby! In His grand plans for our lives, our daughter was conceived that very month. We held her in our arms nine months later.

As a perfectionist, I have a hard time releasing things, especially when the loudest voice speaking to us at times is shame. Relaxing is very difficult, but Jesus is teaching me how to relax in Him. I still have to practice this constantly, but the journey of infertility has been a brutal invitation to rest deeper in the sovereignty of God. Even in the healing journey, the fear, and the pain of feeling like I failed, God has continued to show and comfort me with His nature as my sovereign God.

God is in control of all things. If He wanted things to be done differently, He could make it happen. God can raise the ruins; I can't. I haven't failed. I can give way to a sweet place of surrender, not to just accepting the way things are but surrendering my story to God's big story.

He has already finished all our stories well! In that surrender, there's nothing left to do but relax and enjoy what I have as a gift.

I don't know that I would have embraced this concept so deeply if I had biological children. My complete inability to bear a life has made me more aware, dependent, and surrendered to the life He wants to bear through me.

Our adoption journey was not strewn with roses, either. After giving birth, the birth mom began to waver on her commitment. Because we had accepted this baby as our daughter, we knew we would grieve the loss just as parents grieve the loss of their child following a stillbirth.

A supernatural gift of grace from God helped us to go see our "daughter" the next morning, with no assurance from our adoption agency that we would be leaving with our baby. As I held her, I spoke her name and prayed over her, asking Jesus to let her walk with Him every day of her life. Unfortunately though, we did leave without that beautiful baby girl. Isaiah and I both cried bitterly as we drove away, empty car seat in the back. But less than an hour later came the call that changed everything! We would be able to adopt our beautiful child after all. We took our daughter home that night and appreciated that this was the biggest gift anyone could give us. We would get calls to bring her back, then keep her, then bring her back for a few weeks yet, but throughout all of this, my hope has become firmly planted in God's hands.

Jesus said in John 15:5 that He is the vine and we are the branches...if we abide in Him and He in us, we will bear much fruit. Without Him, we can do nothing. God was telling me, "Focus on My family, and I will take care of yours." This took my eyes off of growing my own family and focused them on seeing how can I help God's family grow. I am a card-carrying member of the "Motherhood Club" as long as I am helping with God's plan for the regeneration of hearts. I can bear "life" because of the seed of the Gospel within me. There is no shelf-life for the capacity to be a "mother"—we just need to continue to tell younger women our stories.

CHAPTER 28

The Sacrifice of Praise

"Therefore by Him let us continually offer the sacrifice of praise to God, that is, the fruit of our lips, giving thanks to His name." (Hebrews 13:15)

"Thus says the Lord: 'Again there shall be heard in this place...the voice of joy and the voice of gladness, the voice of the bridegroom and the voice of the bride, the voice of those who will say: 'Praise the Lord of hosts, for the Lord is good, for His mercy endures forever'—and of those who will bring the sacrifice of praise into the house of the Lord. For I will cause the captives of the land to return as at the first,' says the Lord." (Jeremiah 33:10-11)

"Be anxious for nothing, but in everything by prayer and supplication, with thanksgiving, let your requests be made known to God; and the peace of God, which surpasses all understanding, will guard your hearts and minds through Christ Jesus." (Philippians 4:6-7)

Day 28. It's here. What now?

If you're on a regular cycle, this is the make-it-or-break-it day that brings joy or pain every month. Or maybe it's the day you'll find out whether or not your adoption application has been chosen by a birth mom.

For infertile women, it's the day of reckoning...you go through this every month, waiting for its arrival.

You stand on a game show stage, wait your turn, watch the emcee spin the wheel, hold your breath until it comes to a halt. Will you find out if you're pregnant? Will you win the sweepstakes? Will a little child become part of your home?

Or will the wheel come to a halt on the "not a winner" slot again?

As you face this day, or whatever day your period returns, you brace yourself for the unwanted consequences, the pain, the desolation, the discouragement. You hope against hope that this time will be different, that this will be the moment when you finally experience the heart-melting joy of pregnancy.

How do you deal with the uncertainty of month-to-month waiting?

As you've seen in previous chapters, you have opportunities for help.

This is the time to lean on your husband for his support, to grieve together as a couple if this turns out to be yet another time of disappointment for both of you. Do not neglect him or his comfort...use this as a time to draw closer.

It's a time you can lean on your closest friends and family, those who know you best, and welcome their sympathy. A good friend will share your sorrow and attempt to cheer you at the same time. You need both of those encouragements, and those who have walked this road with you will shriek the loudest in their joy if your dreams are realized.

Your mentors will challenge you to rise above despondency and strengthen your faith, to help you carry on and not fall apart.

Your Bible reading refreshes your faith and reminds you that God will keep His promises—to prosper you, redeem you, restore you—through mercies that are new every morning.

Most importantly, this is a moment for spending time alone with God. This is the time to offer your praises to Him for this trial.

What?!? Sing praises to God if another heartache comes today? How is it possible to offer praise and thanksgiving to Him in the midst of a going-through-the-hormone-blender day?

Sure, it will be easy to throw a big party and do a happy dance for God when He answers your prayers. But how can you even think of worshipping and applauding God when your world is on the brink of another collapse?

But praise, like joy and love, is not a matter of the heart—it is a matter of the will. That sounds illogical. Modern culture says that these human experiences are based on feelings, that joy and praise especially are the results of happy events. These responses aren't naturally associated with grief.

The writer to the Hebrews disagrees. Praise, in the Scripture text above, is viewed as a sacrifice, an offering to God. This kind of praise means giving up something that we want to keep.

Praise means turning our eyes off ourselves, away from the things we want, away from all earthly desires. Praise means looking only at God, full in His beautiful face, and giving our total, complete love to Him.

Praise is the sacrifice of raising our arms before God and declaring that He is in charge of our lives. Praise is lifting our eyes to heaven and acknowledging His power, His glory, and His dominion. Praise is kneeling on the ground, bowing before our incredible God, submitting ourselves to His authority.

The sacrifice of praise is relinquishing our hold on that which we want on earth yet will never keep. It is grasping the truth that our treasure lies in heaven and will never rust or perish there. It is a fragrant offering that pleases God in honor to Him.

In her book, *31 Days of Praise*, Ruth Myers asks her readers to develop the practice of praising God and giving thanks to Him in times of blessing and times of trial:

"In genuine spiritual worship, we bow before the Most High God, the most merciful and reliable and winsome of all beings, and we crown Him as Lord of all that we are. We consent to His gracious, transforming work in our lives; we agree that He can work in us, so that we'll be willing and able to do His will. In other words, we choose to let Him be God in our lives. This is our greatest privilege, the highest thing we can do."[1]

If we do not praise Him, if we keep silent, God will be praised nonetheless—Jesus Christ, during His Palm Sunday procession, said that even the very stones will immediately cry out their Hosannas! Join the mighty chorus of those who continually sing praises to Him in heaven!

As you ride the emotional seesaw of infertility, find your balance in the praises of God. Praise Him for this trial. Praise Him for His sovereign plans, that what He does is always right. Praise Him for His love and sacrifice for you.

Bryan Stevenson is an advocate/attorney for lost causes—prison inmates on "death row." Stevenson found his voice of praise in the brokenness around him.

"I do what I do because I'm broken, too," he wrote. "My years of struggling against inequality, abusive power, poverty, oppression, and injustice had finally revealed something to me about myself. Being close to suffering, death, executions, and cruel punishments didn't just illuminate the brokenness of others; in a moment of anguish and heartbreak, it also exposed my own brokenness....

"We have a choice. We can embrace our humanness, which means embracing our broken natures and the compassion that remains our best hope for healing. Or we can deny our brokenness, forswear compassion, and, as a result, deny our own humanity....

"When you experience mercy, you learn things that are hard to learn otherwise....You begin to recognize the humanity that resides in each of us."[2]

As you focus on praise, you'll find that the sting of grief is softened, the burden is lighter, and your path for the future grows clearer. You'll find it easier to give Him thanks when other things go badly, and you'll find strength to avoid succumbing to hopelessness.

You'll find your eyes opened to a new reality—that Jesus Himself is walking beside you, holding your hand or carrying you as a precious lamb. You'll find rest in His loving arms and awaken each day in a renewed friendship with your Shepherd.

Most of all, you'll know peace, true peace...a peace beyond understanding, a peace that no worldly situation can provide...with no more anxiety, only thanksgiving in your heart and mind, now guarded by the Commander of angels, Jesus Christ.

Day 28? Praise Him. For everything.

PRAYER:

Oh, let me sing praises to You! Let me shout joyfully to the Rock of my salvation. Let me come before Your presence with thanksgiving and shouting with psalms. For You are the great God and the great King above all gods.

In Your hand are the deep places of the earth, the heights of the hills, the sea, and the dry land—You made them all. I worship and bow down before You, kneeling before You, my Maker and my God; I am a sheep of Your pasture, held tenderly in Your hands.

Bless the Lord, O my soul; and all that is within me, bless His holy name! O God, let me never forget all Your benefits: You forgive all my iniquities, heal all my diseases, redeem my life from destruction, crown me with lovingkindness and tender mercies, and satisfy my mouth with good things so that my youth is renewed like the eagle's.

You are so great and greatly to be praised! I praise You in Your sanctuary, in Your mighty heaven, for Your mighty acts, according to Your excellent greatness! I praise You at the sound of music and dance for joy! Let everything that has breath praise You!

I will bless You at all times, even in the midst of my trials and difficulties; Your praise shall continually be in my mouth. You are my strength and song, and You have become my salvation.

I will praise You, O Lord, with my whole heart; I will tell of all Your marvelous works. The poor shall eat and be satisfied; those who seek You will praise You.

You are my praise, and You are my God, who has done for me these great and awesome things which my eyes have seen. I will exalt You, I will praise Your name, for You have done wonderful things; Your counsels of old are faithfulness and truth. You are my Strength and my Shield; my heart trusted in You, and I am helped.

I will praise You forever, because You have done it, and in the presence of Your saints I will wait on Your name, for it is good. I will praise You, for You have answered me and have become my salvation. I will freely sacrifice to You!

Lift up my head above my enemies all around me; therefore I will offer sacrifices of joy in Your tabernacle; I will sing, yes, I will sing praises to You. To You, O my Strength, I will sing praises; for You are my Defense, my God of Mercy. Put a new song in my mouth—praise to You—so that many will see it and fear, and will trust in You. Let my praise be upright before You...and beautiful in Your sight.

Why are you cast down, O my soul? And why are you disquieted within me? God, let me hope in You, for I shall yet praise You for the help of Your countenance. Heal me, O Lord, and I shall be healed; save me, and I shall be saved, for You are my praise.

You console me when I mourn, You give me beauty for ashes, the oil of joy for mourning, the garment of praise for the spirit of heaviness; let me be called one of Your trees of righteousness, the "planting of the Lord," that You may be glorified.

Call me out of darkness into Your marvelous light, that I may proclaim Your praises. And if I should have children someday, please help me to raise them up to a faith in You—that the generation to come, that a people yet to be created may praise You, too.

O God and Father of our Lord Jesus Christ, You have blessed us with every spiritual blessing in the heavenly places in Christ...just as You chose us in Him before the foundation of the world, that we should be holy and without blame before You in love.

Blessed be Your name, O Lord God, from everlasting to everlasting! And let all the people say, "Amen!" Praise the Lord!

(Psalm 95:1-7; Psalm 103:1-5; 1 Chronicles 16:25; Psalm 150; Psalm 34:1; Exodus 15:2; Psalm 9:1; Psalm 22:26; Deuteronomy 10:21; Isaiah 25:1; Psalm 28:7; Psalm 52:9; Psalm 118:21; Psalm 54:6; Psalm 27:6; Psalm 59:17; Psalm 40:3; Psalm 33:1; Psalm 42:5; Jeremiah 17:14; Isaiah 61:3; 1 Peter 2:9; Psalm 102:18; Psalm 106:48)

FOR REFLECTION:

❖ Choose one trial you are currently enduring (besides infertility), and write a prayer of praise here to God about it, even if it's difficult. Even so, He calls us to praise Him in everything...give it a try.

❖ Think of a past problem, crisis, or challenge that was resolved without your having to do anything…in other words, God reconciled the issue for you. Pause here to lift it up as a sacrifice of praise to Him for His goodness.

_____

_____

_____

❖ What other sacrifices can you offer to God? Is there anything in your life right now you could give up, something that comes between you and a deeper relationship with Him? An attitude, an idol, a habit, a lack of something? Resolve to push this aside temporarily (or permanently), and list it here…make it a gift that will give pleasure to God and you as well.

_____

_____

_____

❦ ❦ ❦

KIMBERLY'S STORY:

Growing up, I always expected that one day I would have children of my own. But years of singleness crept by, with no husband in sight. Finally, in my early 30s, I met a wonderful guy named Chris and married him. The future looked bright again for motherhood.

More time passed, with no pregnancy. In the process of investigating my own physical issues, which included endometriosis, we discovered a devastating truth—my husband was infertile. It wouldn't matter now how many fertility treatments I received; nothing would change my husband's condition.

What those who have never experienced infertility don't realize is that it's an "us" thing, not just a woman's issue. The reality is that both wife and husband are affected. Chris still bemoans the fact that guys don't want to talk about infertility or acknowledge it. And while Mother's Day is hard for me, Father's Day is difficult for him as well.

Finding out about Chris's problem was a full stop to our parenthood. It was actually good because many people go years without making a decision or finding out the truth. Adoption wasn't going to be the best idea for us, either. We accepted that we would be a family of just two.

Early on, I struggled with how my childless life would be different. While my husband was a wonderful support and encouragement, I didn't know another older woman—either in church or elsewhere—who had no kids. Only on the Internet did I find any support groups.

Now, I have reached the point where I can go "public" with my infertility. As I look back, I realize God really has the best plans for us.

We have expectations about how life will go, but then things can fall apart. One woman might get cancer or have a miscarriage, another woman might just be trying to get married, or yet another could get divorced without ever having children. Life doesn't go as we expect. Even so, God is in control. I still have a good life because this is where God has me and He has good things for me.

It doesn't mean it's pain-free. Children are not a guarantee from God. That's enough to shake your theology and understanding of how God works. Does this mean He's unfaithful to us because we don't have kids? No, it means that we live in a broken world, but He is faithful to walk us through it anyway.

I wouldn't go back and change my life. I would still marry Chris because my love for him is still the same. God gave me my husband first, and my first role is being his wife. You can't want a child more than your husband.

It's also important to know that adoption is not necessarily a "cure" for infertility...it's not how you "fix" things, because you still have to grieve the loss of what might have been. God has to put adoption on your heart. And, while I do okay with other kids, I have also come to a point where I know that working in the church nursery is not my thing.

Not every woman has to do something with children. And I don't feel obligated to go to baby showers.

After searching for direction in my Christian efforts, I have found a new ministry in working with other women, both within and outside of my church. I have loved it! Now I'm getting additional training in teaching. One of the blessings of growing older is finding out what you're good at and what you enjoy doing.

The reality is that my life is rich and fulfilling without children. My prayer life has grown, because God has given me His hope. His plans for me are beyond my wildest imagination. His enduring love has assured me that I am worthy, that I can come to Him in complete trust in His good plans for me. He has given me grace to praise Him with complete abandon!

CHAPTER 29

The Beauty of Christian Contentment

"I form the light and create darkness, I make peace and create calamity; I, the Lord, do all these things." (Isaiah 45:7)

"Now godliness with contentment is great gain." (1 Timothy 6:6)

"But let all those rejoice who put their trust in You; let them ever shout for joy, because You defend them; let those also who love Your name be joyful in You." (Psalm 5:11)

"Let Your work appear to Your servants, and Your glory to their children. And let the beauty of the Lord our God be upon us, and establish the work of our hands for us; yes, establish the work of our hands." (Psalm 90:16-17)

Who is in control of everything in times of calamity? It's not us. God is completely sovereign of our world, our lives, our experiences, our sorrows and griefs, our joys and triumphs. Nothing happens to us by accident but purely by His plan for us.

Missionary trainer Ann Austin speaks to women's groups on the secrets and blessings of Christian contentment. Much of the following content is drawn directly from her comments:

"God is good, and He does good things," Austin asserts. "His eternal perspective is different from our 'good'—He has His own definition. We live in a fallen world with a good God. He works all things together for our good."

When we are assaulted with problems, our tendency is to ask God "why??" But would we be satisfied if we knew the whys? Probably not. We have to walk in trust.

We can tether our storm-tossed boat to two anchors: God's sovereignty and His goodness. God's comfort can be real, like a rock, in spite of our pain. We need to reach out and grasp His goodness, praying to Him that He will not let us fall into a pit of depression.

As Austin said, the emergency room is not the place to figure out our theology. We need to go deep now, before the storms hit, to taste and see that the Lord is good, to know that His good hand is upon us. Austin knows this well because her first husband died young, unexpectedly from a heart attack.

"We need to base our faith and daily spiritual walk on God and His attributes, not on our current circumstances," she said. "Circumstances change more frequently for women than for men. We are often more tied to our seasons of life...changes in family situations, physical changes, and so forth.

"If we are tied to our changing circumstances, we'll be on a constant rollercoaster of emotions. But God does not change. Whether we are walking through a sunlit glade or walking through a raging fire, our walk will be steady if our minds and hearts (this is the struggle of personal discipline) are fixed on *who* God is and *what* He has already done for us. He has kept us thus far, and He will carry me through the future only He can see, especially in the small things."

Dr. Bryan Chapell, pastor and former president/chancellor of Covenant Theological Seminary, proposes that trusting in God's sovereignty, dependability, and goodness is essential for personal contentment:

"Biblical faith affirms that our God is able to rescue," Chapell said. "But that is not enough reason to trust Him. If He can rescue but is undependable, unkind, or untrustworthy, then faith in Him would be worthless. To trust God as He desires, we must believe we can entrust ourselves to His care. To do this we need to know that God is worthy of our trust. Biblical faith is not merely the confidence that our God is able; it also requires the confidence that our God is good."[1]

What exactly does Christian contentment look like? It is *beautiful*. It sweetens the spirit of the young and lends dignity to the old. It reflects a correct relationship between the creature and the Creator. It is an inward form of worship to God.

In contrast, discontent is *ugly*. Discontent reflects a lack of gratitude and a distrust of God. It is accompanied by complaining and grumbling. It is dangerous to our spiritual well-being.

As Paul wrote to the Philippians, in verses 4:11-13, contentment is something to be learned. It is not natural to us. It requires that we learn not to become mastered by our circumstances:

"Not that I speak in regard to need, for I have learned in whatever state I am, to be content: I know how to be abased, and I know how to abound. Everywhere and in all things I have learned both to be full and to be hungry, both to abound and to suffer need. I can do all things through Christ who strengthens me."

Learning contentment during times of plenty is a good start, but it's not enough. It won't protect us from discontent during not-so-great times...we will not be satisfied, always hungering for more.

Discontent adds to our worries and concerns. In the Garden of Eden, Eve had everything she could want. So remember from her downfall—"plenty" can fan the flames of discontent. We run the risk of valuing the gifts over the Giver, when our happiness or joy is focused on the blessings instead of on God.

Psalm 131, a short prayer from King David, gives a good "word picture" of contentment. He starts with humility, placing himself before the Lord without pretense or pride.

"Surely I have calmed and quieted my soul, like a weaned child with his mother; like a weaned child is my soul within me" (Psalm 131:2).

This image of a satisfied child cradled in a mother's arms is akin to crawling into the lap of our heavenly Father and taking comfort in His love. It shows our inward attitude...a calm, still soul.

But the weaning process can be distressing to child and mother. It's a process of loss—a great mystery. When what seemed indispensable is lost, what is left is a new dependency on God. It means finding ease with what God puts in our lives.

Is there a place for grief in contentment? God is compassionate...He doesn't tell us to "buck up" and get over it. Jesus has walked on this earth and has felt the hurts of the flesh. He knows our pain.

Jesus Christ was a Man of Sorrows, well acquainted with grief. Godly grief opens up our hearts to God and to the body of fellowship here on earth for comfort. Ungodly grief becomes hard and bitter, and it cannot accept comfort from others.

Reminding ourselves of this truth takes mental discipline, though, because we fall into circular thinking or get bogged down in the usual clutter of wrong messages from the world.

True contentment comes through sanctification, which is a work of God's grace in our lives. We need that grace, to keep watch over our hearts.

When we ask God to pour His contentment into our souls, we should begin with a gracious humility, a lowliness before God, not demanding our own way. We need to strive not only to do what pleases God, but strive also to be pleased by what God is doing in our hearts.

We need to continually remind ourselves about God's character, what He has done, and what He has said He will do. And we need to practice the daily routine of recognizing His presence in our lives.

Brother Lawrence (Nicholas Herman) was a cook and sandal fixer in a monastery near Paris in the 1600s. His conversations about his "practice of the presence of God" with his friend Joseph de Beaufort gave evidence that this consistent habit brought Brother Lawrence great peace and contentment.

"Brother Lawrence said that the worst that could happen to him was to lose that sense of God which he had enjoyed so long," Beaufort wrote. "Yet the goodness of God assured him He would not forsake him utterly and that He would give him strength to bear whatever evil He permitted to happen to him. Brother Lawrence, therefore, said he feared nothing.

"'I worshipped Him the oftenest I could, keeping my mind in His holy presence and recalling it as often as I found it wandered from Him,' Brother Lawrence said. 'I made this my business, not only at the appointed times of prayer but all the time; every hour, every minute, even in the height of my work, I drove from my mind everything that interrupted my thoughts of God.'"[2]

All learning takes practice. So how do we practice contentment? Start with small things to find contentment in big things. For example, if you're considering a purchase, ask yourself, "Will this bring me contentment in the Lord?" When little losses and disappointments show up, discipline your mind to say, "Where is God in this?"

As she described in her book *Seated with Christ*, author Heather Holleman has discovered a true satisfaction in receiving the spiritual riches that accompany being "seated" in the heavenly realms in Christ Jesus (Ephesians 2:6).

"I love that our desires are *satisfied*—not just whetted," Holleman wrote about Psalm 103.

"Jesus continues to redefine for me the definition of 'riches' or 'treasures.' For example, in Proverbs 24:3-4, we read this: 'By wisdom a house is built, and through understanding it is established; through knowledge its rooms are filled with rare and beautiful treasures.' I wanted rare and beautiful treasures....

"We hosted a big Christmas party for students recently....I remember how, years ago, I worried about the old carpets, outdated and damaged furniture, and mismatched plates. I wanted a stunning home, filled with all kinds of breathtaking things....But that night, with all the people filling our living room and caroling, I remember that the 'rare and beautiful treasures' are *people*....

"The Lord is my home. He is where I dwell. I'm with Christ and and *in* Him at the royal table...I have all of Him. I have all I need and want at all times." Holleman concludes, "I'm indeed the richest one at the party."[3]

Ultimately, contentment and practicing it brings the healing power of God into our lives. It makes us hopeful. God is making us more like

Christ, who humbled Himself to the point of death. Through abundance and want, we are learning to be more Christ-like.

Hearkening back to Romans 8:28-29, we know that all things work together for good to those who love God, *"to those who are the called according to His purpose. For whom He foreknew, He also predestined to be conformed to the image of His Son, that He might be the firstborn among many brethren."*

Take heart, friends, even in the midst of infertility and despair. God is good. God is love. God is sovereign. God is able to do *"exceedingly abundantly above all that we ask or think, according to the power that works in us (Ephesians 3:20)."* We are not there yet on our journey of life, but we have hope...that God is working in us, for us and for His own glory.

May He bless you today with a taste of His goodness and contentment. May He take you in His heavenly arms, give you great comfort and peace, and fill you with joy as you see His banner of love waving over you.

May you see how He is making you more beautiful, every single day. May His beauty shine upon you always.

PRAYER:

Good Father, Gracious Lord Jesus Christ, Gladsome Holy Spirit—blessed be Your name, Three in One! I lift up my praise to You, the Father of mercies and God of all comfort. You comfort me in all my tribulation, that I may likewise be able to comfort those who are in any trouble. Give me the same grace to rejoice with those who rejoice and to weep with those who weep.

Father, as I come before You now, let me be as a child in Your lap, comforted by Your loving arms, sheltered beneath Your banner of love over me. Let me rest in You, without agenda, without demands, without complaining...satisfied by Your grace. Let me behold again, in wonder, Your honor and majesty. Let me see the strength and gladness that are found in You.

Strengthen my faith...that I might have peace with You in Jesus Christ, through Whom also I have access by faith into this grace in which I stand. Help me to rejoice in hope of seeing Your glory. And not only that, help me also to glory in tribulations, knowing that tribulation produces perseverance; and perseverance, character; and character, hope. I know that hope does not disappoint, because Your love has been poured out in my heart by the Holy Spirit You have given to me.

Show me the path of life; give me the mental self-discipline to practice contentment, in plenty and in want. Remind me to focus on Your attributes of goodness, the fullness of joy in Your presence, the pleasures forevermore at Your right hand. Your anger is but for a moment, but Your favor is for life; my weeping may endure for a night, but Your joy comes in the morning.

Let me rejoice with all those who put their trust in You. Let me ever shout for joy, because You defend me. Let me love Your name more and more, and let me be joyful in You.

As I seek to rejoice in that hope, give me patience in this tribulation of infertility. Let me not give up the practice of continuing steadfastly in prayer; please let this be a lifeline between us.

And even though I have never 'seen' You, I have seen Your hand at work in my life...let me continue to see Your handiwork as my journey with You unfolds. I thank You for granting me a place with You in heaven, where I may see You finally, face to face, and then fall down in total worship.

I praise You, finally, for all of Your wonderful promises in the here and now...for the words of Your Son Jesus Christ, that You have spoken these things to me, that Your joy may remain in me, and that my joy may be full.

In the promise, hope, and coming revelation of the glory of Your Son Jesus, Amen.

(2 Corinthians 1:3-4; Romans 12:15; 1 Chronicles 16:27; Romans 5:1-5; Psalm 16:11; Psalm 30:5; Psalm 5:11; Romans 12:12; 1 Peter 1:8; John 15:11)

🍎 🍎 🍎

FOR REFLECTION:

❖ Consider your circumstances for a moment...what gives you joy? What gives you grief? How would focusing on God and His goodness change your attitude?

❖ As Ann Austin suggests, try practicing contentment in small blessings and small trials. List one or two here and any success you've received from God in finding contentment in them.

___

___

___

❖ What are some of the barriers in your life right now that are keeping you from embracing contentment? Write a prayer that God will tear them down and open a clear path to immerse yourself in His forgiveness, joy, and peace.

___

___

___

🍓 🍓 🍓

STEPHANIE'S STORY:

I had never really wanted to have children, but my husband did. So, after about four or five years of marriage, I began to pray that God would change my heart to want a family.

God did change my heart, so imagine my surprise when we could not get pregnant after trying for six years. It was painful to see everyone, it seemed, getting pregnant easily. And many of them were ungrateful to be pregnant unexpectedly.

We went through a bit of infertility treatment where I got laparoscopic repairs to my Fallopian tubes to clear the way to pregnancy. However, at the end of six years, we decided that if God wanted us to have a child, it would have happened by now. We had to decide on the ultimate question—if we wanted a child from our own loins or if we wanted a child, period. So, we did not pursue any further fertility treatments.

Honestly, it was hard at this time for me to go to Walmart and see all these people walking around with children, and I was empty.

I wrestled with my own lack of control at this time. I actually remember a person at our church who didn't really want to get together with us for dinner because we didn't have children and they did. That really hurt my feelings. Some people also thought we could not be good teachers if we didn't have our own children. I tried to realize that they were not malicious but just ignorant.

So, after my husband and I met for lunch one day—incidentally, the exact time period that our baby boy was being conceived—we decided that it was not all that important for our child to look just like us.

Our mantra during this adoption was, "God is bigger than our fears!" And it was true. God gifted us with every bit of the $25,000 we needed for the journey through faithful friends who believed in us and believed that God was directing them to bless us. I remembered saying faithfully, that $25,000 was "chump change" for God. And it was!

After adopting our children, I can honestly say that those experiences really made me trust the Lord for His provision for our family. I always tell people that I could not have made a better set of children for myself. And it's true!

The Scripture that has been so important to me through all of this is Psalm 37:3-4–*"Trust in the Lord, and do good; dwell in the land, and feed on His faithfulness. Delight yourself also in the Lord, and He shall give you the desires of your heart."*

The adoption journey has healed my infertility woes and my quiver is full!

Our Story: From Siberia, With Love

The straight-backed bench where we sat waiting was hard and cold. Only a few agonizing minutes more, and the judge would return with the verdict. My husband Mark and I held hands briefly, but their embrace brought no comfort from the icy tension that still numbed our hearts.

I had prayed to God for years, prayed intensely in the past months, prayed constantly in the past few days, and now I was prayed out. I could only sit and wait for His will to be done, whatever the outcome.

How had we arrived here on March 23, 1999, more than halfway around the world, sitting in this 19th-century Russian courthouse? Was it my own selfish desires that had led us here or the relentless prodding of the Holy Spirit?

When, for that matter, had the search for a little boy begun? Perhaps it was eight years earlier, in the chilling words in a doctor's office, words I did not want to hear...infertility...severe endometriosis...cancer. The journey through surgeries and infertility treatments had given Mark and me the unspeakable joy of bearing a beautiful daughter, Elizabeth. But the two years afterward had offered nothing but the looming prospect of a hysterectomy.

On the day before a surgeon's knife would forever remove any chance of conceiving another child, I had cried out to God from my backyard. "Where is he, O Lord? Where's that little boy I've always wanted? Where is Elizabeth's brother? How can I trust You to provide when this door is slamming shut in my face?"

There was no answer from heaven, no angels pulling back the curtain to reveal the future...just the surfacing in my heart of the only Scripture I could lean upon: *"Wives, be submissive to your husbands."* God had provided Mark for me, and now I must trust the wisdom of my physician husband who knew only too well the insidious ravages of ovarian cancer and the uncertainty of my condition.

And so, the door to bearing more children silently closed. But God began to open other doors in our hearts...drawing us to see that He had other plans for our lives.

He began to open our hearts toward adoption. And He led us to Bethany Christian Services, to a wonderful counselor named Nancy Lesslie who held our hands in prayer as we explored our options together. We began to believe that God was guiding us to go to Russia.

Like infertility treatments, the process was long and arduous. Home studies, marriage licenses, birth certificates, statements from the police department, letters from friends, document after document after document...all notarized, then certified, then apostilled, then translated...the paperwork never seemed to end.

And then there were delays because my fingertips, prune-like from too much cooking and cleaning, wouldn't make good prints. The FBI held up the paperwork an extra six months because they rejected my fingerprints twice and then lost the third set. Adoption is not for the faint of heart.

But we were finally approved and put on the waiting list in Russia to receive a referral. And not just Russia...all the way to Siberia! Just saying the names conjured up all kinds of exotic images...secretive, beautiful, stark, defiant, and co-o-o-o-ld! I had taken some Russian language in college and now desperately tried to brush up on tongue-twisting phrases like *zdrahstvooeytyeh* which is "hello" and important words like *morozhenoyeh* (ice cream)!

In only two months, we got the call: "We have a beautiful little boy for you named Alexei." And he *was* beautiful...shy smile, long lashes over green eyes that pierced through the Internet photos and said, "Take me home." The videotape arrived, and we played it over and over...just a few minutes showing Alex catching and throwing a ball. The paperwork showed he had delayed development but was likely to bond with a family. We prayed and then said, "He's ours."

We packed our bags to go...and then they stayed packed for ten months. Adoption laws, passed by the Russian legislature (Duma), had suddenly changed jurisdiction, placing our case with a regional judge who had not previously handled adoptions. We slowly realized we were caught in a legal battle...the judge was holding up the paperwork for a legal statement that our American government was not yet willing to provide.

Our judge-to-be, the only one out of 88 regional judges, was refusing to hear any American adoptions in her court until one specific document was provided. Our Russian adoption liaison, Dr. Alexei Sander, took our case and others to the Russian Supreme Court for assistance. But the judge's ruling was upheld: no adoptions without the document.

We had found out about Alex in May of 1998 and now it was March 1999 with no hope in this stalemate. Would we never get to see our little boy? Would I never get to hold my son? What was God doing here? How could He bring us this far and leave us hanging? We prayed, others prayed...and God answered.

After months of frantic emails, I suddenly received one from Dr. Sander containing the two-sentence statement that the judge was requiring. I sensed that it was now or never and that I had to act. Because my fingerprints were delayed, I had been given an "inside" phone number to the Immigration and Naturalization Service office. One quick prayer: "God, would You please cut through the bureaucratic red tape for us?"

By a true miracle, I was patched straight through to a director's office, and he graciously agreed to write up the statement for us. Now, the Russian judge had the necessary documents...and she gave us our court date. We would be the first to go into her courtroom out of more than 50 American families waiting to adopt children in this region.

Another couple from Johnson City, Scott and Ruthie Evers, were approved to go with us to adopt a boy from another orphanage in the same region. They would become a great blessing to us and good friends in this adventure together.

It took 48 hours in combined travel time to go more than halfway around the world. When we arrived in Irkutsk, which was shrouded in snow, our Russian liaison team greeted us warmly and ushered us to a red brick apartment building that would be home for three weeks. It was a haven of rest for a few hours, and then we went to see Alex at the orphanage.

So tired but so eager to see him, we waited in a recreation room until his caregiver brought him in. Alex was such a tiny, frail little figure who burst into tears at the sight of us. The matronly, buxom Russian caregiver brought him over and set him in my lap, then proceeded to lecture me in Russian on his needs...good discipline, lots of love, naps, walks. All the while, tears were streaming down her face and mine.

This sweet little boy, not quite three years old, shivering with fear in my lap, was our son...our son! Mark got him to calm down and even giggle a little by knocking toy blocks down with him. We said good-bye and went to the apartment to sleep, completely drained of all emotion and energy.

The next day, we saw Alex again as well as some of the other little children at the orphanage. The building housed 11 children in each room, little beds stacked up like those of Snow White's seven dwarfs. There was only one bathroom for every 22 children. But the orphanage looked clean and inviting and smelled of bleach and hot soup.

The caregivers were obviously attached to the children clamoring for their attention. There were such heart-tugging little ones...girls with big gauzy bows clipped into short-cropped hair...boys with more energy than they could expend in a tiny play area...some cross-eyed, some with vacant stares, some with shining smiles...all of them precious in the eyes of Jesus Christ.

Tuesday morning—court day—dawned cold and colorless, a gray day that matched the grayness of our emotional weariness. After dressing in our best Sunday-school-type clothes, Mark and I spent time in prayer together, not assured of the day's outcome but placing it in God's hands.

Dr. Sander took us to the 150-year-old regional justice building and then upstairs to a long, dull-green courtroom. At the head of the room was the judge's desk, flanked on the left by a barred cage for holding defendants…a chilling reminder of the strict Russian justice system.

With Dr. Sander and adoption workers Andrei and Tanya next to us, Mark and I sat on the hard bench together about 15 feet in front of the judge and about two feet below her…a physically imposing arrangement. The stage was set for formalities and calculated discourse, not the warm and fuzzy experience related to me by other adoptive couples who had gone to court in other regions.

At precisely 10 a.m., the judge walked in, a no-nonsense woman wearing a two-piece black suit, almost like a judge's robe, with black high heels. She strode briskly to her desk, taking no notice of us as we all stood and then sat down. For the next two hours, Tanya translated the judge's questions and reading of the documents, often unable to keep up because of the rapid pace.

Mark and I quickly assessed that this judge was not going to make things easy for us—no smiles, no affirmation of acceptable answers, only a serious look in response to each of our answers. Mark was the first one to be interrogated, with questions about his practice experience and his medical opinion of Alexei's conditions.

The judge would then call upon me, alternating my questions with the ones for Mark, although the ones for me were very pointed. What role did religion play in my life? Did I think I would have enough language skills to work with Alex? Had I spent enough time with Alex to be sure he was the child for us? As she quickly read aloud parts of our dossier, pausing to ask questions, she gave us no hint of her opinions about our answers…no smiles, no nods, no humor, no deference to the uncomfortable position we were in.

As the reading of the dossier was finished, I offered our photo album—pictures of our home and family. Picking it up with the rest of the papers, she announced a recess until 2 p.m. and sailed out of the room while we stood at attention.

It was noon, so the adoption crew took Mark and me to lunch at a nearby cafe for *peimeni*, little meat-filled dumplings that are a Russian regional specialty. They turned into rocks in our stomachs by the end of the court proceedings.

After we all returned to the courthouse to wait out the remainder of our recess, Mark and I walked down the hall and stood beside a window to pray aloud quietly and discreetly. Later, we found we had been standing outside the judge's door.

When the judge returned, the focus of the case shifted to information concerning little Alex, his history, and physical. As proceedings drew to a close, the adoption representatives pleaded their case for adoption—that while orphanages provided adequate food and shelter, they could not replace the love and care of a family.

The prosecutor, an attractive blonde in a knee-length black suit with high lace-up boots (she would have looked at home in a James Bond movie) gave some intense, rehearsed remarks at the end that I never quite followed. But it was obvious she was sympathetic to our side. The judge announced a one-minute pause for her verdict and left the room.

Dr. Sander assured us that everything was okay. The judge came back in and read the adoption proclamation. For a moment, despite the vast differences in circumstances and translations, it reminded me of our marriage pronouncement. After so long, after so much, the moment had finally arrived. The well of tears, which I had held back in the proceedings, now flowed silently without shame.

The judge exited with everyone standing silently. Then all pandemonium broke loose...tears, hugs from everyone! Alex was ours and we would be taking him home with us. The Russians said it was a big day for them, too. And we gave thanks to God as well.

Our day in court was finished. The war was essentially over, yet there would be more skirmishes as we advanced toward home. Scott and Ruthie survived their court day to adopt Thad, a 15-month-old from Slyudyanka. On the day before we left Irkutsk, we and the Everses were summoned to return to the judge's office, this time bringing Alex and Thad with us. To our surprise, the judge gave us a warm welcome (this time she was wearing a crisp white suit) and even pronounced a beautiful Russian blessing upon Alex and Thad.

Overall, the Russian people we met were absolutely wonderful and hospitable to us. We fell in love with them and their beautiful country…graceful golden onion-bulb dome churches…ancient log homes with intricate, lacy wood carvings around windows shuttered in blue and green…birch-filled woods deep with snow…and breath-taking Lake Baikal, the world's largest fresh-water lake. We took a walk along the edge of its thick ice surface, watching cars driving around out in the middle. But we could feel the shudders and hear its groans and cracks as the deep giant yawned from its winter slumbers. Spring was coming, promising new beginnings for all of us.

But the peace of the remote lake could not completely erase the gloom of politics. Our U.S. government began bombings that week in Yugoslavia, stirring up anti-American sentiment across the continent. In Irkutsk, downtown demonstrations kept us behind locked doors in our apartment, not willing to risk any confrontations.

In Moscow, angry demonstrators first threw eggshells filled with paint against the American Embassy building and then shot out the windows with machine guns. When we arrived at the Embassy at the end of our trip, the entire place was crawling with Russian SWAT team officers. Kort and Lisa Eggers, friends from home working in Moscow as missionaries, hosted us and kept us safe in their apartment (Lisa made the best spaghetti I've ever eaten…).

Back home, hundreds of people across Tennessee were praying for us…including many people we didn't even know. I worried. Would we get back home safely to Elizabeth? I agonized over the distance and time apart from her. Had we done the right thing? Was it worth it all? In the Russian apartment, as I held little Alex at the window to watch the snow, I whispered, "*Ya tibya looblyoo*," which means, "I love you." Turning with a huge grin to hug me, he whispered back, "*Ya tibya looblyoo*," and kissed my cheek. Oh yes, it was worth it all.

And, we made finally made it home with our new sons, greeted by a midnight welcoming party at the airport. There would be many more battles to be fought on the home front. Alex was a very, very active boy who had received little personal attention and constantly sought it from adults. He had to learn how to eat like a normal kid, and I had to learn how to feed a reluctant eater. He had to learn how to be a brother, and Elizabeth had to tolerate a little brother who could be a pest at times.

And, much to Alex's chagrin, we made it very clear that Mommy and Daddy were in charge, not him.

But Alex has blossomed into a smart, handsome young man currently in training to become a commercial pilot. He is a bright light in our lives, and we have grown together in love...as parents, as a family, as children of a merciful Father. Thad Evers, too, has grown into a confident, winsome fellow who is involved with the Army Reserves in college and hopes to go to medical school.

We know now that our adoption stories started in God's heart, stretching all the way back before Creation, when He planned to put Alex and Thad in our homes. There has been consistent confirmation for us...and Alex looks just like me. Even our feet, hands, and eyes are alike. We don't always see how God's mighty hands skillfully weave together the tapestry of our lives, but we catch little glimpses of His masterpiece in the rays of sunlight that He shines on it from time to time, to say, "See how I am working to make all things beautiful...."

If Alex ever doubts, ever questions God or our love for him...I'll be so happy to look at him and say, "Sit down, son, and let us tell you again about how God answered a whole lotta prayers for you in Siberia...."

A daily walk in the ice and snow from the orphanage in Irkutsk to an outdoor pavilion....

The Good News of God's Grace

The foundation of the Christian life is our faith in the Good News of God's grace. The Living and True God is a God of justice and of mercy. Every person at one time bears the guilt of sinful rebellion against God and is separated by that sin from a relationship with Him. God's holy justice requires punishment for human sin, but out of His love and mercy He gave His Son Jesus Christ to become the Savior of all who will trust in Him.

Christ became a man to fulfill the righteous requirements of God's Law on their behalf, and to bear the punishment of their sins through His death on Calvary's cross so that they can be forgiven and adopted into God's eternal family.

Contrary to much of popular belief, we cannot earn the forgiveness of our sin and the inheritance of eternal life with God by being good enough to merit these blessings. The Bible teaches that as sinners we can never be good enough on our own merit. But God offers us these benefits as a free gift, purchased in love by the holy life and the sacrificial death of Jesus Christ.

We accept this gift by placing our faith in Christ, repenting of our sins and trusting in His death as the means of our forgiveness and acceptance by God, receiving Him as our Savior and Lord. You may express this by praying a prayer in faith like the one that follows:

Dear Father, I believe that Jesus Christ is Your only begotten Son, and that He became a human being, shed His blood and died on the cross to pay the penalty and clean away the sin that has separated me from You. I believe that He rose bodily from the dead to give me new life. Lord Jesus, I invite You and ask You to come into my heart. I confess my sins, and ask You to forgive me. I accept You as my Savior and Lord. I want to turn from my sins and pray that Your Holy Spirit will help me follow Your way. I believe that You have come and are living in me right now. Thank You, Lord. In Your Name I pray, Amen.

(By Dr. James E. Richter, Retired Pastor, Lookout Mountain, Tennessee)

Acknowledgments

Where do I begin to thank my friends and family for their loving help, contributions, and prayers? I have to start with the women who were bold and kind enough for more than two decades to tell me their stories—this is their book, and I am just passing their words along to you. Because I promised anonymity to them, I can't list their names here. But if you are one of them, may your story bless the lives of other women walking this path after you. You have blessed me.

I am thankful for you, my reader, for picking up this book and listening to its message. My prayer is that you will come away refreshed and encouraged in your faith.

My faithful "Moms in Prayer" group—Rebecca Alexander, Traci Begley, Melody Counts, Julie Gouveia, Beth Poland, Cheryl Songster, Mara Torok—have lifted this effort up with me over several years, sometimes weekly. I can never thank them enough for their sweet prayers for my children.

The mountain getaway crew of extremely talented writers, led by the intrepid Pam Johnson, have inspired me at our annual writing retreats. You are responsible for egging me on to get this published. I am in awe of each of you...especially you, Chautona Havig! Thank you, Miyoshi Gardner, for your kind hospitality.

My colleagues and students at Milligan College have been most supportive, too, cheering me onward in this effort. Thanks, Alyssa Boyér Sprouse and Taylor Martin, for your capable assistance in graphic design and social media.

Many, many sisters in Christ have lifted this effort up in prayer and encouragement—unfortunately, I won't remember all of them, but here are a few: Beth Barnes, Allyson Bohlman, Martha Burgin, Melinda de Troye, Lee Anne Duncan, Ruthie Evers, Coleen Falasca, Barb Gemar, Susanne Gentry, Myra Gerlock, Francine Hagg, Dorcas Hill, Mary Hogue, Heather Holleman, Katherine Mansy, Carol McCool, Mary Ellen Miller, Lorrie Smith, Sandy Smith, Carrie Swanay, Sherri Williams, and Heather DeJesus Yates. I love you all dearly.

My editors have been many, too—LeAnne Blackmore, Bible study author/teacher; Betty Brown, counselor/author; Willette Ericson, teacher and C. S. Lewis aficionado; Michele King, family counselor; Dr. Sam Lewis, gynecologist/physician; Anne Phillips, author; and Jim and Linda Richter, our pastor and his wife (who leads women's Bible Studies). All of them have helped refine the message and kindly correct me where needed.

Thank you, Karie Canestrari (K.B. Ballentine), for being a wonderful sister and encouraging me at our writing retreats. You are amazing and talented.

I am especially thankful to my two beautiful, smart children—Elizabeth and Alex—who have blessed me over and over. You are my treasures. I have also been blessed with a wonderful dad, Donald (now in heaven, rejoicing with his Lord), and loving mom, Betty, who have faithfully supported me in every endeavor I've undertaken in life. My mother-in-law, Martha Ann, who loves to laugh with me, has kept up the prayer vigil, too, in the legacy of her late husband, Arnold, a persevering prayer warrior.

Finally, I would never have written this book without the love, commitment, sacrifices, and prayers of my husband, Mark. Thank you for marrying me and living side-by-side with me these three decades. You are my rock, anchor, spiritual warrior, and best friend. You are the best dad our children could ever have.

Thank You, O Jesus Christ, for Your great love and for making this book come to life. This is Your book.

Footnotes

A Letter to My Readers
[1]https://www.mayoclinic.org/diseases-conditions/female-infertility/symptoms-causes/syc-20354308

Introduction
[1]James Strong, *The Exhaustive Concordance of the Bible* (McLean, Va.: MacDonald Publishing Company, 1980), s.v. "Arabah." See also 6160 in the Hebrew and Chaldee Dictionary in same volume.
[2]Ibid., s.v. "rose." See also 2261 in the Hebrew and Chaldee Dictionary in same volume.

Chapter 1
[1]Neil T. Anderson, Victory Over the Darkness: Realize the Power of Your Identity in Christ (Ventura, CA: Regal Books, 2013), pp. 33-34.

Chapter 2
[1]Luder Whitlock, *New Geneva Study Bible*, "God Reigns: Divine Sovereignty" (Nashville: Thomas Nelson Publishers, 1995), p. 1339.

Chapter 3
[1]C. S. Lewis, *A Grief Observed* (New York: The Seabury Press, 1961), pp. 9-10.
[2]Heather DeJesus Yates, *All the Wild Pearls: A Guide for Passing Down Redemptive Stories* (Newberry, FL: Bridge-Logos, 2018), pp. 99-100.

Chapter 6
[1]K. B. Ballentine, "A Reflection on Mother's Day," *Almost Everything, Almost Nothing* (Beulah, CO: Middle Creek Publishing & Audio, 2017), p. 52.
[2]C. S. Lewis, *The Lion, the Witch and the Wardrobe* (New York: Harper Trophy, 1950), p. 158.

Chapter 7
[1]John Bunyan, *The Works of John Bunyan: Allegorical* (Glasgow, Scotland: Blackie and Son, 1855), vol. 3, p. 92.
[2]C. S. Lewis, *The Problem of Pain* (San Francisco: Harper, 1940), p. 91.
[3]Heather Holleman, *Guarded by Christ: Knowing the God Who Rescues and Keeps Us* (Chicago: Moody Publishers, 2016), pp. 101-102.

Chapter 8
[1]Julian Fellowes, *Downton Abbey*, "2011 Christmas Special, Part Two," (Masterpiece Theatre, December 25, 2011), Act III. http://scriptline.livejournal.com/60047.html
[2]Anderson, p 35.

Chapter 9
[1]*Guideposts Classics*, "Corrie ten Boom on Forgiveness" (July 24, 2014). https://www.guideposts.org/inspiration/stories-of-hope/guideposts-classics-corrie-ten-boom-on-forgiveness?nopaging=1

Chapter 10
[1]Anderson, p. 148.

Chapter 11
[1]*Harvard Health Publications*, "Harvard Men's Health Watch: Marriage and Men's Health," (Harvard Medical School, July 1, 2010). http://www.health.harvard.edu/newsletter_article/marriage-and-mens-health

Chapter 13
[1]Ed Wheat, M.D., and Gaye Wheat, *Intended for Pleasure: Sex Technique and Sexual Fulfillment in Christian Marriage*, Fourth Edition (Grand Rapids, MI: Revell Books, 2010), pp. 18-20, 22.
[2]Kyle Idleman, *Not a Fan. Becoming a Completely Committed Follower of Jesus* (Grand Rapids, MI: Zondervan, 2011), pp. 138-139.

Chapter 14
[1]Rick Hove and Heather Holleman, *A Grander Story: An Invitation to Christian Professors* (Orlando, FL: Cru Press, 2017), p. 62.
[2]Stephen Kendrick and Alex Kendrick, with Lawrence Kimbrough, *The Love Dare* (Nashville, TN: B&H Publishing Group, 2008), p. 122.

Chapter 15
[1]Jane Austen, *Emma* (Ann Arbor, MI: Borders Classics, 2004), p. 52.

Chapter 16
[1]Heather Holleman, *Seated with Christ: Living Freely in a Culture of Comparison* (Chicago: Moody Press, 2015), pp. 111-112.
[2]https://www.faithgateway.com/praying-example-susanna-wesley/#.W5McBi2ZOfQ

Chapter 17
[1]Stormie Omartian, *The Power of Praying for Your Adult Children* (Eugene, OR: Harvest House Publishers, 2014), pp. 19-20.

Chapter 18
[1]Dave Ramsey. *BrainyQuote.com*. (Xplore Inc., 2018). http://www.brainyquote.com/quotes/quotes/d/daveramsey520282.html and http://www.brainyquote.com/quotes/quotes/d/daveramsey520303.html
[2]Peter Anderson. *Bible Money Matters*. 2018. http://www.biblemoneymatters.com/bible-verses-about-money-what-does-the-bible-have-to-say-about-our-financial-lives/

Chapter 19
[1]Timothy Keller, *The Prodigal God: Recovering the Heart of the Christian Faith* (New York: Penguin Books, 2008), pp. 139-143.

Chapter 20
[1]C. S. Lewis, *The Four Loves* (New York: Harcourt Brace Jovanovich, 1960), pp. 96-97.

²L. M. Montgomery, *Anne of Green Gables* (London: George G. Harrap & Co., Ltd., 1950), p. 53.
³Elizabeth B. Brown, *Standing Up When Life Falls Down Around You* (Grand Rapids: Revell, 2016), p. 142.

Chapter 21
¹"Phyllis Diller Quotes." BrainyQuote.com. Xplore Inc, 2018. 1 October 2018. https://www.brainyquote.com/quotes/phyllis_diller_400596
²LeAnne Blackmore, *Obscure No More: Life-Shaping Lessons from the Often Overlooked* (Cincinnati: Standard Publishing, 2010), p. 88.

Chapter 22
¹For more information, you can find CMDA's entire position statement on ART ethics on the organization's website, at https://cmda.org/resources/publication/assisted-reproductive-technology-ethics-statement.
²Matthew Walker, *Why We Sleep: Unlocking the Power of Sleep and Dreams* (New York: Scribner, 2017), pp. 178-181, 341-342.

Chapter 25
¹Lewis, A Grief Observed, p. 7.
²http://www.mayoclinic.org/healthy-lifestyle/getting-pregnant/in-depth/pregnancy-after-miscarriage/art-20044134

Chapter 26
¹Brown, p. 20.

Chapter 27
¹Blackmore, p. 187.

Chapter 28
¹Ruth Myers, *31 Days of Praise: Enjoying God Anew* (Colorado Springs, CO: Multnomah Publishers, Inc., 1994), p. 23.
²Bryan Stevenson, *Just Mercy* (New York: Spiegel & Grau, 2014), pp. 289-290.

Chapter 29

¹Bryan Chapell, *Daniel: Faithful in All Circumstances* (Christianity Today, 2012), p. 29. https://www.lifenz.org/upload//groups/Daniel.pdf

²Brother Lawrence, *The Practice of the Presence of God: 2002 Edition*, edited by Lightheart (PracticeGodsPresence.com, August 21, 2012). http://www.gutenberg.org/cache/epub/5657/pg5657-images.html

³Holleman, *Seated with Christ*, pp. 94-97.

About the Author

Nancy Canestrari Williams is a wife, mom, and writer, with a background in corporate communications, news/feature writing, advertising, and marketing for national and regional firms. She has a master's degree in journalism, lives in the mountains of East Tennessee, and teaches public relations at a Christian college. She and her husband, Mark, have two adult children.

To write to Nancy, or for more information, go to lightbournecreative.com.

Notes

Notes

Notes

www.ingramcontent.com/pod-product-compliance
Lightning Source LLC
Chambersburg PA
CBHW020402080526
44584CB00014B/1134